Tradition and the Individual Poem

Tradition and the Individual Poem

AN INQUIRY INTO
ANTHOLOGIES

Anne Ferry

STANFORD UNIVERSITY PRESS
STANFORD, CALIFORNIA

Stanford University Press
Stanford, California
©2001 by the Board of Trustees of the
Leland Stanford Junior University
Printed in the United States of America

Library of Congress Cataloging-in-Publication Data

Ferry, Anne
    Tradition and the individual poem : an inquiry into anthologies / Anne
Ferry.
        p.   cm.
    Includes bibliographical references and index.
    ISBN 0-8047-4235-9 (alk. paper)
        1. English poetry—History and criticism.   2. Anthologies—Editing—History.
3. American poetry—History and criticism.   4. Literature publishing—History.
5. Anthologies—Editing.   6. Canon (Literature).   I. Title.

PR508.A54 F47   2001
821.009—dc21   00-067944

This book is printed on acid-free, archival-quality paper.

Original printing 2001

Last figure below indicates year of this printing:
10   09   08   07   06   05   04   03   02   01

Typeset in 11/14 Garamond

To David
and to Stephen, Elizabeth, David, Sebastian

For their indispensable scholarly and critical contributions toward the making of this book I express my admiration and thanks to Elizabeth Ferry, Stephen Ferry, Dayton Haskin, Richard Poirier, William Pritchard, Christopher Ricks, Dennis Taylor, Herbert Tucker, David Wood.

Chip Coakley, Elizabeth Falsey, Susan Halpern have given invaluable advice and guidance in the use of the Houghton Library's resources.

To David Ferry I owe more than I can express.

A.F.

CONTENTS

"In its countless alveoli space contains
compressed time. That is what space is for."
—Gaston Bachelard

"I read poetry to save time."
—Marilyn Monroe

INTRODUCTION

QUESTIONS AND PREMISES

These days it is guaranteed—and has been since the beginning of the twentieth century—that the phrase *anthology of poetry* would be understood as the ordinary way of referring to a certain familiar kind of book where many readers of poetry first and perhaps most of the time meet poems; or it might even be said that anthologies have become part of the experience of anyone who reads poetry at all. Anthologies, as all sorts of evidence help us to understand, are a powerful force in the situation of poetry now, and have been in different ways and degrees since the earliest extant book of this kind was published in England in the mid-1550s. That span of centuries in the making of printed poetry anthologies in English is the chronological territory explored in the chapters to come.

Like other common terms, *anthology* is commonly taken for granted, so that we are unlikely to ask what makes an anthology, in what conceptual and practical ways it is different from other collections of poetry. Nor are we likely to wonder about the linguistic roots of the word *anthology* or its history in English. The recentness of its common currency turns out to be surprising if we consider the existence for 450 years of English printed books, and even earlier of manuscript collections, fitting the category of what are now called anthologies of poetry; and surprising also given the ancient beginnings, in Greece at least as far back as the fourth century B.C.E., of this kind of book and the present name for it. Part I, "What makes an anthology," opens up these questions about the special dimensions—conceptual, spatial, temporal—and the classifying features of anthologies. It proposes some definitions in Chapter 1 to be tested more fully and in detail in later discussions.

An anthology is a peculiar kind of poetry book: peculiar in the sense of distinctive, in that, unlike an author's own collection or an edited gathering of a poet's work, the choice of poems is not limited by their single authorship. An anthology is peculiar also, both distinctive and odd, for the corollary reason that the choices about the book's contents, except those that went into the making of the poems, are the decisions of someone whose aim is to make something of a very different kind: a selection of several or many poets' work, decided and arranged on principles and using materials different from what would be found in a book of poems by only one author. The anthologist as author of the book supplants the author of the poem in choosing how it should be presented, with interpretive consequences that Chapter 1 illustrates by two contrasting readings of Elizabeth Bishop's "Sestina." The two readings show how the unique role and presence of the anthologist can give a different direction to the experience of reading a poem than if it were read elsewhere. While our awareness of these shaping differences is sometimes vivid, at other times subliminal, the anthologists' awareness of them seems always to have been close to the surface; this self-consciousness is another distinguishing feature of the anthology.

The definitions or defining descriptions proposed in the opening chapter lead in Chapters 2 and 3 to considerations of the ways anthologies are arranged, and of how arrangement of entries and other devices for presenting them—for instance, titling them and revising their language and form—can exercise authority over poems and readers. The detailed illustrations of these practices are concentrated on certain historically influential anthologies—Richard Tottel's *Songes and Sonettes*, Thomas Percy's *Reliques of Ancient English Poetry*, Francis Palgrave's *The Golden Treasury*—and on what happens to certain entries in them: the earliest by Tottel's foremost poets, Sir Thomas Wyatt and Henry Howard, Earl of Surrey; the most recent by William Wordsworth, the poet given the largest space in Palgrave's book.

The focus tilts slightly in Part II, "What makes an anthology-piece," away from the nature of the book toward the choice of its contents, though without contradicting a premise of all these discussions that book and contents are bound in a new whole as a unique entity. Poems that were in the eighteenth-century approvingly called *beauties* and in the nineteenth *gems* are now labeled—neutrally or with various shadings of disapproval—

anthology-pieces. These chosen poems are also derogatorily called *stock pieces* or *chestnuts*. W. H. Auden dismissed them as "old war horses."[1]

To reflect on what makes an anthology-piece is to ask two questions so entwined that they can be taken as inseparable. How did the poems most often included in anthologies get there: in what cultural situations, by what circumstances? And what inherent qualities of these poems—of matter, language, and form—meshed with their situations and circumstances to make them seemingly inevitable choices for inclusion in poetry collections? Discussions in the three parallel chapters of Part II explore these questions, sometimes separately but sometimes simultaneously, asking them about poems written in each of the past five centuries and about their appearances in different periods in the history of anthologies printed in English. While the same kind of question can be asked about every generation of poems and every generation of anthologies, the meanings of the questions themselves can change, as well as the responses to them, with shifting circumstances and situations.

It follows that the chapters in Part II take very different shapes to respond to some of these changes. Chapter 4 tracks the appearances of six very short songs or lyrics of the late sixteenth and earlier seventeenth centuries, chosen after research for this book proved them to be the poems in English with the longest and least discontinuous presences in anthologies. The discussion traces how this came about, and then looks at the forms and language of these anthology-pieces, to understand why poems of the kind these six exemplify would hold their places so securely for so long among the favorites of anthologists and their readers. Chapter 5 reflects on the suitability of public poems, beginning in the eighteenth century, to the special character of anthologies as public spaces. Extended readings of three public poems written during the past three centuries—Oliver Goldsmith's "The Deserted Village," Matthew Arnold's "Dover Beach," Philip Larkin's "Church Going"—suggest ways of thinking about how the changing cultural and aesthetic attitudes toward poetry and readers of it reflected in these poems contributed sooner or later to their status as anthology-pieces. In Chapter 6, how and why Elizabeth Bishop was known as "the poet of 'The Fish'" are the shaping questions that a history of Bishop's reception and reputation, and that a revisionary reading of "The Fish," intend to answer. Questions asked in the two preceding chapters are here addressed to the situation of poetry in the second half of the twentieth century, and to the special circumstances of Bishop's writing life that contributed to making "The Fish" as well known as any single poem of her time.

The emphasis shifts again slightly in Part III, "What poets make of anthologies," to consider more directly the ways that anthologies, in their ever increasing role as a prime source for poetry readers, have intersected with the history of poetry and the history of criticism. Two of the special dimensions of the anthology as a kind of book are most visibly active in these moments: the discontinuousness produced by its many, varied, short entries; and the importance of its spatial orderings and limits, both topics that enter discussions all through this book. These distinguishing dimensions have, since Tottel's venture, promoted songs and sonnets—sixteenth-century shorthand for any poems in short forms—to a higher rank than they had held before. This rearrangement of generic hierarchies constitutes a transformation in literary theory, criticism, and practice so effectively charged that for many readers now the lyric—modern shorthand for any short poems—has become virtually synonymous with poetry.

The reconfiguring, begun in the mid-1500s, was displaced in the eighteenth century by the prevailing interest in discursive poetry but reaffirmed by the early 1800s. Not coincidentally, that was the time when interest in Elizabethan verse was being encouraged by recoverings and reprintings of early anthologies, and when the primacy of the lyric was beginning to be more visible everywhere in contemporary poetry and critical writings. The instances most often cited are *Lyrical Ballads* and John Stuart Mill's definition—made in 1833 in his famous discussion of Wordsworth—of "Lyric poetry" as the kind "more eminently and peculiarly poetry than any other."[2]

This was also the period when the anthology itself, which from the beginning had promoted short poems, was established as an available and preferred source for poetry readers. The wider cultural causes of this situation have been much discussed in studies of reading and readers. The reasons most pertinent here have to do with the spread of literacy, and of the means to buy books, to readers with only brief intervals of time for leisured amusements. For them a collection of discrete short pieces was ideally—that is, practically—suited.

Poets, evidence of mixed sorts shows, have always taken notice of poetry anthologies, and increasingly since the late seventeenth century. By 1800 poets were particularly eager to promote retrospective anthologies, where they could find earlier models at a safer distance who did not have the oppressive influence on their own art and on their readers' preferences that their more immediate eighteenth-century predecessors could still exert. As a form of encouragement to anthologizing of earlier poetry, poets in this period were eager to acknowledge their debts to what they found in such retrospective collections. Wordsworth, and poets of his time sympathetic with his ideals for poetry, celebrated with almost religious fervor the transforming influence of Percy's *Reliques* on English poetry through its revival of Elizabethan lyrics and recovery of old ballads. Their terms of praise suggest that they thought of him as an author, a fellow poet, more than as an anthologist. At the end of the nineteenth century, in 1892 to be precise, Robert Frost bought a copy of *The Golden Treasury*, a discovery of immediate personal importance that became an event in modern poetry and criticism of a magnitude almost equal to the Romantics' encounter with Percy's anthology. In Chapter 7 these enthusiasms of poets as anthology readers are set beside the revolt of some twentieth-century poets against anthologies, vigorously led by Robert Graves.

Chapter 8 looks further into the uneasiness poets have felt at the indisputable power of anthologies to influence the course of poetry and of criticism. It discusses the ways poets have appropriated that power by making anthologies to serve their own interests. Beginning with John Dryden, or even earlier with George Gascoigne in the 1570s, poets have made anthologies as showcases to display work of their own and increasingly of their congenial contemporaries as well. This kind of anthology—Pound called it "a sort of group manifesto"—proliferated in the twentieth century.[3] Those of Pound's era, later of Auden's, again of Larkin's, and still later the so-called anthology war of the 1960s illustrate this pattern.

Also in the twentieth century some poets, most spectacularly W. B. Yeats in *The Oxford Book of Modern Verse* and Larkin in *The Oxford Book of Twentieth Century English Verse*, discovered the possibility of making a retrospective anthology that would reshape literary history to suit their sense of where their own work belonged in it. Detailed attention to their choices and arrangement of entries, including poems of their own, shows the expressive power of this kind of anthology as an instrument of criticism. In the same period, poets appropriated some of that power by practicing old and new ways of controlling the appearances of their poems in anthologies not of their own making.

The last part of this book, "T. S. Eliot's imaginary anthology," I have called Coda (Eliot liked to use musical terms as titles for his poems) in the hope that it will act as the *OED* says a coda should: as a "passage of more or less independent character introduced after the completion of the essential parts of a movement so as to form a more definite and satisfactory conclusion."

Eliot's interweaving of texts—specifically his most often anthologized essay "Tradition and the Individual Talent," his contemporaneous poem "Whispers of Immortality," his review of Sir Herbert Grierson's anthology of metaphysical poets—into what I call an imaginary anthology is an altogether individual and peculiarly telling confirmation of premises this book is predicated on.

One of those premises is that the anthology has always been an effective instrument in shaping the direction of criticism and of poetry, as it seems Eliot, consummate master of both arts, fully recognized. Another is that its effectiveness can be discerned in virtually all the revisionary moments in literary history since the sixteenth century. A third premise is that the conceptual, spatial, and temporal dimensions that define anthologies as belonging to a special class of poetry book have made them both a physical embodiment and a figurative representation of what poets have tended to call *the tradition*—the iconoclast Pound said that the "tradition is a beauty which we preserve and not a set of fetters to bind us"—but which many critics more recently and more often have called *the canon*.[4]

The ways these premises have directed the focus of interest in this book have added other limits to the territory it maps besides its chronological beginning in the sixteenth century. Although the discussions here stress the seeming paradox that anthologies are a unique kind of book capable of taking an uncountable variety of forms to contain very different contents, the focus of this book necessarily reflects only some of that variousness.

The chapters here do not consider what Robert von Hallberg in *American Poetry and Culture 1945–1980* calls the "decentralization" in the recent "quasi-political anthologies of gay poetry, women's poetry, or black, Chicano, and Amerasian poetry" or other collections of this kind, because my interest, paralleling von Hallberg's, is in anthologies of "poetry written with an eye to the center."[5] For the same reason, there is very little attention given here to anthologies devoted to other kinds of concentrations: in an always favorite category like religious or patriotic or love poetry, for instance *A Collection of Moral and Sacred Poems* (1744), *Any Soldier to His Son* (1933, third edition 1944), *Out of the Heart. Poems for Lovers Young and Old* (1891); in more special topics such as *The Home in Poetry* (1884), *The Daffodil* (1949); in occasions like weddings, such as *Into the Garden* (1993) edited by Robert Haas and Stephen Mitchell, for which entries are chosen and re-written to package them for the matrimonial market.[6] There are mentions but no detailed discussions of popular anthologies, using *popular* in the sense of appealing to the broadest segment of the poetry reading public, in-cluding particularly people who may not think of themselves as poetry read-ers. An example of this category, which is of special value for studying the sociology of poetry, is *Popular Poetic Pearls* (1887), containing about 120 po-ems, possibly 50 of them attached to names a reader would recognize now.[7] Also left undiscussed is the kind of poetry Geoffrey Grigson collected in *The Gambit Book of Popular Verse*, using *popular* (as distinct from *literary*) to mean poetry with different origins and modes of transmission from the sorts of written poems usually printed in anthologies.[8] Another variety of socio-logical interest but not particularly pertinent to this study is the anthology explicitly designed to meet the postulated needs or preferences of a special group of readers. Such anthologies would include Oliver Goldsmith's *Po-ems for Young Ladies* (1767), and Marguerite Wilkinson's *Contemporary Po-etry* (1923) for readers to whom the compiler would not "recommend the work of T. S. Eliot, D. H. Lawrence, Maxwell Bodenheim, Ezra Pound, Conrad Aiken, and others who have challenged the serious attention of our reviewers."[9]

While the consideration of poems in this book also aims at variety as well as range, some that have appeared prominently and over a sustained period of time in anthologies "with an eye to the center" have invited most atten-tion because they have played particularly conspicuous parts in the histories of poetry and criticism traced here. Such poems have made themselves visi-ble in every period of poetry from the sixteenth century to the present, though for logistical reasons I have avoided discussing poems by writers still living after the 1980s: many more questions about their presence in anthologies would be unanswerable than is true of poets whose work is complete and who can be viewed from the distance of at least a decade.

Of the remarkably little that has been written about printed anthologies of poetry in English, most is fragmentary and marginal to some other interest. They are briefly considered in histories of readers and reading such as Richard Altick's *The English Common Reader*.[10] Mentions of them crop up in discussions of canon formation such as Craig Abbott's "Modern American Poetry: Anthologies, Classrooms, and Canons," Alastair Fowler's "Genre and the Literary Canon," Alan Golding's *From Outlaw to Classic*, Douglas Patey's "The Eighteenth Century Invents the Canon"; in studies of literature as a commodity in the cultural marketplace, for instance von Hallberg's *American Poetry and Culture* and Frank Lentricchia's *Modernist Quartet*; in discussions of the shift from manuscript to print culture such as Arthur Marotti's *Manuscript, Print, and the English Renaissance Lyric*.[11]

Among the very few studies that use anthologies as their main area of investigation, the majority of the more recent ones treat it as the ground for discussing the same current interests as the various writings listed above. Barbara Benedict's *Making the Modern Reader*, mainly about eighteenth-century collections, argues that "the history of the anthology demonstrates the growing control of the self-definition of readers by a rhetoric turned to mass production in an increasingly anonymous market."[12] Sabine Haass's "Victorian Poetry Anthologies: Their Role and Success in the Nineteenth-Century Book Market" looks at the later period from much the same angle, as do Natalie Houston's "Valuable by Design: Material Features and Cultural Value in Nineteenth-Century Sonnet Anthologies" and Linda Peterson's "Anthologizing Women: Women Poets in Early Victorian Collections of Lyric."[13]

Besides Elizabeth Pomeroy's chronological description, *The Elizabethan Miscellanies*, there are a few articles that look at other segments of the history of anthologies, and from other perspectives.[14] An early example is Raymond Havens's classic "Changing Taste in the Eighteenth Century: A Study of Dryden's and Dodsley's Miscellanies," which has lately been somewhat amended by James Tierney in his "Relics from the cave of Dodsley."[15] Robert McDowell's "The Poetry Anthology" is an account of the contentions among twentieth-century anthologies for which Robert Ross's book-length history *The Georgian Revolt* gives the background.[16] "Hardy's Copy of *The Golden Treasury*," Dennis Taylor's detailed study of annotations, is a very recent and all but unique study of the importance an anthology can have in the making of poems.[17]

Arthur Case's *A Bibliography of English Poetical Miscellanies 1521–1750* is a useful but by no means complete listing of anthologies in this period, not even of those in accessible collections like the Houghton Library, which has been my ever-present help in time of need.[18]

This book has learned from and borrowed from this small body of writings about selective subjects related to poetry anthologies in English, but its own lines of perspective are very different. It is a theoretical, historical, and critical exploration of anthologies that looks in detail at what assumptions they are predicated on; how they are made; how they treat the poems in them; what effects their presentations have on their readers' experiences of those poems; and what roles they have played in the changing situations of poetry and the criticism of it since Richard Tottel, a publisher mainly of law books, gave readers of poetry the earliest extant printed anthology of English verse in 1557.

PART I

WHAT MAKES AN ANTHOLOGY

CHAPTER ONE

ANTHOLOGIES AS A KIND

A compressed history of changing terms used in titles to classify what we now mean by anthologies of poetry will show that these books have assumed a rich variety of forms expressing widely ranging aims and emphases, and making quite different appeals to differently imagined readers. The discovery and rediscovery, the appearing and fading of classifying terms in the titles of anthologies spanning five centuries, mirrors this plenitude of possibilities. Paradoxically, it also suggests that, from almost the beginning, anthology makers sensed that such books might be categorized as a single kind or genre, and have expressed that distinction in titles and many other presentational devices. For all their variousness, anthologies have features in common that inevitably set them apart from other kinds of poetry collections made by authors of their own work or by editors. Most particularly, the anthology is the work of a unique kind of maker, whose presence is felt, inescapably, only in this kind of book.

FORMAL CLASSIFICATIONS

The Greek root for *anthology*—*anthos* (*flower*) + *legein* (*to gather*)—was still fully alive in English in the second half of the eighteenth century. Among definitions in Samuel Johnson's dictionary, "A collection of flowers" comes first, "A collection of poems" last.[1] He certainly knew the most famous gathering of verses by ancient poets, which has come to be known as *The Greek Anthology* at least since the early 1780s (when the *OED* says Joseph Warton used that name for it). Even so, Johnson did not necessarily think of the word mainly the way we do, as the classifying term in English for a special kind of book. It was not fixed in that status until the end of the nineteenth century. In the preceding three and a half centuries readers knew such books by a variety of terms encoding a mixture of signals.

There is a clear reason for the slow, unsteady emergence of *anthology* into its recent familiarity. Since this kind of book has no more fixed requirements than that it be a compiler's gathering of pieces of poetry by more than one or two poets, it has made the most of its many undefined possibilities of form and content. As a consequence, its passage through centuries is not traceable as a linear or other shapely movement: certainly not as a *progress* (a ruling metaphor for literary histories as they were written in the eighteenth and nineteenth centuries); not even as an *evolution* or a *development* (more recent, somewhat more subdued teleological descriptions).

For the same reason, it follows that the changing formal terms for categorizing this special genre of book have been tentative, various, overlapping, sometimes contradictory in their implications. Even so, what has remained a constant in its checkered history is that this kind of book has seemed, soon after its first English appearance in print, to need some special self-definition, explanation, justification.

Successive efforts to classify it, to find a legitimate place for it among other kinds of books, have been responsive to that need, and their most visible outward sign is the title. As we trace them, the changes in these classifying titles, their very inconsistencies, help to fashion a condensed history of anthologies as an emerging kind or genre with its own conventions. Like all conventions, they encode an odd mixture of highly articulated conceptions with largely unexamined assumptions; this history can help us to read them.

The title *Songes and Sonettes*, probably Tottel's choice, does not use a classifying term for the book, or make any reference to it. A reason for this suggested by Martin Elsky is that even "the very idea of the book as a discrete, self-enclosed object does not seem to have been widespread" until print had firmly supplanted manuscript culture.[2] Tottel's title is no more than a simple description of its contents. In a then familiar shorthand, it tells what the "gentle reder" would find inside this little volume: short poems (which was the original meaning of *sonnet*), or as the printer's epistle modestly calls them, "small parcelles" of verse, mainly to do with love.[3]

From a later perspective this unassuming title is surprising because it does not give a self-referential definition of the book itself, but the prefatory paragraph following the title page suggests one reason why not. It makes clear that Tottel, who probably wrote "The Printer to the Reader," did not think of *Songes and Sonettes* as a new kind of book needing special definition in its title to promote it, but as a kind already existing in the form of private manuscript gatherings of poetry: "It resteth now . . . to publish . . . these workes which the ungentle horders up of such treasure have heretofore enuied thee." What was new about his kind of book from his perspective was its public appearance in print.

The sort of private manuscript claimed here as the source for this printed compilation was not titled: an extant example is a contemporaneous gathering of poems from Wyatt and Surrey to living authors begun by John Harington of Stepney.[4] Still, such manuscripts could have suggested the modest, almost casual presentation of *Songes and Sonettes*. It sounds like a notation added by the copier to what might even have been loose sheets, or like a gloss in the margin or heading above a group of poems in a bound manuscript, put there for the guidance of known readers in the private circle where the poems would be passed.

The title *Tottel's Miscellany* prefixed to *Songes and Sonettes* in 1870 by Edward Arber (which is the title the anthology has generally been known by since) was anachronistic. The noun *miscellany* did not come into English until the earlier seventeenth century, when it was used also as an adjective along with *miscellaneous*. It made one of its earliest appearances as a generic term in a title of 1652, *Misselanies Or, fifty Years Gatherings, Out of Sundry Authors in Prose and Verse*. Then beginning in the 1680s, and steadily for the next hundred years, it shared pride of place with *collection* as preferred terms to classify anthologies of poems in their titles, even though these two words had then, as they do now, somewhat different meanings: a *miscellany* is a mixture or medley, a congeries; a *collection* is an act, or the end result of an act, of gathering together related things.

To title a volume of poetry a miscellany was to make a claim for the interesting variety of its contents. This is clearly the task given in 1684 to the title *Miscellany Poems. Containing a New Translation. . . .* [of Virgil, Ovid, Horace, and others] *With Several Original Poems. By the most Eminent Hands*. It is the title of the first volume in a series of six printed by Jacob Tonson with John Dryden's collaboration on the earlier volumes. It made the term *miscellany* common usage by the instantaneous and continued success of the series. The title's neutral-seeming announcement of what was in fact a boldly innovative mixture of translated and original poems insinuates that variety, even before newness or eminence, was the chief principle of selection.

The title of Robert Dodsley's *A Collection of Poems in Six Volumes by Several Hands*, published between 1748 and 1758, describes a gathering of congenial entries chosen to be exhibited in some sort of order, or to give an intelligibly unified impression, which the presentation of the series seems to have been designed to support. Unlike the Dryden/Tonson sequence, where titles of separate volumes differ except for the constant term *Miscellany*, Dodsley's successive volumes repeat the same title. In the earlier series, particularly in the first volumes, the order of entries is not clearly articulated, and all through the sequence the proportions of translations (of both ancient and modern works) to original verse vary considerably from one volume to the next, while the entries in Dodsley's *Collection* are consistently grouped by authorship of a comparatively narrower range of poetic kinds, although their styles kept changing as new poets appeared on the scene. In the retrospective "Postscript" to the last of the six volumes, Dodsley stated what had been his plan for the collection: to "select and preserve" those examples worthy of remembrance out of the "loose and fugitive pieces, some printed, others in manuscript, which for forty or fifty years past have been thrown into the world, and carelessly left to perish."[5]

These differences in emphasis in the shapings of the two most widely read and admired compilations of verse seem to have gone largely unnoticed in their own time, as is clear in the use sometimes of both generic terms in the same title: for instance in 1685 in *Miscellany, Being a Collection of Poems by several Hands*.

What was then the most obvious common feature of these terms was the tone of moderation they gave to titles. They sounded politely measured by contrast with the entrepreneurial exaggerations typical of titling for late-sixteenth-century compilations such as *A gorgious Gallery of gallant Inuentions*; their manner was unpedantically judicious after the wisecracking of mid-seventeenth-century titles like *Recreation for Ingenious Head-peeces. Or, A Pleasant Grove for their Wits to walke in* (1645). Belonging to the vocabulary of educated social circles, the preferred terms carried an added suggestion of being au courant. *Miscellany* had only recently arrived in English, and *collection* was being put to current use in connection with the newly fashionable interest in accumulating and cataloguing books, statues, medals, coins, and other curiosities such as attracted John Evelyn and provoked Pope to satire. Being up-to-date was increasingly a desirable feature of a book and matching attribute of a reader: Johnson advised Boswell, "We must read what the world reads at the moment"; Sir Joshua Reynolds agreed that "it was his place to have read what every person else has read."[6]

The clearest evidence of the shared appeal these anthologies had for their similar and eventually overlapping audiences is in the references to them made in the same or interchanging terms. A specially telling example is in Thomas Warton's preface to *The Union: Or, Select Scots and English Poems*, published in 1753 contemporaneously with Dodsley's later volumes. Warton began by giving a history of the genre from the point of view of his generation, which was almost as much ignorant of the poetry of former periods as it was indifferent to it, particularly to the shorter kinds that were perpetuated in early printed anthologies. In the 1770s these were still not represented in the multivolume collections of poets being introduced to the widening public of readers. The series accompanied by Johnson's lives of the poets begins with Cowley; John Bell's *The Poets of Great Britain* looks farther back only at Chaucer, Spenser, and Donne.

Warton's historical minisurvey of anthologies reflected contemporary perspective: "The first miscellaneous collection of poems, that ever appear'd in Great-Britain with any reputation, is that publish'd by Mr Dryden: which was afterwards continued by Tonson."[7] Excluding the series "known by the name of Mr. Pope" as not truly a "collection of poems by different hands" (since most of the pieces were Pope's), Warton brought his historical summary to a prompt conclusion: "The best miscellany at this day extant in our language, and the first complete one of the kind which we have seen, is that lately publish'd by R. Dodsley, which boasts the greatest names of the present age among its contributors." Although partial in more than one sense, this exclusive claim for the historical importance of Dryden's *Miscellany Poems* and Dodsley's *Collection* was not all exaggeration.

Together the two series raised the status of anthologies designed both to gather poems worthy of being preserved, and to introduce and promote a variety of new verse, making them respected volumes that could take their place beside the works of single poets in a respectable library, as we know from surviving records of private libraries and lists of books suitable to include in them.[8] John Clarke's *An Essay Upon Study* of 1731 gave directions for building a personal library that included specific recommendations of books to acquire in each of the parts of learning. The last and least category,

"Books of English Poetry," includes miscellanies along with separate volumes by Waller, Dryden, and Pope, and whole *Works* by Spenser, Milton, Cowley, and the Duke of Buckingham.[9]

J. Partridge's *The treasurie of commodious Conceits* (1584) and John Cotgrave's *The English Treasury of Wit and Language* (1655) are among the earliest uses in the title of an anthology of the word *treasury*, which became a generic term after it was revived in 1861 for what is still the most famous of all anthologies of poetry in English, Palgrave's *The Golden Treasury*. While Partridge and Cotgrave almost certainly used the classifying word to mean what we would call a thesaurus, a storehouse of words, Palgrave's pairing with *golden* gave *treasury* the more glamorous meaning of a repository of treasures. In this sense, the term incorporated currently popular metaphors for the contents of an anthology: *gems, brilliants, jewels, heir-looms, patrimony*. Palgrave's title added more weighty importance to *Treasury* as the name, already with a long history, for the department or building that takes charge of public revenue; the term also had a special association with museums in titles such as *Art Treasures of the United Kingdom* (1858). By incorporating this richness, *The Golden Treasury* figured at once a private and a public space where personal and national wealth is carefully guarded and held in trust for the future.

The immediate success and awesome reputation of Palgrave's collection both in England and America would alone have ensured that the comparison of a poetry anthology to the repository of treasures would enter the language. The association was reinforced by Macmillan's ongoing use of the title *The Golden Treasury* for a prestigious series of books, and by many imitations of the title formula such as *The Golden Pomp, Golden Leaves, Golden Numbers, Garnered Treasures from the Poets*.

Although Shakespeare's Slender spoke in *The Merry Wives of Windsor* (I,i,199) of Tottel's anthology as a "Book of Songs and Sonnets," neither *book* nor any other reference to the volume itself (as distinct from the poems it contained) was added to Tottel's title in eight successive Elizabethan editions. The unassumingly ordinary word *book* was generally ignored in presentations of verse collections in this period in favor of a more excited vocabulary. A Scottish collection of ballads moralized of 1567, *Ane Compendious Buik of Godly and Spirituall Soungis*, and a compilation of English and

Latin verses titled *A Booke of Epitaphes* dated 1583 seem to have been quite unusual in calling themselves a book. The spare term matched their sober contents.

Later the word *book* might have seemed too loose a term to publishers of anthologies, when classifying itself had become a more orderly habit of mind, making *miscellany* and *collection* the preferred terms for what was then thought to be an essentially new or newly respectable kind of book. The association of those words with specifically modern interests gave another advantage to using them in preference to *book*, which survived in this period of titling mainly for traditional religious compilations: *The Book of Common Prayer*, *The Book of Psalms*. Not coincidentally, then, the appearance of the word *book* in titles for anthologies coincided with the virtual demise of the former favorites, *miscellany* and *collection*.

The homely familiarity of the word *book* seems to have been what made it attractive to use in titles for anthologies of poetry beginning in the early nineteenth century. Being what any person would most likely call any volume, the noun *book* could make an anthology seem to be a more personal possession, as on the title page of a collection published in America in 1835: *The Young Man's Book of Elegant Poetry* ("By the Author of 'The Young Man's Own Book'"). A volume called a book might be found in any home—and small collections of them were more and more common in the nineteenth century—or so potential readers were told by American titles like *The Household Book of Poetry* (1858) and English titles like *A Household Book of English Poetry* (1868). Amelia Edwards made this point explicitly in a polite apology for the "exceeding homeliness" of the title for her anthology of 1878, *A Poetry-Book of Elder Poets*: "But the taste for high-sounding titles has passed away; and the changes have been wrung so long and so often upon 'Gems,' 'Beauties,' 'Wreaths,' 'Caskets,'" that it seemed "the old plain, familiar nursery name by which we have all designated the 'poetry-books' of our childhood would find more favour."[10]

These anthologies were apparently designed to reach the larger and more socially diverse reading public that had grown since the poet William Shenstone wrote in a letter to a friend in 1753 that poems printed in Dodsley's *Collection* would "be read by the polite World," and to Thomas Percy in 1760 that his ballad collection, *Reliques of Ancient English Poetry*, would be well received by "All People of Taste."[11] *Beeton's Great Book of Poetry*, dated 1870 in its often reprinted preface, belonged to a popular series that included an equally fat volume on *Household Management*.

Nineteen hundred was the year *The Oxford Book of English Verse* appeared in England, and initiated a respected series of successors: a revised edition in 1939 of the first, with this same title and the same editor, Sir Arthur Quiller-Couch; *The New Oxford Book of English Verse* in 1972, compiled by Helen Gardner; Christopher Ricks's edition of 1999, which resumes the original title. The publication of a comprehensive retrospective anthology was a new venture for the Oxford press, while collections of English verse all or mainly by Oxford poets that appropriate the hallowed name of the institution in their titles go back as early as 1798 to Elijah Fenton's *Oxford and Cambridge Miscellany Poems* of 1708. *The Oxford Sausage* of 1764, edited anonymously by Thomas Warton, combines its borrowed prestige with a clubby joke.[12]

The first editor of the series, Quiller-Couch, had no reputation as a scholar then, or perhaps ever, but had edited a retrospective anthology of poets from Surrey to Shirley in 1895 and had a friend, Charles Cannon, at the Oxford press.[13] The name *Oxford Book* quickly won almost generic status. By 1912, according to *The Oxford Magazine*, "no civilized person in Great Britain, the Dominions or the United States is 'married or given in marriage' without being presented with one or more copies of the *Oxford Book*."[14] During the Great War, it was the constant companion of English soldiers in the trenches, and may have been the source of one of the songs most popular with front-line soldiers, "The Bells of Hell."[15]

Officers of the Press instructed Quiller-Couch what sort of collection was wanted. It was to rival *The Golden Treasury*, which continued to be widely read in editions somewhat revised and enlarged since its first printing in 1861. Still, the promoters of the new venture thought or wanted to persuade prospective readers to think that Palgrave's anthology was "passé."[16] This rivalry for its readers was to be won because the recent invention of India paper would allow a more broadly ranging, fuller, and more complete collection of "old favorites the public would expect to find" in "a handy little volume."[17] The new anthology would then be able to avoid the heaviness and awkward double-column pages of another rival, Charles Mackay's *A Thousand and One Gems of English Poetry* of 1867, which still had the appeal of a good buy for "Containing Nearly Two Thousand of the Best Pieces in the English Language" packed into one volume.

The choice of title was Quiller-Couch's, and not an easy one since it had to match or surpass the appeal of *The Golden Treasury*, with its brilliantly fused evocations of classical and Elizabethan, national and imperial, aesthetic and financial interests. Essentially the title was to attract readers with admiration for, if not direct experience of, a classical education, along with respect for other traditions and for institutions that embodied them—Britannia, Oxford. These were much the same readers as those who were continuing to buy *The Golden Treasury*, but who might prefer more poems more recently chosen (Quiller-Couch was born two years after Palgrave's anthology was first published).

Quiller-Couch's preference for the title *The Oxford Book of English Verse* was the final choice of the Oxford editors in spite of some uneasiness that the inevitable abbreviation *The Oxford Book* would be appropriate only for the Bible.[18] Even though this objection was overruled, the very fact that it was seriously made and discussed suggests that the accepted title may have been intended to evoke some vague reverence for its resemblance to religious books. The India paper (first used in 1875, for Bibles and prayer books) combined with the dark color and gilt lettering of the cover might have encouraged the association. These slightest suggestions of sanctity would have helped to free the venture from the taint of commercialism, and contributed to giving new dignity to the word *book* in titles for anthologies.

The precise calculations of detail were, it seems, not lost on the makers of titles for anthologies in England, where *book* is still largely preferred even though in all other forms of writing that kind of book is regularly called an anthology. *Book* is even used in England for titles that admit to being the work of a trade publisher, *The Faber Book of Modern Verse* (1936) being an influential example. In the United States, *The Harvard Book of Contemporary American Poetry* (1985) is an unabashed appropriation of the encoded meanings in this title formula.

Simultaneously with the publication of *The Oxford Book of English Verse* at the end of the nineteenth century, the ancient term *anthology* was revived in America, where it is still the preferred classifying term in titles. It had once appeared, it may be for the first time, transposed into Latin in a title for a volume of verses in honor of King Charles in 1632, but seems not to have been used as a generic term in English titles until the end of the eighteenth century. Then it made a brief appearance in the titles of two verse compilations of very different kinds. In 1793 it was put to use by the idiosyncratic antiquarian Joseph Ritson for a gathering of verse with what was at the time an idiosyncratic title, *The English Anthology*. Its allusion to *The Greek Anthology* was an encoded claim for the classical status of the collection, which was unusual at that date for including authors from Chaucer and Langland to the living. In 1799 Robert Southey brought out the first volume of what he called *The Annual Anthology*, which displayed the work of contemporaneous poets, liberally including himself. His choice of the unusual classifying term may have been a way of avoiding *miscellany* and *collection*, which had neoclassical associations out of harmony with the prevailing verses in the anthology. Southey's annual was discontinued after the second volume, and Ritson's unfinished collection—unlike its only contemporaneous rivals, Henry Headley's *Select Beauties of Ancient English Poetry* (1787) and George Ellis's *Specimens of the Early English Poets* (1790)—was left out of nineteenth-century lists of admired earlier collections. The word *anthology* had not yet won approval as a classifying title for that kind of book; it virtually disappeared again, not coming into its own for another hundred years.

Then it was revived by Edmund Clarence Stedman, one of the most influential American critics of his generation. In 1895 he produced *A Victorian Anthology*, a collection of shorter poems written by British poets during the preceding sixty years. The anthologist's reputation as an authority was matched by the established air of the anthology itself. Opening this imposingly thick volume, the reader sees on the title page—opposite a picture of Queen Victoria—a photograph of the Poets' Corner in Westminster Abbey. The encoded comparison of the space in an anthology to that national shrine where poets' names are gathered to be immortalized prepares for the tone of Stedman's introduction. Posterity, he predicted, will know the "reign" whose verse is gathered in the book "for an imaginative fertility unequalled since the 'spacious days' of the Virgin Queen," holding out the likelihood that the "present reign may find no historical equal in centuries to come."[19]

Stedman's equally capacious compilation published the same centennial year as *The Oxford Book of English Verse* with the title *An American Anthology* imagines an even grander possibility for itself: that it might become "the voice of a time, of a generation, of a people,—all of extraordinary import to the world's future."[20] Together Stedman's two widely known anthologies helped to establish the classifying term in their titles as the familiar generic name for the kind of book they so confidently represent, and the preferred term in titles of American collections such as *The Norton Anthology of Poetry*. Since its first edition of 1970, it has succeeded along with other collections by the same trade publisher in making almost as big a space in our vocabulary for *Norton Anthology* as *Oxford Book* takes up in British English.

The titles are otherwise altogether unlike in their expressiveness: *Oxford* is associated with an ancient national shrine to learning, and *book* with a cherished private possession, a double appeal; *Norton* carries the respect that success brings to a modern commercial operation, and *anthology* evokes the authority of the classroom or lecture hall, a combined attraction.

SPATIAL AND TEMPORAL DIMENSIONS

Shakespeare's Slender all unknowingly conformed *Songes and Sonettes* to what became the paradigm for titling an anthology when he spoke of it as his "Book of Songs and Sonnets." The grammar of this phrase, typical of the anthology title, makes a distinction—though here not as emphatic as some—between the book itself and the entries in it. Simply, the preposition *of* allows the phrase to signify this double status: *a book consisting of or made out of songs and sonnets*, but also *a book not made out of but filled with or containing songs and sonnets*. That being so, Slender's phrase can be read in one sense as analogous to *a package of songs and sonnets*. Understood this way, the separation of nouns by the preposition *of* diagrams the case that a *book* does not belong exclusively to the sphere of discourse. It also occupies space in the world of physical objects, like a package, and within that class it belongs, like a package, to the subset of objects that are themselves containing spaces.

The twofold ontological status of objects in this category has been described with helpful concreteness by Gaston Bachelard:

Chests, especially small caskets, . . . are objects *that may be opened*. When a casket is closed, it is returned to the general community of objects; it takes its place in exterior space. But it opens! . . . The outside has no more meaning. . . . for the reason that a new dimension—the dimension of intimacy—has just opened up.[21]

Of course this description applies to all other containing objects as well as books, and to books of all kinds, which have in common that the dimension of intimacy is constituted by language. Still, the special application of the argument to the anthology as a distinct sort of book is suggested by Bachelard's chosen examples, "especially small caskets." These belong to the very objects and to the precise type of container often used in titles for and writings about anthologies to figure the nature of that kind of book. Quiller-Couch proposed *Casket* as a possible alternative to *Book* in the title of his Oxford anthology; *A Cabinet of Choice Jewels, A Cabinet of Gems* are examples of a much used title form. These show a sense of need to point to the anthology as a book not wholly identifiable with or wholly describable by its contents, a need not suggested by *The Poetical Works of Christina Rossetti* or *Prufrock and Other Observations*.

Heightened awareness of the book as a containing space is also shown in the vast number of seventeenth- and eighteenth-century titles for anthologies that use rather than *of* the more strictly defined connective *containing*: *A Poetical Rapsody Containing, Elegies, Madrigalls, and other Poesies* . . . (1602); *Miscellany Poems. Containing* . . . *Several Original Poems* (1684); *A Choice Collection of Poetry* . . . *Containing Poems* . . . *&c.* (1738); *The Warbling Muses, Or Treasure of Lyric Poetry: Containing Seven Hundred and Thirty-one Songs* (1749).

While all books are containing objects, it is a distinguishing mark of anthologies, by contrast with authorial collections or those made by editors, that their titles have almost from the beginning typically called special attention to that spatial dimension by wording that both sets apart and links together container and contained. This conventional form of presentation is the first sign the anthology makes of self-consciousness about its peculiar character among other collections of poems: that it makes a new whole which is not identifiable with its contents. A consequence is that anthologies demand special attention to the fitness of the containing space to what is fitted into it.

The size of any book is always constrained by practical considerations, for instance: how heavy it is to hold, how portable, how conveniently sized to display or store, all possibilities inseparable from the consideration of what price it will sell for. Then the physical dimensions and cost are determined by paper, type face, format, binding, illustrations, and so on, as well as by how much material the containing space is asked to hold.

According to Roger Chartier, the hierarchy of sizes was established when books were copied by hand. The folio was used for serious subjects because a book of that size—*book* was used equally for manuscript as well as printed volumes—could be laid flat for sustained study; the medium size of the quarto was suited for easier reading of humanist texts, both classical and recent, which could be held in the hand; the portable octavo and still smaller duodecimo were fit for lighter matter suitable in "a pocketbook" or "bedside book" with various uses and many more readers.[22] The first edition of *Songes and Sonettes* was an unusually small quarto, but anthologies soon after began to be printed in octavo or duodecimo.[23]

For the maker of an anthology, its size is a specially pressing issue because the choices of what and how much material it should contain are not predetermined to the degree that they are in collections limited to poems of a single author. The question of how many entries to include, as well as which ones, is more freely left to the discretion of the compiler acting in agreement with the publisher (who in early anthologies might be the compiler himself). This makes the number of lines in a poem an important feature to take into account for the simple reason that it determines how many can fit into the containing space of the book.

Quotations from preface after preface show some anthologists promoting a *complete* (larger) collection over a *selected* (smaller) treasury, or using a title that boosts quantity as a value (making more poems accessible for instruction or pleasure at a good price), as in *A Thousand and One Gems* by contrast with *Fifty Perfect Poems*. For compilers who have advertised the selectivity of their anthologies, the shortness of their chosen entries has also had special value. It has allowed them to be gathered in slimmer and therefore usually more elegant volumes, encouraging anthologists to promote the shortness of poems not as economically advantageous but as aesthetically desirable. For instance, the explicit excuse usually made for cutting stanzas from longer entries is that the shortened version can more powerfully affect the reader. Implicit is the notion that what is most *poetical* is experienced in small proportions.

By the second half of the nineteenth century this view was openly argued, as in William Cullen Bryant's preface to *A Library of Poetry and Song Being Choice Selections from the Best Poetry* of 1874: "It seems to me that it is only poems of a moderate length," or extracts from poems of "greater" length, that "produce the effect upon the mind and heart which make the charm of this kind of writing."[24]

Another benefit in the shortness of poems preferred in anthologies, besides the fact that they fill short spaces on the page, is that they take a shorter time to read than other literary forms. The conflation of spatial and temporal measurements in this vocabulary for describing the dimensions of such poems—in different periods called *small, little*, now usually *short*—is an instance of what W. J. T. Mitchell has argued is true of our language in general: "All our temporal language is contaminated by spatial imagery," and, it follows, all our spatial vocabulary has temporal implications. Inescapably, "we speak of 'long' and 'short' times, of 'intervals' (literally 'spaces between'), of 'before' and 'after'—all implicit metaphors which depend upon a mental picture of time as a linear continuum."[25] The conflation of time and space in metaphor, then, conflates our phenomenal and conceptual ways of speaking about them.

This general feature of our language, the argument here claims, is specially visible in writings about anthologies because they are conceptually spatialized in distinctive ways, and because they have practical, physical requirements of space peculiar to their kind of book. An instance is the poet Thomas Campbell's prefatory defense of his *Specimens of the British Poets* of 1819: "Books, it is said, take up little room. In the library this may be the case; but it is not so in the minds and time of those who peruse them."[26] Its main point is that anthologies save time, but the epigrammatic statement of it hints that they also save space by condensing many books into one. Chapter four will show other instances of this argument associated with the uniqueness of the anthology, and with the aesthetic and practical values of its preferred size of poem.

Before the period when interest in classifying informed many vocabularies including the titles of miscellanies and collections, anthologies were presented more colorfully as quasi-mythological spaces. The titles describing them in these enticing terms attracted at least as much if not more attention to the containing books than to what they contained. Some examples are: *The Paradyse of daynty deuises* (1576); *A gorgious Gallery of gallant Inuentions* (1578); *Brittons Bowre of Delights* (1591); *The Arbor of amorous Deuises* (c.1592); *Bel-védere Or The Garden of the Mvses* (1600).[27]

Each of these books is imagined by its title as an idealized space glamorized by its associations with courtly poems and imitations of them, which the anthologies contained. Each is imagined as an enclosure of natural growth shaped by art, a paradisal garden filled with flowers (or posies, a common pun on *poesy*) to delight the viewer. Or it is an encircling arbor, bower, gallery in the garden where courtly or mythological figures are entertained as they are in Sir Philip Sidney's *The Countesse of Pembrokes Arcadia* or Edmund Spenser's *The Faerie Queene*.

Although opened to the reader, these enclosed spaces are at the same time exclusive, adding to their attraction for the fortunate guest (who was in fact a member of a small class able to read and to have access to such books). The book is at once an idealized natural space for the display of its contents and an idealized social gathering place where its readers may share the pleasures enjoyed by fine company. The gatherer of the poems who invented the rationale for those to be included and how to arrange them is the planter and cultivator of the space where they are displayed, and its title an invitation to the reader to enter it.

The self-advertising features of many early anthology titles reflect some uncertainties about the acceptance of such books. Although the large number of them, and in many editions, shows they sold well, there is no clear evidence that as a kind they filled a much respected place in the hierarchy of books where poems might be read. They were not, like Thynne's edited collection of Chaucer, printed in folio, which was the size that granted a book most honor as late as the 1780s when George Crabbe in his poem *The Library* satirized the ranking of books in a social hierarchy headed by the "mighty" or "lordly" folio.[28]

The mythologized pastoral spaces in the titles of Elizabethan and earlier seventeenth-century anthologies went out of fashion with the poems they were borrowed from, to be replaced by more concretely imagined spatial figures that give more emphasis to the book as an object in the physical world. Something like the same awareness may be reflected in John Baskerville's uses of type to suggest—in Bertrand Bronson's view—"marble colonnades" defining architectural spaces in his designs for eighteenth-century title pages.[29] The spaces named in titles of anthologies of this period locate the cultural ideals of post-Restoration society in its actual cultural situations.

The shift in perspective is illustrated in the publisher Dodsley's way of stating his comparison of shaping a book to gardening. In 1748 he wrote to Joseph Spence, it seems with some amusement at his own fancy: "I don't know but I may sometimes be as much entertain'd in planning a Book, as you are in laying the Plan of a Garden," and of all the books he designed, the volumes containing and arranging poems by various authors in various kinds gave him the fullest occasions for this entertainment.[30] He pictured his work space not as a paradisal garden but as a gentleman's plot of ground planted and cultivated to realize the ideal mapped in the owner's plan of it.

It was not at all unusual for titles of verse collections published around the same time as Dodsley's to give off similar signals. They invited their readers to enter a hypothetical but not mythological space that might be actually replicated, if not in their own everyday circumstances, then in social circles they knew about, a form of appeal repeated with variations all through the nineteenth century. This shift in the way the spatial dimensions of these books were conceptualized suggests a change in their social situation, as reading for pleasure in periods of leisure was becoming a more common pastime among more classes.

The concrete localizing of the anthological space can be illustrated if we compare the titles *The Garden of the Muses* of 1610 and *The Muses Library*, compiled by Elizabeth Cooper and published in 1637, when interest among the upper classes in forming private collections of books was full grown. In the earlier title, the space of the anthology is wholly idealized and mythologized; it is filled with immortal flowers. In the second, the fiction is grounded because a library is in fact a place where poems are kept. The *Muses* decorate it as do ornaments on the doorway of the room or building that stand for and compliment what is inside. What is inside the anthology is then described on its title page as if it were a library: "A General Collection of almost all the old valuable Poetry extant, now so industriously enquir'd after, tho' rarely to be found, but in the Studies of the Curious, and affording Entertainment on all Subjects" then listed in categories.[31] In this instance it is possible that the very concreteness of the title figure contributed to the poor success of *The Muses Library*. For although libraries were actual spaces frequented by some members of early eighteenth-century society, there were many others who would not have been likely to imagine themselves in the "Studies of the Curious," reading antiquated poems "From the Saxons to the Reign of King Charles II."

In the titles of eighteenth-century anthologies it was commoner to figure them as places more enticing and imaginatively realizable to more classes of readers than a library. An instance is the title *The Theatre of Ingenuity: Or, The Gentleman's and Lady's Pleasing Recreation and Delightful Pastime at Leisure Hours* of 1704, which invited among its readers would-be gentlemen and ladies who wanted to learn what were the fashionable amusements, reading increasingly among them. Some uneasy sense that the anthology must compete with other places of entertainment, and even other forms of reading may explain the hint in this title that anthologies have the advantage in containing discontinuous, short pieces suited to the desultory mode of reading that had come to be called *dipping*.

By the mid-nineteenth century, the localizing figure of a library had become a persuasive way to imagine an anthology in the changed cultural situation when home libraries on a much humbler scale than the private collections amassed after the Restoration had become familiar and comfortable spaces. The novelist Walter Besant remembered in his *Autobiography* the "small library" of his childhood "provided for me by Fortune!" where he read Pope, Goldsmith, Byron, Wordsworth, and "two volumes, very useful to me, called *Elegant Extracts*."[32] This cultural shift is reflected in the contrast between *The Muses Library* and *The Family Library of British Poetry from Chaucer to the Present Time*, the title of an anthology of 1878.

When titles compared anthologies to spaces that might be actually realized in the reader's world, they located the book itself somewhere in that world. An evidently popular eighteenth-century example, *Wits Cabinet Or, A Companion for Young Men and Ladies*, was first printed in 1684 and in at least seventeen later editions. The fashionable word *cabinet* could in that period refer to a small room or boudoir, usually furnished with books and works of art, or to an ornamental piece of furniture with compartments for the display of books and other curious or precious objects. Here the meaning is not precisely pinned down as it is in *A Cabinet of Choice Jewels* of 1688, but either definition of *cabinet* locates the anthology in a house where readers of different social classes could have, or could imagine having, access to its entertainments. Some titles take a further step in placing the anthology within reach of the reader by telling in the title exactly where in the house, any house, the book might be found: *The Tea-Table Miscellany* (1724); *A Book for a Corner* (1849); *The Fireside Encyclopedia of Poetry* (1878).

The titles of anthologies, examples have illustrated, change with the fashions of their times in more obvious and quite often more exaggeratedly faddish ways than titles for poets' gatherings of their own work (while typical titles for edited collections of single authors have stayed virtually unchanged for centuries). Their continual restyling is another sign of the self-consciousness that attaches to the anthology as a less well established kind of poetry book.

This pattern also shows some uncomfortable sense that anthologies of poetry would have a shorter shelf-life, that it was necessary for them to seize the day. In a letter of 1808, Charles Lamb wrote of having completed "out of old plays at the Museum and out of Dodsley's collection" an anthology titled *Specimens of English Dramatic Poets contemporary with Shakespear*: "Specimens are becoming fashionable. We have—'Specimens of Ancient English Poets,' 'Specimens of Modern English Poets,' 'Specimens of Ancient English Prose Writers' without end. They used to be called 'Beauties.'"[33] Then the fashionable breezes shifted, bringing another style of title: *The Book of Gems* (1836); *Gems of the Modern Poets* and *Gems from American Female Poets* (1842); *Gems of the Poets* (1860); *A Thousand and One Gems of English Poetry* (1867). Both *Specimens* and *Gems* imply the likeness of the containing book to a cabinet where such treasures would be on show, or to a museum displaying rarities or curiosities.

Anthologies changed styles of titling to compete from the beginning with other kinds of poetry collections, but increasingly also among themselves to catch the attention of a growing body of readers with more various as well as more quickly changing reasons for buying books. And capturing attention is a specialty of titles. Their choices of adjectives to describe what the anthology held reflect the typical appeals of their titles to special and varied—to the point of contradictory—interests: *ancient* along with *new*, *modern* poems; nationally important, public *English, British* pieces and also homely, domestic *fireside, family* verse; distinctively tasteful *choice, select, elegant* entries beside *famous, best-known, familiar* poems that have become *household words*; *rare* selections that are not the *representative* or *favorite* pieces to be found in every other anthology.

THE ANTHOLOGIST'S PRESENCE

A partial definition of what makes an anthology is implied by the terms used to classify it and by its distinguishing features as a containing space. A further distinction to be considered in defining this kind of book is the special character of its maker. What is recognizable as an anthology is an assemblage of pieces (usually short): written by more than one or two authors; gathered and chosen to be together in a book by someone who did not write what it contains, or not all; arranged and presented by the compiler according to any number of principles except single authorship, which the nature of the contents rules out. These predications for admission to this special category of book distinguish an anthology from a body of poems put together by their author, and, in a lesser way, from a collection of a single poet's work presented by an editor.

A poet's own self-presentation in a volume like Stevie Smith's *The Frog Prince and Other Poems* can be simply distinguished from an anthology in two of its dimensions. To begin with, it offers, without having to say so in its title or elsewhere, a self-explanatory reason—single authorship—why these poems were put together in one book. Secondly, the style of presentation signals that no compiler other than the poet chose them to be together, decided their arrangement, or made changes in their form. These conditions allow a straightforward identification of a book like Smith's with its contents. It does not have to explain itself *as a book*: that is, it does not have to justify what is in it and what is not; does not have to persuade readers to recognize the authority of whoever made those choices.

Or to state the distinction simply another way, in a collection made by the author of the poems in it there is no other person whose controlling presence is acknowledged and whose decisions mediate between the poems and the reader. Of course we know from experience, and from what has been shown recently by the many invaluable studies of the materiality of the book, that nonlinguistic features like size, format, type face, among many presentational devices are the work of others not the poet, and that they affect our experiences of reading. To borrow D. F. McKenzie's summary of this observation: "the material forms of books, the non-verbal elements of the typographic notations within them, the very disposition of the space itself, have an expressive function in conveying meaning."[34] Still, the relevant point here is that although in all kinds of books including anthologies the designer, compositor, and others contribute to the production, they are not figures we know by name and feel to be actively or personally present as we read. They do not address us directly, even speak to us as anthologists typically do: openly in introductions, headings, annotations; elsewhere without admitting to other performances of their role.

Since the anthologist's decisions about the presentation of the poet's work, and the effects of that mediation on readers' experiences of poems, are among the dominant concerns in this book, I want to give here at the start an illustration (partly hypothetical) of how a reader's responses to a poem can differ depending on the nature of its setting in an anthology. The particular example is an instance of explicit guidance by annotation; the poem is by Elizabeth Bishop, originally titled "Early Sorrow."

Sometime before its publication in *Questions of Travel* she made the radical substitution of the much less directive, even inscrutable title "Sestina":

> September rain falls on the house.
> In the failing light, the old grandmother
> sits in the kitchen with the child
> beside the Little Marvel Stove,
> reading the jokes from the almanac,
> laughing and talking to hide her tears.

Then "The iron kettle sings on the stove" and "the grandmother" drinks from her cup of "dark brown tears" while "the child" watches the kettle's "small hard tears" fall on the stove, and makes a crayon drawing of "a rigid house" and a man in front of it wearing "buttons like tears":

> But secretly, while the grandmother
> busies herself about the stove,
> the little moons fall down like tears
> from between the pages of the almanac
> into the flower bed the child
> has carefully placed in front of the house.

> *Time to plant tears*, says the almanac.
> The grandmother sings to the marvellous stove
> and the child draws another inscrutable house.[35]

The poem has the clear shapes and outlines of a children's book about "the old grandmother" and "the child" who live in "the house." In "the kitchen" are "the Marvel Stove" and "the almanac." They begin to speak, like objects in a fairy tale where, as here, "marvellous" events simply happen and are simply told in the same even tone as are ordinary actions.

The way of telling shifts between, or mixes, two styles. There is the childlike matter-of-factness of repeated article-noun phrases, and a different, more adult manner in descriptive expressions like "failing light," "equinoctial tears," and in the flashes of interpretation of what the grandmother "thinks" that go beyond matters of observable fact.

A parallel mixing of childlike and adult language takes place in Bishop's later poem in *Geography III*, "In the Waiting Room," but with an altogether unlike effect. In it the narrative is in the past tense and first-person of memory, the narrator's memory of a terrifying moment in her childhood. It is geographically located by the poem's opening words, "In Worcester, Massachusetts," and placed in daily experience by the description of the "dentist's waiting room" where a child named Elizabeth waits for her aunt. The last lines date it historically—"The War was on"—and in biographical time—"the fifth/ of February, 1918."[36]

In extreme contrast, "Sestina" is told in the present tense as if by someone at the scene, but in the third person, it seems by no one there. The happenings are suspended in time: "September" (in Bishop's copy of *Questions of Travel* it is crossed out and "October ?" written in) is not a date but an "equinoctial" recurrence, which the repetitions built into the sestina form echo. The actual "house" is as unlocated as "another inscrutable house" in the child's drawing.

The effect is as if the poem itself tells what is happening. It speaks impersonally, unambiguously, "But secretly," in language that is utterly out of the ordinary, like the happenings in the kitchen. We are made to feel the terrible sadness of something unexplained and inexplicable. That silence, which the grandmother covers up, the child does not break, and the telling leaves unfilled, is at the very heart of the poem.

Suppose we had met "Sestina" for the first time in one of the many anthologies where the selection from each author's work is introduced by a biographical annotation, a pattern particularly common in anthologies designed to introduce students to poetry. The practice is generally explained as an informative rather than interpretive contribution by the anthologist to the experience of reading the poems.

The editor of *The Harper Anthology of Poetry*, John Frederick Nims, followed that practice. A poet himself, he considerately sent to living contributors for comment his choice of their poems, with his introduction and notes to them. Before Bishop's entries he wrote: "Miss Bishop's own rephrasing of her biographical note reads as follows [there are no mentions of other contributors having rewritten theirs]:

Born in Massachusetts in 1911 but spent some childhood years with her Canadian grandparents in Nova Scotia. Graduated from Vassar; lived in New York and Key West and later for 17 years in Brazil, translated a volume of modern Brazilian poetry. . . . She has taught briefly at the University of Washington, at Harvard for seven years, and recently at New York University and MIT, one term each.[37]

From this resolutely neutral recital of facts we can conclude that what Bishop excised from Nim's original version was personal material she considered an offense to her habitual reticence and an intrusion on the poems.

Nims faithfully reported that she also rejected his proposed footnotes, in her own words "rather violently," for giving the reader too much direction. Frost made this same complaint to Louis Untermeyer about other anthologists who will not let the "beautiful bare text" speak for itself; Wallace Stevens repeated the objection, in his own style, when he complained to a compiler whose "notes on my poems rather bewig their innocence."[38]

It is likely that the offending biographical material Bishop cut was something like this sentence from the introduction to her poems in Helen Vendler's *The Harvard Book of Contemporary American Poetry*: "Elizabeth Bishop's childhood was spent with her grandparents in Nova Scotia, after her father died and her mother was declared insane."[39] If a first reading of "Sestina" were prepared for by this presentation, readers would easily assume that the biographical facts were given to cast light on the poem for them in advance. If so, the anthologist's sentence would be there to explain what the poem could be said to be about not explaining.

In this setting, the overwhelming sense the poem evokes of something unspoken, agonizingly felt and contained by the form, language, and title of the poem would be likely to dim or to be explained away. Readers would be encouraged to respond to "Sestina" as if it were to be taken the way "In the Waiting Room" invites us to read it, as an adult's recalling of a childhood terror painfully assimilated by the power of memory into the making of the poem, when "Sestina" is a very different, radically odder kind of poem. The introduction to Bishop's poems in *The Longman Anthology of Contemporary American Poetry*, edited by Stuart Freibert and David Young, in fact encourages precisely this misleading response by following the biographical facts about Bishop's parents with the apparently nondirective statement: "Poems like 'Sestina' and 'In the Waiting Room' have a strong biographical basis."[40]

So strong is the sense of the anthologist's guiding presence that it seems impossible to avoid, even by makers of anthologies who try to make it disappear. An illustration of this inescapable situation is *The Rattle Bag*, an anthology published in 1982. Its compilers, Seamus Heaney and Ted Hughes, claimed in their introduction—itself a declaration of their inevitable presence—that the collection "amassed itself," and that they arrived late at the "thought of shaping it":

We hope that our decision to impose an arbitrary alphabetical order allows the contents to discover themselves as we ourselves discovered them—each poem full of its singular appeal, transmitting its own signals, taking its chances in a big, voluble world.[41]

Their hope is not realized in their readers' experience, at least not in mine.

Paradoxically, the supposedly arbitrary (by which the editors seem to have meant unideological) order is itself an idiosyncratic choice, like many of the poems selected, and, like them, calls attention to the anthologists doing the choosing. Beyond that, the conventions of anthologies have habituated readers of them to more explicitly purposeful arrangements, so that we automatically register contrived connections among the choices of poems, and attribute them to some intelligence rather than to the mechanism of chance. This happens as soon as a reader opens *The Rattle Bag* to the first three alphabetized entries: "Adieu, farewell earth's bliss," "After his death," "Afterwards."

Since a collection of a poet's work made by an editor has in common with an anthology that both books are presented by someone who did not write the contents, the figure of the editor was from the beginning of printed anthologies a model for the maker of a verse collection by various hands. While the early compilers of anthologies were identified as the printer or publisher (often titles for the same person), soon after they were called editors: the *OED* gives 1649 for the first use of *editor*, but no instances of *anthologist* until the early nineteenth century.

Tottel, as it has become accepted practice to call the compiler of *Songes and Sonettes*, could look to a few editors of English poets, mainly of Chaucer, who set an example for what the maker of a verse collection might do. In 1532 in William Thynne's *The workes of Geffray Chaucer*, the presence of the editor was visible in many features that are repeated in Tottel's anthology. The editor was responsible for prefatory remarks presenting himself as the gatherer of the book's contents; for ordering the entries and giving headings or endnotes to articulate their arrangement; for fashioning titles given to separate pieces; and for listing the contents in a table (in all editions of *Songes and Sonettes* after the first).

In the first sections of *Songes and Sonettes* given separately to Surrey and Wyatt, the compiler acted as an editor. That is, it seems he tried to gather and arrange all the poems—never before collected in print—that he could find by each of these poets (he added at the end of the book some presumably found after the first arrangement was made); grouped them separately, roughly according to formal kinds; and gave a title to every one of the entries attributed to each poet. In the section at the end of *Songes and Sonettes* consisting of a miscellaneous gathering of separate pieces by many unidentified authors, the compiler acted as an anthologist.

Although the sections are markedly different in these ways, all through the book the compiler reproduced poems according to his own ideas of how their texts should be presented. This practice suggests that he had another model in the copyist, who transcribed poems by any number of authors into a commonplace book, rather than the editor of a printed collection of a single poet's work. In this new venture of printing the work of many poets together, Tottel conflated the different procedures of the editor and the copyist.

English editors in the early sixteenth century, aiming to gain for their authors public recognition as classics, tried to match the more formal care that continental humanist editions had given to presenting ancient authors. Thynne, for "loue to my countrey," set out to recover Chaucer's writings and to restore their texts free of the "many errours, falsyties and depraua-cions" that defaced them in previous versions.[42] By contrast, the manuscript collection was a private space (whether the copyist was the owner wanting to preserve poems that interested him, or a paid scribe). This character made its contents personal property and encouraged more freedom in the way the copyist reproduced a poem than was typically exercised by editors.

The compiler of *Songes and Sonettes* was not interested in reproducing the poems in it, not those attributed to Surrey and Wyatt any more than the anonymous entries, according to even the relatively lax standards of authenticity and accuracy that operated in English editing of this period. Instead, the anthologist acted freely as an adapter, a modernizer, whose ren-derings involved restructuring poems, regularizing meter, smoothing out grammatical ambiguities and archaisms, and bringing vocabulary up to date.

Such freedoms with the poems in both sections of *Songes and Sonettes* suggest that the maker of it, like the owner of a manuscript collection, con-sidered it his book, but with the difference that while the private collector shaped his gathering to suit his own taste, the anthologist could justify his selection and arrangement of its contents only by its appeal to his imagined readers.

These days readers are likely to be surprised by the ways the texts of po-ems in early English anthologies were handled. Much more surprising is that such mistreatments went on being perpetrated even long after vastly stricter notions of textual authenticity and editorial accuracy were firmly in place. These continuing abuses by anthologists of the poems in their charge will be illustrated and discussed in detail in Chapter 3. The usefulness of mentioning them here is to support the point that the compiler of an an-thology does not do all the kinds of work that we think of as defining an editor, indeed has often acted in ways counter to editorial standards, even while anthologists have often called themselves *editor* in their prefaces, and many are so described on title pages.

Palgrave made this distinction in performance in a letter of 1863 in re-sponse to objections to his omission of a stanza from a poem by Shelley in

The Golden Treasury: "If Shelley had lived to give an authentic edition of his works, or if I were printing one, or quoting the poem as a part of his biography, I should not think of omitting stanza v."[43] His justification as anthologist (though he called himself "editor" in the preface) was that without the omission, Shelley's poem would not have fitted into "the class of poems which Tennyson and I wished to unite in the selection."[44]

The distinction between the anthologist's role and the editor's or the author's is expressed in the titles of their different kinds of book. Titles for edited collections to this day copy the paradigm used by Thynne, stating what the contents are and naming their author in the third person to signal the presence of an editor. Titles for books of poems put together by their author mostly focus on their contents: on their formal variety, as in *Eglogs, Epytaphes, and Sonettes*; on their formal unity, as in *Pastorals*, or *Sonnets from the Portuguese*, or *Observations*; on their unifying interest, such as *Men and Women, Modern Love, Seeing Things*; on some metaphor for the poems like *Amoretti, Poetical Blossoms, Leaves of Grass, Black Magic*.[45] By contrast, soon after Tottel's venture, it became the convention for the form of title used for an anthology to characterize it as a containing space inseparable from, but not identifiable with, its content.

CHAPTER TWO

THE DISPOSITION OF THE SPACE

Selection and arrangement are the broadest signals of the anthologist's role and presence, as Palgrave was the first to realize fully in both senses of *realizing*. That is, he was the first maker of such a collection to be aware of the richest possibilities built into these functions, and the first to make them work in an anthology as finely tuned instruments for educating readers of poetry, even perhaps the makers of it. It is of course not coincidental that he came to these realizations at the time when anthologies had accumulated their own history and tradition, which allowed them to be accepted among respectable sources of poetry by its most educated readers, and welcomed as the usual and perhaps only place where the less experienced looked for poems they would enjoy. This situation encouraged the multiplication of anthologies in a variety of forms, while it raised the self-consciousness of their makers. Their uneasiness intensified with the triumph of *The Golden Treasury*.

PREFATORY CLAIMS

In the nineteenth century it became virtually obligatory for the maker of an anthology to open it with an apology for inflicting another such book on readers of poetry, an apology that had then to be turned into a self-justifying explanation of the new anthology's reason for being. Such a conventional justification opens the preface to the philologist Richard Chenevix Trench's *A Household Book of English Poetry*, published seven years after the first appearance of Palgrave's *The Golden Treasury of the Best Songs and Lyrical Poems in the English Language* in 1861. Trench's was the earliest collection after that shaping event in the history of anthologies to take itself, and to be taken, seriously enough (Palgrave called it "excellent" in his own preface to *The Treasury of Sacred Song* in 1889) to be worthy of comparison with *The Golden Treasury*.[1]

In presenting his book, Trench felt the need to add to the expected general apology a special excuse for making a new anthology after Palgrave's, a particular formula of justification which itself became a convention for anthologies to come. His preface begins with the "first question which I asked myself," which was "whether Mr. Palgrave's *Golden Treasury* had not so occupied the ground that there was no room for one who should come after. ... But if Mr. Palgrave had not forestalled me, I certainly did not feel that any other had done so."[2]

His claim to deserve a share of "the ground" was that he did not limit his entries to one particular kind of poetry, that he did not exclude poems by living authors, that of more than three hundred of his chosen pieces, fewer than seventy duplicated Palgrave's. Even well into the twentieth century, "Palgrave" (his name eventually came to be used as a metonym for his book) was still the point of reference in justifications of new anthologies.

Ferdinand Earle, the editor of *The Lyric Year* (1912), set his collection apart from the "famous series of Francis T. Palgrave's" for the then novel reason that, of its "three hundred and thirty-nine poems, covering over three centuries, only five pieces are credited to women—whereas their work constitutes more than forty per cent. of this collection."[3] In 1914 Ernest Rhys blatantly appropriated Palgrave's title for *The New Golden Treasury of Songs and Lyrics* in order to advertise his anthology as "a companion book to the old *Golden Treasury*, ranging farther back in time and farther forward, and adding many poets who have enriched the lyric tongue, omitted in those pages."[4] T. Earle Welby explained that his borrowing from Palgrave's title for *The Silver Treasury of English Lyrics* (1925) did not reflect an intention to revise or "supersede" but merely to supplement his model: "My hope is, simply, that the possessor of Palgrave and of this book may feel he has as much of the best of English lyrical poetry as can be put between the covers of two small volumes."[5]

Later editors located their collections in relation to Palgrave's directly or by references to Quiller-Couch's most famous imitation of it. An instance is Louis Untermeyer's "excuse for thrusting yet another anthology upon the world" in the preface to *The Book of Living Verse* (1932): "I am, naturally, conscious of my debt . . . especially to Palgrave's *The Golden Treasury* and Quiller-Couch's *The Oxford Book of English Verse*" which "revalued Palgrave's collection." Untermeyer's "canons" for the selection of poems were

Palgrave's (as indeed were Quiller-Couch's).[6] Helen Gardner implied the need to bring *The New Oxford Book of English Verse* of 1972 up to date by calling attention to the fact that Quiller-Couch's two previous books in the series had their roots in a century-old model: "the most famous of Victorian anthologies, Palgrave's *Golden Treasury*."[7]

Other editors could avoid having to circumvent Palgrave's pre-eminence by simply reprinting his anthology in its entirety, adding their own introduction and supplementary section of poems by authors living after the closing date of around 1850 originally set by Palgrave. C. Day Lewis brought out an edition of this kind in 1954 (reprinted in 1973), justifying it in his own short introduction on the grounds that "Ninety years later, it ["Palgrave"] still holds its own among the flood of anthologies which have followed it" as a "selection of poems which as a whole transcends literary foibles and fashions, giving the reader the delight that comes from seeing something superlatively well done."[8] Essentially similar expanded reprints using Palgrave's title were brought out by Laurence Binyon in 1924, by Oscar Williams in 1953, by John Press in 1964 and 1994 (along with many editions advertising extended notes for use in schools, such as Walter Barnes's *Palgrave's Golden Treasury* of 1915).[9]

The decision of these twentieth-century editors to preserve Palgrave's own selection and arrangement a century later reflects a sense of *The Golden Treasury* as something more than an anthology or a piece of criticism, although of course it is both, but as a work of literature with an integrity of its own. C. Day Lewis suggested as much in his introduction, speaking of Palgrave's supreme gift as an anthology maker: "A satisfying arrangement of poems requires a special talent which can be fairly called 'creative.'"[10] Ricks brought out *The Golden Treasury* in 1991 in an annotated edition of the kind usually devoted to work by a single author rather than a gatherer of many.[11]

This chapter will consider Palgrave's gathering of poems as an imaginative creation as well as a remarkable event in the history of criticism. It will focus on the first edition, which displays Palgrave's designs in their original and clearest form, above all in his arrangement of poems in each of the four books. In 1883, in the earliest of his three revised editions, he added thirteen entries, probably in response to specific suggestions from friends and to meet criticisms of the first edition, for instance by adding a poem each by Blake and Smart, who had been excluded from it.

All the added poems were printed together in chronological sequence at the back of the volume, just after the last poem of the last book and continuing its numbering without a break. In the revised editions of 1890 and 1891, Palgrave gave up this odd format and inserted each of the much more numerous additions (eventually there were sixty, while ten entries were cut out) into the appropriate space in the order established for each book in 1861.

In the 1883 edition there is a hint in the paragraph Palgrave appended at the end of the original preface that the curious handling of the added poems was entirely in the interest of leaving the original arrangement of the anthology undisturbed. Paying tribute to the recommendations from friends and to reprints of "rare early writers" for poems to include, he explained his reasons for deciding to include so few new choices: "To have added all these pieces" would not only have made "a cumbrous enlargement," but would have given "a novel aspect to the selection."[12] This seems to suggest that what the maker of *The Golden Treasury* valued was not only the quality and range of the poetry it contained but also its arrangement according to his carefully considered original design.

Palgrave's preface to *The Golden Treasury* in the first edition opens with the conventional self-justifying claim that this "little Collection differs, it is believed, from others," one difference in the claim itself being that it is true.[13] His modest wording—"little Collection," "it is believed"—is also conventional, but the four short pages of the preface staking out the grounds of difference show Palgrave first subtly and then boldly making large claims for his book, fully confident of its distinguishing excellences.

This confidence was entirely justified, as even his early readers could recognize. In the words of the usually cantankerous critic John Churton Collins: "it would hardly be an exaggeration to say that the appearance of the *Golden Treasury of Songs and Lyrics* in 1861 initiated an era in popular taste."[14] We would expect this kind of statement to be reserved for the work of a greatly original artist.

The first of the two carefully crafted sentences that make up the opening paragraph of Palgrave's preface compresses several differences between this anthology and "others" politely unspecified:

This little Collection differs, it is believed, from others in the attempt made to include in it all the best original Lyrical pieces and Songs in our language, by writers not living,—and none beside the best.[15]

As a gathering of poems at once inclusive and selective, it offered a unique combination of advantages. It had the historical scope of comprehensive anthologies (though it was not as inclusive as "[Alexander] Chalmers' vast collection," *The Works of the English Poets* (1810), the only source Palgrave named in the preface along with "the best Anthologies of different periods").[16] At the same time, its focus on one kind of poem allowed it to fit into an elegant and convenient "little" volume (Chalmers's filled twenty-one), while its admission of "none beside the best" allowed it to escape the indiscriminateness of the many contemporaneous popular anthologies like Charles Mackay's *The Home Affections* (1858) and *Gems from the Poets Illustrated* (1860).

It was this difference of selectivity between *The Golden Treasury* and its less fastidious contemporaries that earned it the most praise in the nineteenth century, for instance from Churton Collins:

Whoever will turn to nine out of the ten Anthologies, most in vogue before 1861, will understand, that the same instinct which in the Dark Ages led man to prefer Sedulius and Avitus to Catullus and Horace, Statius to Virgil, and Hroswitha to Terence, led these editors to analogous selections.[17]

The second sentence of Palgrave's opening paragraph begins as if it were going to be a conventional self-defense against the accusation often aimed at anthologies, that this one includes many poems readers will inevitably have found in other such books:

Many familiar verses will hence be met with; many also which should be familiar:—the Editor will regard as his fittest readers those who love Poetry so well, that he can offer them nothing not already known and valued.[18]

Skillfully, what might be an apology turns into another claim for the book's special character: that it will satisfy a range of readers.

The "fittest" described in this sentence would be those who would recognize here Palgrave's revision of Milton's claim to have "fit audience . . . though few" (*P.L.* VII, 31). They would be readers educated in the same classical tradition as Palgrave himself, who could recognize and translate the untranslated and unidentified fragment from Euripides added as an epigraph to the volume in the printing of December 1861, and the mottoes from Virgil proposed for each section which, Palgrave noted in the manuscript, Macmillan wanted to omit "lest they should give the book a learned look."[19] These readers would be prepared to enjoy the pleasure of recognition in meeting their favorite poems conveniently gathered unmixed with dross, and the satisfaction of having their own judgments confirmed by an editor at home in the classical and literary culture they themselves were brought up in.

Palgrave's substitution of "fittest" for Milton's "fit" could be taken simply for snobbish exclusiveness, but turns into an invitation to readers of different social classes, differently educated. That is, the grammatical superlative "fittest" implies that he expected several sorts of readers, all in some sense *fit* but some, comparatively, *fitter* than others (in contrast with the more homogeneous audience for retrospective anthologies in the eighteenth century). Besides those readers who shared the gentleman's education to be had at public and some grammar schools and at the two universities, Palgrave's anthology addresses a smaller, more highly learned group who would "take up the book in a serious and scholarly spirit," but also others of a very much more numerous class who respect a classical education without having experienced it.[20]

These are the readers who would enlarge their understanding of poetry with the help of Palgrave's notes glossing mythological references ("*Amphion's lyre*," "*twins of Jove*") and explicating figures of speech ("*Time's chest*" "*Nature's Eremite*"); who might be helped by his selection and commentary to recognize "highwrought and conventional Elizabethan Pastoralism" or the "simple pathos" mixed in with the "mannerism" of William Cowper's verse.[21] The range of readers, according to Palgrave's expressed hope in the dedication to the anthology, might even include those he uneasily hypostatized there as "Labour" and "Poverty."[22]

Whether or not that vague hope was quite realized, it is another sign of uniqueness that Palgrave's anthology attempted to fulfill it, showing respect for readers of every degree of fitness by offering those of each kind what might enhance their enjoyment, and doing so without condescension. In the preface he said that he had "found the vague general verdict of popular Fame more just than those have thought, who, with too severe a criticism, would confine judgments on Poetry to 'the selected few of many generations.'"[23]

Availability to all these hoped-for readers was made possible by the modest price of *The Golden Treasury*, which originally sold, and sold astonishingly well, for 4s 6d (by contrast, for instance, with a volume of a single poet's new verse such as Elizabeth Browning's popular *Aurora Leigh*, which cost 12s in 1856).[24]

The appearance of the volume was also finely calibrated to appeal specially to certain groups of readers without putting off any. It was a pleasing size to hold and carry, bound in dark cloth, the face of the cover framed in two gold lines with Macmillan's emblematic medallion in the middle. On its title page was its only illustration, a vignette portraying in simple lines a naked youth playing a pipe, seated on a grassy knoll, a dog at this feet, a tree behind him with a bird perched among its branches.

The looks of the anthology defined it in contrast with a popular collection like Mackay's *The Home Affections* (1858), which its compiler's introduction addressed to "the most refined and fastidious as well as to the simple tastes of those who are not critical, provided their hearts be touched and their generous sentiments aroused."[25] This was a larger volume than Palgrave's, with an ornamental design in an elaborate frame on its cover; a full-page frontispiece like an illustration in a ladies' magazine, showing young lovers in vaguely medieval or Elizabethan dress on a grassy spot arched over by a tree, the youth piping to the maiden; the text sprinkled with other illustrations (the title page advertised one hundred engravings) ranging from stormy landscapes to cozy scenes of mid-Victorian family life such as parents reading to children at the parlor table. In a deliberate contrast of styles, *The Golden Treasury* represented classical simplicity that avoided both ostentation and pedantry. Plainly, it was classy without being expensive.

There must have been varieties among its readers to account for their numbers, or so Palgrave's daughter was convinced:

The first edition of the 'Golden Treasury' . . . was recognized from the beginning as the best anthology of its kind. . . . There is no doubt that this little book has taught many—in all ranks of life—to know and love much of our best lyrical poetry which might otherwise have always remained untrodden ground.[26]

Certainly the reception of *The Golden Treasury* was remarkable: four printings the year it came out; twenty-four more before the end of the century; countless reprintings and expansions since.

The claims to difference that Palgrave made for the anthology in the opening of its preface are cloaked in conventional modesty that disappears altogether in the penultimate paragraph where he made his grandest claim for his collection's uniqueness (which he took out of the preface in 1883):

In the arrangement, the most poetically-effective order has been attempted. . . . within each book the pieces have therefore been arranged in gradations of feeling or subject. The development of the symphonies of Mozart and Beethoven has been here thought of as a model, and nothing placed without careful considera-tion. And it is hoped that the contents of this Anthology will thus be found to present a certain unity, 'as episodes,' in the noble language of Shelley, 'to that great Poem which all poets, like the cooperating thoughts of one great mind, have built up since the beginning of the world.'[27]

Here the anthology is not a "little Collection" but a finished and unified work of art, modeled not merely on symphonic form but, astonishingly, on heroic symphonies, and taking its place in the "great" tradition of poetry. This anthologist's role is not to compile but to compose. He is not an editor but an author, and his *Treasury* itself has the essential qualities required of each piece allowed a space in it: "the most poetically-effective order," "unity," "an arrangement" with the aim of "pleasure, and the Wisdom which comes through Pleasure."

In a letter of 1862 to Sir Alexander Grant, Palgrave hid his pride of achievement in his "little Anthology" behind a playfully off-hand man-ner—"I hope you liked the arrangement and my notes &c. In this sort of paste-and-scissors authorship these trifles are all one can call one's own"— but "authorship" gives him away in spite of the conventional self-depreca-tion of his "trifles."[28]

An unidentified reviewer of *The Golden Treasury* writing within a few months of its first printing called it "the most precious casket that ever ac-companied traveller in his roamings, or laid beside the pillow, or on the ta-ble at home."[29] His enthusiasm was grounded in the recognition that "Mr. Palgrave's labour has not been that of an ordinary compiler" because of his choice to print "entire pieces" rather than the snippets found in "a common volume of 'Beauties' or 'Elegant Extracts,'" and because of his care in weighing the value of each chosen piece on "golden scales." The review merely mentions the arrangement of the contents, describing it briefly by virtually repeating Palgrave's own words in the preface.

The focus of praise on the quality of the selections is typical of remarks about *The Golden Treasury* in its own time, unsurprisingly since the choice of its entries was guided by Tennyson (the one among his three advisers to whom Palgrave submitted each poem for final judgment). It reflected mid-Victorian taste in poetry, also largely shaped by Tennyson, at its most discriminating.

What still makes *The Golden Treasury* one of a kind is the brilliant originality of its arrangement, about which there have been no detailed discussions, but only some sentences of generalized praise. The fullest comment is by C. Day Lewis in the introduction to his expanded edition of Palgrave's collection:

His grouping of his material into successive but overlapping themes, within the period that each of his four books covers, was done with great delicacy, is never obtrusive, and enables the reader both to get more from individual poems and to receive general impressions about the style and poetic interest of each period.[30]

The only observation about the placing of particular poems still seems to be one by Matthew Arnold, who admired Palgrave's "plan of arrangement which he devised for that work," especially in "the juxtaposition, in pursuance of it, of two such pieces as those of Wordsworth and Shelley" ("My heart leaps up" and "O World! O Life! O Time!") that shows "a delicacy of feeling in these matters which is quite indisputable and very rare."[31]

THE ARRANGEMENT

Palgrave described in his preface the division of the collection into four books measuring the passage of time from the second quarter of the sixteenth century to about 1616; then to 1700; to 1800; and through the first half of the nineteenth century. The divisions, though marked off by convenient dates, are justified by the distinguishing "character" given each of them successively by Shakespeare, Milton, Gray, and Wordsworth. While the books are in temporal order, within each the poems are not arranged in "rigidly chronological sequence," but "in gradations of feeling or subject," to reflect "the natural growth and evolution of our Poetry," creating an organic "unity" rather than tracing a linear path.[32]

Implied are contrasts on the one hand with strictly chronological anthologies such as Campbell's *Specimens of the British Poets* (1819) and John Aiken's *Select Works of the British Poets* (1826); on the other with more popular collections arranged by topic, for instance Mackay's *The Home Af-*

fections. The first of this type serious enough to aim at historical range while rejecting the merely chronological model was *The Household Book of Poetry* of 1858, edited by the American journalist Charles Anderson Dana.

In Dana's preface he made the obligatory claim to difference:

The editor . . . flatters himself that in classifying so many immortal productions of genius according to their own ideas and motives, rather than according to their chronology, the nativity and sex of their authors, or any other merely external order, he has exhibited the incomparable richness of our language in this department of literature, quite as successfully as if he had followed a method more usual in such collections.[33]

Following the preface is an index of the topics such as "Nature," "Childhood," "Imagination," "Sentiment and Reflection," with poems listed alphabetically by title under each topic, while in the text entries are grouped according to more narrow categories, mixed out of chronological order. Among "Poems of Nature" on facing pages under the running head "Early Summer" are entries by—in this order—Beaumont and Fletcher, Denis Florence McCarthy, Alexander Montgomery, Wordsworth, Anonymous about 1250, William Motherwell. Grouping poems in this fashion to fit their compiler's chosen categories—several of Dana's are borrowed from Wordsworth—of common "ideas and motives" is as obviously a "merely external order" as is a sequence based on the date of birth of their authors or any other such single, simple principle of arrangement.

If Palgrave did have in mind any model for his different way to order the entries in an anthology, it was one he carefully left unmentioned in his preface. In 1860 the poet William Allingham had published under a pseudonym a gathering of slightly more than two hundred poems he had been working on for at least five years: *Nightingale Valley. A Collection, Including a Great Number of the Choicest Lyrics and Short Poems in the English Language.* Palgrave had seen Allingham's book, we learn from a letter written by their mutual friend Thomas Woolner, a sculptor and poet who was one of the judges of entries for *The Golden Treasury*, who invented its brilliant title and designed the vignette for its title page.[34] Woolner wrote in 1860 to Tennyson's wife that "Palgrave called in this evening; he is busy reading all the Poets for the purpose of making a collection to publish which he intends to beat that of Allingham."[35]

Nightingale Valley may have been a partial model for Palgrave's anthology both for its focus on *The Choicest Lyrics and Short Poems* and for ideas about arrangement suggested in Allingham's preface to this "little volume": "an arrangement of a limited number of short poems with some eye to grouping and general effect" aimed only to "delight."[36] This description of the arrangement makes it sound casual and uninsistent, and indeed it seems to be. The entries appear in the sequence listed in the table of contents with no divisions to suggest chronological or topical order, following one another in a flow of pleasing associations.

The anthology opens, as befits its title, with Milton's sonnet "To the Nightingale," where a lover invokes the bird to sing before night silences its "liquid notes that close the eye of day." Next, in a poem by Joanna Baillie, a lover exhorts his lady to rise and greet the day: "Up! quit thy bower, late wears the hour, / Long have the rooks caw'd round the tower; / O'er flower and tree loud hums the bee." Then comes Samuel Coleridge's "Inscription / For a Fountain on a Heath" where we hear again the "hum of murmuring bees!" A poem by Thomas Hood and the anonymous anthology-piece "Sic Vita" are followed by Wordsworth's sonnet upon sonnets ("Nuns fret not"), a seemingly abrupt shift in focus and in diction, except that again "bees" are heard to "murmur by the hour in foxglove bells." Linkings of this kind appear intermittently, with what seem like medleys interposed among them, so that the "general effect" is pleasantly idiosyncratic and therefore arbitrary, an expression of the anthologist's personal pleasure in browsing.

Since Palgrave thought Allingham's collection worth challenging, he must have found its selection attractive—eventually he included close to fifty of his rival's choices in the first edition of *The Golden Treasury*—and its placing of poems suggestive. Even so, arbitrariness, whether of topics or of personal preferences, is precisely what he set himself to avoid, at least in appearance. While adapting groupings like some of Allingham's to his own design, he tried to save his readers from the rather bewildering impression of serendipity that *Nightingale Valley* risks.

This undesirable effect seems to have been specifically in Palgrave's mind when in his preface he explained his own decision to divide entries in sections:

The English mind has passed through phases of thought and cultivation so various and so interopposed during these three centuries of Poetry, that a rapid passage between Old and New, like rapid alteration of the eye's focus in looking at the landscape, will always be wearisome and hurtful to the sense of Beauty.[37]

By Palgrave's different decision to distribute poetry of three centuries in books marking off sweeps of time generous enough to show large differences, he hoped the poems could be seen to express interests and features reflecting historical processes of "natural growth and evolution." In ordering poems within those books by a different, atemporal principle, their "gradations of feeling or subject," his aim was to show their shared interests and characteristics in multiple, overlapping details of language.[38] That way, the reasons for their positioning could seem to have been generated from within. At the same time each poem would be seen to belong to a historical context created by the connections its inherent qualities make with the poems around it in the same book. Each poem, each book, the whole of *The Golden Treasury* would then reflect the "evolution" of English poetry, a process not arbitrary but inevitable.

To begin with, this intensely self-conscious design depends for its effectiveness, paradoxically, on its appearance of self-effacing simplicity. After Palgrave's very short preface is a table of contents which lists the four books by number only, but not their contents. Then the self-styled "editor" seems to remove himself, not reappearing until the notes, which the reader would come to after some three hundred pages of verse closed with a kind of colophon, "End of the Golden Treasury." At the very back are an index of authors, with their entries otherwise identified only by page and the Roman numeral above each in the text, followed by a separate index solely of first lines.

This postponement of explicit editorial guidance except for the brief prefatory apologia was a silent revolt against the conventional plan of nineteenth-century anthologies, which dictated that they list their entries in advance. Presumably, that format was for the convenience of possible buyers who would want a preview of what they might be getting, and for readers who would enjoy browsing, one of them being Woolner. He described in a letter his own enjoyment of anthologies, of being able to "dip from gem to gem without the trouble of getting up to take books down from the shelves," which was one of the often advertised conveniences of such books that determined their conventional format.[39]

Besides the prefixed table of authors and poems, anthologists often prepared readers by a critical or historical survey of the span of poetry their collections included, either in an introduction or in summaries heading each group of entries. Palgrave delayed that kind of guidance by placing his brief summaries of the four sections that divide the poems at the back of the volume, as lead-paragraphs for the notes to each section. Since the radically abridged table of contents gave no preliminary clue to that plan, readers first looking into *The Golden Treasury* would not have thought to start by turning to the back pages for summaries to guide them through the collection.

FRAMING POEMS

This unexpected spatial arrangement seems designed to allow an unmediated experience of reading poetry—"she speaks best for herself," Palgrave said in closing the preface—as if the reader were a house-guest left alone to enjoy the host's private library.[40] By analogy with this social situation, the reader opens *The Golden Treasury* to page one, to find without further preliminary "Book First," Roman numeral I, and the title "Spring" above three four-line stanzas signed below "T. Nash," as they might have been in a sixteenth-century gentleman's commonplace book:

> Spring, the sweet Spring, is the year's pleasant king;
> Then blooms each thing, then maids dance in a ring,
> Cold doth not sting, the pretty birds do sing,
>   Cuckoo, jug-jug, pu-we, to-witta-woo!
>
> The palm and may make country houses gay,
> Lambs frisk and play, the shepherds pipe all day,
> And we hear aye birds tune this merry lay,
>   Cuckoo, jug-jug, pu-we, to-witta-woo!
>
> The fields breathe sweet, the daisies kiss our feet,
> Young lovers meet, old wives a sunning sit,
> In every street these tunes our ears do greet,
>   Cuckoo, jug-jug, pu-we, to-witta-woo!
>   Spring! the sweet Spring!

This choice of opening poem is as fresh as the poem itself, which makes no other demands than that the reader be delighted and amused by it, as it seems to be delighted and amused by its own sweetly knowing simplicity. It is not an anthology-piece that readers would recognize, or a poem by an

author whose work would inevitably be included among English classics—
for instance Spenser or Sidney, who were trotted out to open Elizabethan
collections for the enticement of readers. The reader is left, with as little apparent guidance as possible from prior knowledge or editorial intrusion, to
experience the verses immediately, on their own terms.

Besides its unencumbered immediacy, this first poem, without carrying
much conceptual weight of its own, serves several more of Palgrave's designs. The most obvious is that it opens *The Golden Treasury* the way the
mythologized natural world of pastoral begins, in "sweet Spring," an analogy expanded in the next, little-known poem, "Summons to Love" (II),
which starts up the morning: "Phoebus, arise!"; "Spread forth thy golden
hair"; "The clouds with orient gold spangle their blue." The world of the
Golden Age is invoked by a vocabulary that unifies the first book, and in its
later transformations the whole of Palgrave's collection.

This consistency is a reflection of both personal and mid-Victorian
taste, but Palgrave, apparently trying to avoid the impression of arbitrary
preference, offered a more general, even philosophical justification for it by
conceptualizing the pastoral harmony among the selections all through his
anthology in a sentence on the first page of the notes (in editions before
1890):

Great Excellence, in human art as in human character, has from the beginning
of things been even more uniform than Mediocrity, by virtue of the closeness of
its approach to Nature:—and so far as the standard of Excellence kept in view
has been attained in this volume, a comparative absence of extreme or temporary
phases in style, a similarity of tone and manner, will be found throughout:—
something neither modern nor ancient, but true in all ages, and like the works
of Creation, perfect as on the first day.[41]

Nashe's poem opens Book I in a way that coincides with another of
Palgrave's conceptual schemes as he described it in the notes. Elizabethan
poetry, he said there, exhibits "a wide range of style;—from simplicity
expressed in a language hardly yet broken in to verse, through the pastoral
fancies and Italian conceits" to poems by Shakespeare and William Drummond where "the 'purple light of Love' is tempered by a spirit of sterner
reflection."[42]

The style of naively artless simplicity typical of popular songs and ballads of the period is not actually represented among his selections, but Nashe's stanzas are a playful imitation of such a song. The poem placed at the end of the first book fits more closely Palgrave's description of the "spirit of sterner reflection" that brings the Elizabethan period to a close: a sonnet by Drummond (LXI) that closes both book and period with the darkened pastoral refrain of "echoes . . ./Rung from their flinty caves, Repent! Repent!"

The way the summary of the period maps out the general plan of the book is unmistakable. At the same time it is played down because the reader experiences the poems first in no announced or visibly explicit arrangement, and only later the explanatory description of their order. In its delayed position, the summary is offered as an account of poems in an already existing, as it were natural pattern which the compiler of the notes has discovered, rather than presenting itself as an outline of his making that he then put the poems in place to exemplify.

While first and last poems mark off the periods they frame, they also show continuities with other books. Book II opens, as Book I closes, with a Christian poem, Milton's "Ode/On the Morning of Christ's Nativity" (LXII). It is at the same time, like Nashe's song, a poem of beginnings, though the new season it celebrates is not "sweet Spring" but "winter wild," when "Nature . . . /Had doff'd her gaudy trim," as if laying aside the fictions of pastoral. The ode has replaced the song to reproduce the sound of "heaven's deep organ" rather than the piping of shepherds and the merry tunes of birds, but its music reinvokes the golden pastoral world transformed by "that Light unsufferable" of the Incarnation: "For if such holy song/Enwrap our fancy long,/Time will run back, and fetch the age of gold."

The rich pattern of connections made by this choice of first poem coincides with Palgrave's summarizing note on Book II, the "latter eighty years of the seventeenth century," which experienced "the close of our Early poetical style" in Milton, and "the commencement of the Modern" in Dryden, whose "Alexander's Feast, Or, the Power of Music" ends Book II.[43] Even so, chronology does not strictly dictate the disposition of poems within this frame: "Ode/On the Morning of Christ's Nativity" is immediately followed by Dryden's "Song for Saint Cecilia's Day, 1687," and "Alexander's Feast" is immediately preceded by Milton's "At a Solemn Music" in order to show how their "splendid Odes" together "exhibit the wider and grander range which years and experience of the struggles of the time conferred on Poetry."[44]

Continuity and difference are more simply represented in the opening poem of Book III, Gray's smoothly measured—in the vocabulary of Palgrave's note "cultivated"—"Ode on the Pleasure Arising from Vicissitude" (CXVII). Pastoral nature is reawakened—"Now the golden Morn aloft/ Waves her dew-bespangled wing"—making the poem clearly parallel to the openings of the two earlier books, but with Nashe's exuberance and Milton's power muted by the distancing poetic diction that gives the ode what it calls "A melancholy grace."[45]

A less graceful melancholy note is struck in the last poem of this third book, Anna Laetitia Barbauld's "Life! I know not what thou art," while in between are a few groupings—political or heroic poems, poems titled with common names like "John Anderson"—more disparate and discrete than many of the sequences elsewhere, which are bound together by more intricate affinities. Palgrave in his summarizing note confessed to this difference between Book III and the others. He found it "more difficult to characterize the English Poetry of the eighteenth century than any other," not because he was guilty of accepting the prevailing clichés that it is "artificial" or "tame and wanting in originality," but because of its "varieties in style," its "diversities in aim," and its "subjects so far apart."[46]

The pattern of framing poems set in the first three books makes Palgrave's choice of opening entry for the last book the most surprising, even though the poem was already well enough known to be a likely entry in an anthology: Keats's "On First Looking into Chapman's Homer" (CLVI). Readers following the order that unfolds in *The Golden Treasury* would have more reason to expect one among the many poems in Book IV that invoke, celebrate, or reflect on nature's beginnings in a vocabulary rich in continuities with earlier pastoral poems such as Wordworth's "Ode On Intimations of Immortality from Recollections of Early Childhood" (placed just before the closing poem of Book IV). In a critical article published the year after *The Golden Treasury*, Palgrave chose that ode to represent the "household delights" provided to mid-Victorian readers by Wordsworth's "favoured generation" of poets.[47] Instead, the more unlikely choice of Keats's sonnet gives the reader of Palgrave's anthology, who comes on it in its unexpected place, a surprise analogous to the traveler's in the poem who hears Chapman's Homer for the first time.

In Keats's title, "First" makes one connection of the sonnet with the entries in the parallel spaces in earlier books as another poem of beginnings. A reader of *The Golden Treasury* who has reached the beginning of Book IV would be prepared to recognize an analogy between that initiating passage into the spatial territory of the book and the poet's journey in the sonnet: "Much have I travell'd in the realms of gold." The associations of "gold" in this opening line with the title of the anthology, and with the pastoral diction that gives the contents its intended unity are clear enough. They are made even stronger by a sentence in the exalted closing of the preface: "Poetry gives treasures 'more golden than gold,' leading us in higher and healthier ways than those of the world, and interpreting to us the lessons of Nature."[48]

Keats's traveler describes his often repeated experience of visiting the richly civilized "realms of gold" held by "bards in fealty to Apollo" in a vocabulary that would not disturb the harmony created in the first three books. Then line eight is interrupted by a voice—Homer's, Chapman's, Keats's—that we hear "speak out loud and bold" in loud and bold monosyllables, a break Palgrave emphasized by adding a dash at the beginning of line nine. A new kind of diction invokes a new world: a "wide expanse" of "skies" and ocean, uninhabited and unvisited until the worldly tourist turned discoverer and explorer first saw it spread before him. It is a premythologized world, not the pastoral Golden Age but primordial nature, on a scale that shrinks the many "western islands" crowded into well-traveled waters, and therefore might seem to diminish the poetry of Apollo's bards that fills the earlier books of *The Golden Treasury* and the opening lines of this poem.

If the sonnet could be read as a dismissal or even a denigration of "golden" poetry, it would have been better placed in a closing space, but Palgrave's positioning of it in the evolving design of his collection as a poem of beginnings encourages a fuller and more precise reading of it. While the poem reaches back into what it pictures as a deep and wild precivilized past, into the beginnings of poetry, it gives living voice to the ancient Greek poet through the voice of the Elizabethan translator in the sonnet's own voice. It speaks from within a highly organized literary form, first practiced to perfection by Shakespeare and renewed in the nineteenth century as part of the revival of interest in what was called (for instance by Thomas Warton in 1774, Robert Southey in 1807, John Churton Collins in 1905) *the Golden Age* of Elizabethan literature.[49] In the summary of Book IV, Palgrave praised "our own age in Poetry" for renewing "the half-forgotten melody and depth of tone" of that earlier period, where his selection begins.[50]

In the context Palgrave made for it, Keats's poem can be read to be a history of poetry revealed in visionary moments as a process both temporal and timeless, like nature's cycles. The sonnet celebrates private moments that became great historical events: when the astronomer (Sir William Herschel who discovered Uranus in 1781, but Galileo also seems to be meant, Milton's "Tuscan Artist") first saw a new planet through his "Optic Glass" (*P.L.* I, 288); when Cortez (mistaken for Balboa) stared for the first time at the Pacific.[51]

They take place—in the timeless grammar of similes—in the visionary moment when the poet could first "breathe" inspiration from Homer speaking through Chapman. Perhaps having in mind the choice of Keats's sonnet to open the last book, Palgrave in his summary of it characterized the "modern" genius of the age as stirred by "that far wider and greater spirit which . . . sweeps mankind round the circles of its gradual development."[52] It seems likely that Palgrave intended what he described as the symphonic "development" of *The Golden Treasury* to be an instrument for expressing this modern spirit.

SEQUENCES

Within the temporal frame of each book, the pieces of the whole spatial design are in connected sequences consisting of from two or three to more than a dozen entries, occasionally with one of them titled to suggest their common focus: "Time and Love," "The Poetry of Dress." They are not disposed according to a single principle like strictly chronological dating, or the logic of topical categories like Dana's Wordsworthian "Poems of the Imagination" or "of Sentiment and Reflection."

In the summarizing notes Palgrave described the contents of the four divisions as variously displaying range of style, of subject, of feeling and thought, of moods or tendencies, but since the books are not subdivided, the transitions from one sequence to the next as well as the shadings within a series can be gradual, like those from book to book. For the same reason, the connections among them can be both multiple and detailed, sometimes only subtly suggested by key words and phrases.

An instance where Palgrave brings to bear on a single poem the context of two differently ordered sequences of entries in the last book (much the longest, containing 122 poems written within only fifty years) illustrates another form of implicit interpretive direction. It shows how Palgrave's placing of an individual poem can make subtle suggestions that color the reader's sense of it, giving it slightly different lights and shadows than it might be cast in apart from his carefully composed context.

Starting with Wordsworth's "To the Skylark" are five poems (CCXL–CCXLIV) that form an immediately recognizable group. Defined by its focus on the image of a bird as a figure for poetic inspiration, it comments on a group of four poems in Book III with a similar focus: Thomas Gray's "The Progress of Poesy / A Pindaric Ode"; William Collins's "The Passions / An Ode for Music"; Gray's "Ode on the Spring"; William Cowper's "The Poplar Field" (CXL–CXLIII). The sequence comes to an end as the bird's song "fades" ("The blackbird has fled from "The Poplar Field") in the poem situated last in this arrangement of the five poems, Keats's "Ode to a Nightingale." Next are four birdless poems that might be thought to have been put together for their formal likeness, since they are all sonnets, three of them by Wordsworth: "Upon Westminster Bridge, Sept. 3, 1802"; Shelley's "Ozymandias of Egypt"; "Composed at Neidpath Castle, / The Property of Lord Queensberry, / 1803"; "Admonition to a Traveller." All but the first are clearly bound together by their double focus—on a figure identified generically as a "traveller" (like Keats's), and on an object of "decay," an actual or perhaps imminent ruin.

This double focus is not so clearly visible in "Upon Westminster Bridge" without a closer look at it in the context of the poems grouped just before and after it:

> Earth has not anything to show more fair:
> Dull would he be of soul who could pass by
> A sight so touching in its majesty:
> This City now doth like a garment wear
>
> The beauty of the morning: silent, bare,
> Ships, towers, domes, theatres, and temples lie

Open unto the fields, and to the sky,
All bright and glittering in the smokeless air.

Never did sun more beautifully steep
In his first splendour valley, rock, or hill;
Ne'er saw I, never felt, a calm so deep!
The river glideth at his own sweet will:
Dear God! the very houses seem asleep;
And all that mighty heart is lying still!

The "sight" of the city, like the birds in the preceding poems, inspires a vision: "All bright and glittering in the smokeless air," it enchants the viewer. Like all the birds, the view of the city seems to be suspended in "air," so that it enjoys, as birds do, some other than human reciprocity with the "sky," while it also belongs to the "Earth" as distinct from the mortal "world" that Keats's nightingale has "never known."

The last lines of Keats's ode are the immediate link with "Upon Westminster Bridge": "Was it a vision, or a waking dream? / Fled is that music;— do I wake or sleep?" Wordsworth's sonnet in the end may imply a version of the same questioning: "the very houses seem asleep." Reverberations here of Keats's last line bring out the new tentativeness in the poet's voice: what he sees may only "seem" to be a "vision," may be as fragile and ephemeral as sleep. The tentativeness is in contrast with absolute assertions earlier in the sonnet that "Earth has not anything . . . ," "Never did sun . . . ," "Ne'er saw I . . . ," affirmations but all in the negative, as if to fend off uncertainty.

This reading of "Upon Westminster Bridge" is compatible with the further interpretive suggestions made by the group of three sonnets immediately following it. Because a traveler figures in all three, they make the poet standing on the bridge more clearly recognizable as another transient viewer distanced from what he looks at, a traveler through the city seeing it as a stranger, as if from outside it rather than from his stopping place at the "heart" of its ordinary busy life.

Adding to the sense of this poet as a traveler from far away, he first describes "this City" as if it did not belong to the modern, industrial world of 1802, with its banks, shops, prisons, houses of parliament, but were a city in an "antique land," the home from which Shelley's mythologized traveler has come, with structures like the "ancient dome, and towers" of Neidpath

Castle. Then the city seems to dissolve into a ruin, its loftiest structures melting into "the fields," their roofs "Open ... to the sky," "silent, bare" like the "boundless and bare" sands that surround the ruined colossus of Ozymandias. Even the bridge the traveler stops to look from seems to "melt away" like the "abode" imagined in "Admonition to a Traveller" if it were to be violated by human touch. All that remains is the untrammeled river, nature returned to its primordial state (as in "On First Looking into Chapman's Homer"), reclaiming what belongs to it. If the sight of the city is more than a waking dream, it is a momentary glimpse of a visionary world from which the viewer, who is like all human beings merely a passerby, must inevitably be excluded.

TEMPORAL AND SPATIAL ORDER

To consider the implications of the expressive use of physical and conceptual space and time in this anthology—Palgrave's placing of poems according to "gradations of feeling or subject" within books laid out in chronological order—we will look back at the poems grouped around bird images, which echo one another so closely that the slightest variation can express shadings of mood and feeling.

Wordsworth's "To a Skylark" is placed first of the five, each addressing or contemplating a bird as a visionary figure: "Ethereal minstrel," "blithe Spirit," "Presiding Spirit," "blithe-newcomer," "blessed bird," "immortal Bird." The ecstatic pitch of Wordsworth's apostrophe to the skylark harmonizes with the song of the bird: "To the last point of vision, and beyond, / Mount, daring warbler," to that height "Whence thou dost pour upon the world a flood / Of harmony, with instinct more divine." Shelley also greets a skylark "That from heaven, or near it / Pourest thy full heart / In profuse strains of unpremeditated art." Then, midway in the poem, he begins to doubt his own figure: "What thou art we know not." In the last poem, Keats's "Ode to a Nightingale," the poet, listening "While thou art pouring forth thy soul abroad / In such an ecstasy!," thinks of his own mortality, and that reflection leads him to accuse the "immortal Bird" as a "deceiving elf" to be distrusted as a figure for poetic inspiration: "Was it a vision, or a waking dream?"

Because this poem is positioned last in the spatial sequence, allowing its closing lines to act also as a conclusion to the earlier four in this closely bound group (as "The Poplar Field" completes its sequence), together they trace a defined curve of mood or feeling that emerges from Palgrave's ordering of them. This design makes the application of the word *earlier* to poems that come before Keats's in the sequence seem to have a special temporal reference, as if they somehow happened before, and not only in the time scheme of the reader turning the pages one after another.

As a group they have a kind of internal development that creates the illusion of a psychological narrative, as if their interwoven details expressed successive changes of mood and feelings, the evolution of a poet's inward experience. This fiction, entirely of Palgrave's making as an unobtrusive instrument for shaping the reader's sense of the poems, is not true to the actual experiences of the poets who wrote them: to their experiences of making their own and of reading each other's poems. That is, Keats composed "Ode to a Nightingale" six years before Wordsworth wrote his poem on a skylark, one year before Shelley wrote his. The same poems rearranged in the chronological order of their composition would tell a different story.

The illusion of temporality is created by the way the poems are arranged spatially, all equally present on the pages of the anthology while to the reader, coming on them one after another as they are ordered there, they form a psychological narrative of which Palgrave is the author.

The larger implication is that Palgrave orchestrated the expressively ordered sequences of poems within the framework of chronologically ordered books to reflect his conception of poetic tradition. It is simultaneously and equally historical and timeless, like Shelley's "great poem . . . built up since the beginning of the world," or like T. S. Eliot's imagining of it a century later as "a living whole of all the poetry that has ever been written."[53] The accumulation of poems in sequences within each book of the anthology, and from book to book, reflects the idea of tradition and the individual poem that Palgrave wanted to embody in *The Golden Treasury*.

FOLLOWERS AND CONSEQUENCES

Palgrave became an honored literary figure as the maker of *The Golden Treasury*—he was appointed Professor of Poetry at Oxford largely on the strength of its reputation—and the anthology was very early considered a kind of national treasure, a modern classic to set beside the works of distinguished English poets in every respectable library. No book of this kind had ever before won that kind of general recognition, and none since except perhaps *The Oxford Book of English Verse*, which Robert Graves called "the Establishment's first choice for well-educated men and women."[54] In fact, its success enhanced the status of *The Golden Treasury*, which Quiller-Couch had meant to supersede, by being so recognizably an imitation of it.

Of course Quiller-Couch's preface begins by pointing out his collection's distinguishing features, though without actually saying they are precisely the ones that make it different from Palgrave's: the longer span of its contents from the thirteenth to the end of the nineteenth century; a wider range of poetry in English not restricted to "these Islands only"; the inclusion of epigrams as well as lyric poetry; a simpler scheme of arranging poets in order of their birth; the omission of notes to keep the larger number of entries from making the book "unwieldy."[55]

Still, these differences did not prevent the book from looking like a copy of *The Golden Treasury*. The dark binding ornamented only by letters and border-frame in gold, the unencumbered presentation of poems with no table of contents or other introductory editorial paraphernalia than its preface (as brief as Palgrave's), the uncrowded spacing of entries, are all designed to give the impression of unostentatiously elegant simplicity, while avoiding the learned look that would drive away some readers Palgrave had tactfully invited.

Again without saying so, Quiller-Couch fashioned himself as Palgrave's successor, sharing the classical education and editorial seriousness untainted by pedantry or condescension that gave Palgrave his unique status: at once a much respected man of letters and a maker of an anthology with an exceptionally wide and various audience. Particularly in the closing paragraph of his preface Quiller-Couch shaped himself in Palgrave's image:

For the anthologist's is not quite the *dilettante* business for which it is too often and ignorantly derided. I say this, and immediately repent; since my wish is that the reader should in his own pleasure quite forget the editor's labour, which too has been pleasant: that, standing aside, I may believe this book has made the Muses' access easier when, in the right hour, they come to him to uplift or to console—[56]

following which are two lines, unidentified and untranslated, of Greek verse.

What Quiller-Couch missed in Palgrave's presentation of himself was that, unlike other anthologists, he cast himself as an author, and his book as a creative arrangement displaying the unity and harmony of a work of art. The possibility of seeing an anthology in this strange and enhancing light as a heroic symphony escaped Quiller-Couch's capacity for imagining, but not some few twentieth-century poets who tried their hands at making original books out of compilations. Chief among them were Robert Bridges and Walter de la Mare; what they made were not logical but eccentric extensions of Palgrave's conception.

In 1907 Bridges said in a letter to Yeats, "I have a great abhorrence of these anthologists, tho' I now and then get something out of them. But I believe that the multiplication of their poetry books does really hinder the sale of poems."[57] Then six years later he wrote again to ask if he might include certain of Yeats's poems in what he variously called his "anthology," "so-called anthology," "queer . . . book."[58]

Longman the Publisher who lost his son early in the war asked me to make him up a volume of consolatory poetry. . . . I told him that I did not believe in the benefits of consolatory poems, but that if he liked I wd make a book that I thought people in distress would like to read. He came round to my notion of the book and putting it together has been a great distraction. . . . It is a very serious performance and I think unlike anything that has been done before.[59]

Then to overcome what he sensed might be Yeats's resistance, he added in closing his appeal, "I am quite sure that the way in which I set your poems will do them a lot of good."[60]

The title page announces a performance that is very serious indeed, on a grand scale, for a universal audience: *The Spirit of Man/An Anthology in English and French from the Philosophers & Poets*. Below the title a vignette shows the hand of God stretched out to Michelangelo's Adam. At the same time the unusual calligraphic design of the type face looks like handwriting, as if the book were a record of private reading. Altogether the title page, by its unconventional aspect, presents the anthology as a personal act of creation, which is what its very short preface—otherwise given over to a public denunciation of Prussia—claims for it. It is described there as "the work of one mind at one time; and its being such implies the presence of the peculiarities and blemishes that mark any personality and any time," which the compiler did not seek to avoid.[61]

The table of contents, probably in imitation of Palgrave's, gives only the division into four books without listing entries or authors, but it does name topics under each: for Book One, "Dissatisfaction"—"Retirement"—"Spiritual Desire"—"Idea of God"—"Spiritual Love & Praise." In the text these are further narrowed in running heads beginning with: "Sadness," "Dismay," "Weariness," "Dejection," "Sorrow's Springs," "Clouds."

Otherwise Bridges outdid Palgrave in suppressing explicit editorial guidance. He delayed giving titles for the entries and names or dates of their authors until the index at the back of the book, to allow "the demonstration of various moods of mind, which are allowed free play":

First then, the reader is invited to bathe rather than to fish in these waters: that is to say, the several pieces are to be read in context; and it is for this reason that no titles nor names of authors are inserted in the text, because they would distract the attention and lead away the thought and even overrule consideration.[62]

The waters the reader is left to sink or swim in are arrangements like this sequence of entries, numbered 274 through 280: a prose passage from Coleridge's "Lay Sermons," Blake's "The Tyger," lines from *Paradise Lost*, an extract from George Darley's allegorical poem "Nepenthe," sentences from St. Paul's Epistle to the Romans, a couplet from John Masefield's "The Everlasting Mercy," a passage of prose untranslated from Henri-Frederic Amiel's *Fragments d'un Journal Intime*.

Walter de la Mare wrote a review of *The Spirit of Man* for the *Times Literary Supplement* in 1916, praising the anthology mainly for its arrangement: no "mere succession of self-contained poems and fragments of prose," but an order designed to bring out their "interrelation and intercommunion one with another."[63] In the next sentence he compared the entries to "a host of candles" that illumine "the mind that set them in their places." The review lists some of the groupings that make these illuminating corollaries, but, de la Mare advised, "only a close study of the book can show the indefatigable pains of the artist to express an idea and an ideal with the world's masterpieces for his material."

There is no explicit evidence that Bridges was stirred to think about unconventional ways of arranging a compilation from studying *The Golden Treasury*, but we learn that he did study it closely from his endnote on Wordworth's "It is a beauteous evening." It records laconically: "Palgrave prints *is on* for *broods o'er*."[64] We also learn from de la Mare's review that he too studied Palgrave's collection with special attention to his editorial presence by comparison with Bridges's, which suggests that de la Mare sensed some likeness in their designs. He praised Bridges for restricting his intrusions on the reader's experience to an occasional marginal gloss of explanation and to sparing endnotes in the index: "Help is freely given, but not indulgently. Digression into æsthetic appreciation—which sometimes enlightens and sometimes frets the reader in 'The Golden Treasury'—is rare, and, whenever present, terse."[65]

The portrait of the anthologist as an artist that de la Mare drew in his review of *The Spirit of Man* may have encouraged his own unconventionally personal version of an anthology, *Come Hither*, published first in 1923 and then in 1957 in a much expanded version. His inclusion of light verse, certainly not suggested by Bridges, may have been modeled on Allingham's *Nightingale Valley*, which de la Mare owned in a much worn copy.[66] It also seems possible that his study of *The Golden Treasury* suggested the notion of the anthologist as a literary critic. C. Day Lewis saw both Palgrave and de la Mare in that role when in the introduction to his expanded edition of *The Golden Treasury* he likened them in their "creative" gift for designing such books, "a rare talent: in our own day, Mr. de la Mare possesses it: Palgrave had it too."[67]

The introduction to *Come Hither*, called "The Story of this Book," is cast in narrative form as a quasi-allegorical fable of the author as a child finding "an enormous, thick, home-made-looking volume covered in a greenish shagreen or shark-skin" and filled with scrawled writings that he copied out into what eventually became the book in the reader's hand. In it nursery rhymes, popular songs, ballads, many anonymous verses, literary poems (especially lyrics), and extracts are grouped under mysterious topics like "Elphin, Ouph and Fay," or "Far."[68] The entries are identified by title and author but they follow one another without commentary, so that the reader experiences recurring patterns of diction and specially of rhythm. The accumulated effects are simple and sensory, almost like charms. They create an "air of mystery," Elizabeth Bishop wrote in 1957 in her review of the revised edition, that de la Mare's own poetry is famous for.[69] It is this unity and harmony of effect that gives the compilation the integrity of a created work.

Tucked here and there in "The Story of this Book" and everywhere in the chattily voluminous notes are simply expressed principles and examples of literary criticism, fitting for what the subtitle calls *A Collection of Rhymes and Poems for the Young of All Ages*. The reader comes on a rewriting of "Old King Cole" that demonstrates what would be lost by changing its meter and lineation; instructions about reading aloud and where to put the accent in a word; comments on the expressive value of archaisms and dialect. There are also unspoken critical criteria at work in the selection of entries: obscurely allusive or difficult poems are avoided; light verse is valued as much as high poetry; listening is promoted as essential to the experience of reading.

Like *The Golden Treasury*, *Come Hither* is a serious work of literary criticism for which poets have specially valued it. Auden was indebted to it for introducing him to light verse and to poems by Frost, one of his early masters.[70] Frost himself seems to have approvingly associated a collection of his own poems for children, *Come In*, with de la Mare's anthology (even while contrasting his own colloquial title with de la Mare's archaizing). Bishop revealed what was the special attraction of *Come Hither* for her when she wrote in her review of it: "He loves 'little articles', home-made objects whose value increases with age, Robinson Crusoe's lists of his belongings, homely employments, charms and herbs. As a result he naturally chose for his book many of what Randall Jarrell once called 'thing-y' poems, and never the pompous, abstract, or formal."[71]

Bishop also valued *Come Hither* more generally—she called it "the best anthology I know of"—as a work of criticism:

De la Mare has some practical things to say about meters (which he used so beautifully himself), and even suggests how to read certain of the poems; but he never speaks directly of any of the usual concerns of critics; for one, let's say, 'imagery.'[72]

High praise from a habitual critic of critics and anthologies.

De la Mare's book may also have been a model for the use by other writers of a personal compilation as a platform for their own critical views. Examples are: George Moore's *An Anthology of Pure Poetry* (1924); Pound's

Profile (1932); Aldous Huxley's *Texts & Pretexts* (1933); Auden's "commonplace book" or "sort of anthology," *A Certain World* (1970).[73]

Conventions of anthology making from quite early dictated that anthologists, like other makers of products to be marketed, must define their work by criticizing rivals. In this situation there have always been some who have argued their differences as expressions of their sense of literary history and of their commitment to well-defined critical principles or attitudes.

This kind of distancing organizes F. O. Matthiessen's introduction to his edition of *The Oxford Book of American Verse* of 1950. He designed it to distinguish his collection most obviously from Bliss Carman's earlier anthology in this Oxford series, published in 1927 (which included some 175 poets, a hundred of them now virtually unknown). Behind Matthiessen's revised reading of American poetic tradition was Conrad Aiken's *American Poetry 1617–1928*, where diminished spaces had already been given to such nineteenth-century favorites as Oliver Wendell Holmes, Sidney Lanier, James Russell Lowell, and John Greenleaf Whittier in order to make appropriately proportioned spaces for Emily Dickinson, Walt Whitman, and poets since 1910.

Matthiessen's ultimate target was not Carman's *Oxford Book* but *The Golden Treasury*. Like Palgrave, Matthiessen laid down rules for his choice of poems, most of his meant to revise the expectations of readers brought up on *The Golden Treasury* and its imitators: "fewer poets, with more space for each"; "not too many sonnets"; "no excerpts"; and one rule—on which the others pivot—that "runs counter to all Golden Treasuries by holding that, whenever practicable, a poet should be represented by poems of some length." Matthiessen overturned Palgrave's influential tenets so that his collection would not perpetuate what he saw as one of the most damaging among the "effects of anthologies upon popular taste," their tendency to "overemphasize the lyric at the expense of all other genres, to the point of establishing in unreflective minds the notion that the short lyric is the chief surviving poetic form."[74]

Matthiessen was no doubt thinking specifically of Palgrave's anthology, which focused an interest he did not invent. It had been fostered by the work of early-nineteenth-century poets, encouraged by the revival of interest in Elizabethan poetry, and expressed in words that could easily have been

Palgrave's in 1833 in an influential essay by Mill:

Lyric poetry as it was the earliest kind, is also . . . more eminently and peculiarly poetry than any other: it is the poetry most natural to a really poetic temperament, and least capable of being imitated by one not so endowed by nature.[75]

Poetic—meaning beautiful, mellifluous, elevated—was a favorite adjective used everywhere to describe the kind of poem readers of anthologies all through the nineteenth century liked and expected to find there.

Helen Gardner in *The New Oxford Book of English Verse* distanced herself from her predecessor in that series, Quiller-Couch, and by implication from his model, Palgrave, along lines that followed Matthiessen's from a slightly different angle: "Q's bias was towards the lyrical and the poem of personal joys and sorrows. This anthology balances against poems of the private life poems that deal with public events and historic occasions, or express convictions, religious, moral, or political."[76] In other words, she set out to rectify the neglect, encouraged by the two still most influential retrospective anthologies, of "the tradition of satiric, political, epistolary, and didactic verse"; to correct their "virtual exclusion of Pope" and much else of the best eighteenth-century poetry.[77]

The charge is deserved against both Quiller-Couch and Palgrave: their criteria for kinds of poems to be admitted imposed a powerfully distorted shape on the history of English poetry, most grotesquely on the eighteenth century. Pope is represented in Quiller-Couch's collection only by "On a Certain Lady at Court," "Elegy to the Memory of an Unfortunate Lady," "The Dying Christian to his Soul." Palgrave, whose even more exclusive criteria left out epigrams and religious verse, gave space only to "Ode on Solitude" (retitled "The Quiet Life"), which, besides being a short lyric, was in harmony with the overwhelmingly pastoral cast of his eighteenth-century selection. In consequence, Palgrave's anthology made an inadvertent but inevitable contribution to the devaluing of the eighteenth century "in the criticism now popular" that he himself set out to correct in the article on "English Poetry from Dryden to Cowper," published the year after *The Golden Treasury*.[78] The article reinforced the revisionist remarks he had already inserted for the same corrective purpose into the summary of Book III about the eighteenth century as "an age not only of spontaneous transition, but of bold experiment," characterized by "a nobleness of thought, a courageous aim at high, and in a strict sense manly, excellence in many of the writers": "—nor can that period be justly termed tame and wanting in originality, which produced such poems as Pope's Satires, Gray's Odes and Elegy, the ballads of Gay and Carey, the songs of Burns and Cowper."[79]

Palgrave, it seems, believed, or hoped, that his clearly articulated focus on the best lyrics and songs in English would be understood to absolve his collection of the responsibility to be more inclusive, more representative of the best of all possible poems in the English language. To remind readers of that restriction, carefully explained in the preface to the anthology, he repeated it at the back of the book on the first page of the notes. He cautioned there that the summaries are meant mainly to describe the contents of his collection, "in which (besides its restriction to Lyrical Poetry) a strictly representative or historical Anthology has not been aimed at," but rather a "standard of Excellence . . . true in all ages."[80]

Besides his conviction that his narrowing of focus was legitimate and an inducement to discriminating critical judgment, Palgrave's wonderfully achieved aim of creating a unified work of art out of harmoniously arranged elements must also have encouraged him in thinking that his exclusion of disparate kinds of poetry was justified by that high purpose.

Above all, his prescription for the "Lyrical conditions" that a poem was required to meet to be admitted to his anthology so closely matched the mid-Victorian ideal for what constituted the truly poetic, that his readers, and probably Palgrave himself, could almost forget that the "best" poems in English are not all in *The Golden Treasury*. The grand finale to his preface, declaring that "Poetry gives treasures 'more golden than gold'" suggests that he did forget.

Sonettes as a gathering of courtly and would-be courtly verse would promote his own, and with it his social ambitions. Writing as the mere compiler of the manuscript (signing himself "G.T."), Gascoigne claimed only to have "with long travayle confusedly gathered together" and put in order the contents, "adding nothing of myne owne onely a tytle to euery Poeme, wherby the cause of writing the same maye the more euidently appear."[1]

Gascoigne's assumptions here are clear, and tell us something of the situation in which *Songes and Sonettes* was made, and how it was read. He assumed what we know to be true of the literary system in his time: that poets themselves were not usually the titlers of their poems; that this was a proper task for the compiler of a collection; that titles to "euery Poeme" were a defining mark of the anthologist's presence; that this person was in the position of the owner or copier of a poetry manuscript, the publisher or printer of a verse collection; that this position entitled anthologists by right of possession to choose the forms of presentation for the poems gathered. A hundred years later, when the social taboo against self-promotion by such poets (titling their own poems was considered one of its forms) was largely lifted, a title was no longer assumed to have been put in place by someone not the author. Even so, that practice of nonauthorial titling continued in many anthologies for some two hundred years after it had disappeared from other kinds of poetry collections.

A now common agreement among scholars is that Tottel himself, or someone acting for him in getting the poems in his collection ready to print, gave the titles placed above them in successive editions. I would qualify this view slightly by saying that most of the entries in a brief section attributed to Nicholas Grimald, as well as scattered poems in the miscellany of uncertain authors, have titles stylistically somewhat different from a much larger number of those assigned to Surrey, Wyatt, and most of the unknown contributors. The likelihood is that those exceptional entries were copied from manuscripts where at least some of the poems already had titles. Still, the local variations do not disturb the strong impression that whoever prepared Tottel's collection gave titles with a consistency of style quite remarkable in this early period.

The unassuming title of *Songes and Sonettes* may have been chosen partly for its prestigious likeness to headings in private manuscripts, partly for its alliteration (in fashion for book titles, such as *A Myrrovre For Magistrates* of

CHAPTER THREE

THE ANTHOLOGIST IN THE POEM

Cultural historians have lately shown interest in anthologies by focusing on their compilers' choices of poems—what they leave out sometimes even more than what they include—as instances of canon formation; and selection is ultimately the most important sign of the anthologist's presence. Even so, this is not what many readers are or have ever been likeliest to be aware of as a sign of direction by the maker of an anthology. The simple reason is that a large proportion of anthology readers know only the poems they find there, which means they are not prepared to judge alternative choices. Even signs in the texts of the poems of changes made in them by the anthologist are likely to go unnoticed by readers who have not seen other versions. Still, anthologists since the beginning, and at least until quite recently, have left their imprint on poems by adding or changing their titles, correcting or modernizing their language, even restructuring their forms. Inevitably, to some degree or other, these revisions lead to reinterpretations of the poems so treated.

TITLING

In 1573, a year before Tottel's *Songes and Sonettes* appeared in its seventh edition, the poet George Gascoigne brought out a book of poems to be discussed in detail in Chapter 8, under the title *A Hundreth sundrie Flowres bounde vp in one small Poesie*. Its allusion to the then current definition of *anthologia* as flower gathering was designed to pass the book off—how seriously is unclear—as a printed gathering of poems by various authors retrieved from privately circulating manuscript collections or loose sheets. At this date Gascoigne could only have been thinking of—and expecting that his readers would be reminded of—Tottel's book as the English model for the kind he pretended to offer, perhaps hoping the success of *Songes and*

1559). Its most practical function was to tell readers they should expect only poems in short forms (Gascoigne in a treatise of 1575 took exception to the lax view that "all Poemes (being short) may be called Sonets").[2] That such poems were not usually to be found in printed books is suggested by the printer's prefatory recommendation to the reader's attention of verses in "small parcelles," on the grounds of praiseworthy precedents among the "workes of diuers Latines, Italians, and other."

Beyond that, the book's title signaled that entries would include poems about love and others about topics conventional to epigrams, epitaphs, epistles, riddles: virtue, fortune, the courtly life, honor, death. This is the sort of mixture typical in private collections of Tudor poetry like the Arundel Harington manuscript, which reflected what was being done in short forms during the period when the selections in *Songes and Sonettes* were being written. In that manuscript, many entries are titled but many not, and the titles themselves do not follow a consistent style or styles.

Humanist editors of classical poets could have set an example for Tottel of consistency in titling, and he in fact usually followed their title forms for poems not having to do with love. His titles beginning with *of, against, to, upon* copy the conventions for titling classical short forms like the epigram, the epistle, and the epitaph. Because humanist editors did not have a distinct system Tottel could imitate for titling love poems, which far outnumber entries on other topics in *Songes and Sonettes*, he had more freedom to invent title forms for them or to choose from among existing types those best suited to the arrangement of his book. Since there was variety among typical forms of titling for love poems, the concentration of certain repeated constructions in *Songes and Sonettes* had to be a matter of choice, and one suggesting considerable self-consciousness about the special role and presence of the anthologist. An aim of consistency might have been to raise the status of love poems as a genre among other short forms already dignified by traditional title formulas.

All through the pages of Tottel's anthology are reappearances of the same and closely similar title forms, the most often repeated—forty-four times in the Wyatt section alone—beginning with the formula "The louer." In the larger sections given to Wyatt and to unnamed authors, groups of three, four, even twelve entries in a row have titles beginning that way. Of course such consistency itself takes for granted the presence of an arranger, but if the title were in the personless form of "A true loue" (the title given to the first entry by Grimald), the sense of presence would not be as immediate as when the recurrent phrase in the space above the poem is "The louer." This third-person form announces the titler referring to the lover who speaks of himself in the poem as *I*. Besides the titler and the lover, there is the reader addressed in the title, and sometimes another person listening in the poem, spoken to as "you." This multiplicity of persons evoked grammatically by the title gives a strong social cast to the poem, by contrast with a title in the personless grammatical form of "A true loue," which seems more like a sign hung above the verses than like someone telling the reader something about another person.

Another sign in *A Hundreth sundrie Flowers* that seems to point to *Songes and Sonettes* as its model is the description of the book given to the reader by one of Gascoigne's fictional intermediaries: a "poeticall posie" containing "manie trifling fantasies, humorall passions, and straunge affects of a Louer," "invented uppon sundrie occasions by, sundrie gentlemen."[3] This ascribes to Gascoigne's book the emphasis of Tottel's collection, and points to another function of its repeated title forms. They prepare the reader in advance to recognize the "occasions" of the poems, locating the lover in situations created by the uniquely close proximity of ladies and gentlemen in courtly society, or the fiction of such a world that the conventions of courtly poetry evoke.

Although many of the occasions named in Tottel's titles are set forth clearly enough in the poems to be understandable without the titles, they are still not redundant. They insist on the social origins, manners, and language of the world the poems actually belonged to, or else of the world they pretended to belong to by imitation. The titles induct readers into that society by addressing them in a formulaic language suited to the conventional expressive mode of the courtly lovers performing in the poems.

When we look closely at a particular poem and its title in the context made for it in *Songes and Sonettes*, and then at the same poem in the space and with the title given it by a much later anthologist, we can see how the anthology maker's choice of title can influence the reader's response to the poem. One example can make the point here, the sonnet by Surrey placed as the second entry in Tottel's book.[4] Among all the poems in *Songes and Son-*

ettes, it is the one that has most often been given space in later anthologies since it was first reprinted in 1737 in *The Muses Library*.

Here it is the way Surrey's sonnet appeared in Tottel's book:

Description of Spring,wherin eche
thing renewes,saue one-
lie the louer.

The soote season, that bud and blome furth bringes,
With grene hath clad the hill and eke the vale:
The nightingale with fethers new she singes:
The turtle to her make hath tolde her tale:
Somer is come, for euery spray nowe springes,
The hart hath hong his olde hed on the pale:
The buck in brake his winter cote he flinges:
The fishes flote with newe repaired scale:
The adder all her sloughe awaye she slinges:
The swift swalow pursueth the flyes smale:
The busy bee her honye now she minges:
Winter is worne that was the flowers bale:
And thus I see among these pleasant thinges
Eche care decayes, and yet my sorow springes. (2)

The sonnet is surrounded by more than twenty entries also on the topic of love, all with formulaic titles. The pattern is set just before this sonnet in the title for the opening poem: "Descripcion of the restlesse state of a louer,with sute to his lady, to rue on his diyng hart." Then the second title repeats the formula so that repetition itself becomes a signifier: courtly situations, like the lover's almost legal "sute," are rituals regulated by conventions mirrored in courtly verse. The poem is, like the suit, a game the poet plays according to rules: the readers without privileged knowledge of courtly conventions learn them here from the anthologist's presentation.

The title of the sonnet, though insistently formulaic, also fits the poem it introduces in particular details that have a decisive influence on the way the reader responds to it. After identifying the sonnet as a "Description," a performance of the poet in that chosen form, the title goes on to predict the shape of the lines to come: a catalogue of "eche thing" in the natural world renewing itself in accordance with the ritual of the seasons, then disturbed by the lover who "onelie" is out of order. We can see as well as hear this structural design diagrammed below the title on the printed page—its imbalance of two closing lines set against twelve—because the scheme is built on only two rhyme sounds here spelled (with a consistency rare in this period) so that the two rhyming words look as well as sound the same in every pair of lines until the last, which has only one rhyme sound.

This play with the sonnet form has the expressive value of allowing multiple repetitions of all sorts. The catalogue is made of twelve lines, all but the opening pair parallel end-stopped clauses, all but two marked with a colon. Within each line are patterns of repeated consonant and vowel sounds so elaborate and pronounced that they make all things in nature seem to rhyme. Besides these internal rhymes, the end-rhymes have their own pattern: the first paired word is always a verb signifying a burst of energetic activity, the second a noun bringing the motion to rest. These exaggeratedly stylized uses of repetition are an artful representation of nature's cyclical patterns, returning always to the spring, as springs do, and like them always holding motion in stasis, always in the present.

The catalogue itself would therefore have no internal reason, conceptual or structural, to end, but because the title has made readers aware from the start of an impending disturbance, that too is recognizable as a feature of the poet's carefully designed performance. The couplet, by doubling the final rhyme sound ("thinges" / "springes"), jolts the pattern of paired lines with contrasting rhyme sounds ("inges" / "ale"), but the jolt is less violent than if the last two lines introduced a new rhyme, as couplets regularly do in Shakespearean sonnets.

If the couplet were set apart that way, it would altogether seal the lover off from the enduring cyclical patterns of nature, a danger Shakespeare pitted his art against in the couplets of his eternizing sonnets. Surrey's closing pair of lines works differently by continuing one of the two rhyme sounds in the catalogue of nature's renewals: the end rhyme of line 14 ("springes") repeats the sound of the end rhyme of line 1 ("bringes") and the end word of line 5 (again "springes"). Repetitions represent the inward state of the lover as well as they do the motions of the seasons, the difference being—as the title says—that the lover's rituals are not renewals bringing freshness, energy, and rest, but stale repetitions that imprison him in what the titles for the poems bracketing this one define as his endlessly recurring "restlesse state." That is what separates him from other things in nature.

The elaborate artfulness of the lover's performance here plays a game with the form and language of a "Description of Spring," and of a sonnet, so that it handles his inward situation with the lightness of touch demanded by courtly manners. Because readers are allowed to know the game and to recognize the rules for it laid down in the title, they can respond to the couplet as the inevitable decorous closing move. Their experience is different when they read the poem as it is placed in another context with another title by a much later anthologist, whose presence is nevertheless felt, but by different signals.

Here are the titles originally printed in Tottel's book above the three love poems of Surrey's included by Gardner in *The New Oxford Book of English Verse*: "Description of Spring,wherin eche thing renewes,saue onelie the louer"; "The louer comforteth himself with the worthinesse of his loue"; "Complaint of the absence of her louer being vpon the sea." Gardner substituted the titles "Spring"; "Consolation"; "The Seafarer." The design of Tottel's titles for love poems embedded them in a social context that made historical claims: that they belonged to a courtly world readers could believe had existed outside the pages of the anthology. Gardner's titles ignore social and historical associations, as well as the temporality built into the quasi-narrative grammatical forms of Tottel's titles.

Gardner preceded the notes to her book with a slightly defensive rationale for assigning some titles of her own making, a signal that editorial titling had come under criticism: *The Norton Anthology of Poetry* of 1970 used only the first words of the opening line in the title space above any poem thought to have been originally left untitled. Gardner admitted to giving titles not only to extracts from longer works but also to "the many poems up to the beginning of the seventeenth century which their authors left untitled," but went on to defend herself that "when the practice of giving titles to lyrics had become established, titles have not been supplied to poems their authors thought fit to leave without them."[5]

The tartness of the last sentence must have been aimed at the titling practices of earlier anthology makers: Quiller-Couch but more particularly Palgrave. He often imposed his own titles on untitled poems of all periods,

even on poems by recent authors like Wordsworth that were already familiar to readers of anthologies. To "I wandered lonely as a cloud" he gave the
title "The Daffodils" (which Gardner, presumably thinking it authorial, repeated in the variant form of "Daffodils"); "It is a beauteous evening" he
called "By the Sea"; on "Three years she grew" he imposed the title "The
Education of Nature."

Gardner's personless noun title "Spring" for Surrey's sonnet asks only
that we enjoy for their own sake the evocative details that constitute the es-
sence of spring: their small, energetic, crisp distinctness comprising a
cheerful harmony. By leaving out reference to the form of the poem, the title directs attention away from the sonnet as a carefully wrought artifice,
though a reader could scarcely miss how finely it is made. Still less does
Gardner's title point to the poem as a social performance, which readers un-
used to sixteenth-century writings might not recognize. Least of all does her
title suggest that the sonnet is expressive of inward experience conventionally contained by the rules of an artful game.

The effect of these suppressions is that the title "Spring," saying nothing
about the shape of the poem, gives no conceptual or formal reason for the
couplet. An explanation for it might be that it is a sudden, uncontrolled
outburst, except that it does not sound like one; another that it is a trick, except that it does not feel like one. The design of the whole sonnet is so satis-
fyingly completed by the couplet that neither of these suggested explana-
tions rings true. What I think was the effect in my own experience of having
read the poem first with the title "Spring" is that, without looking for these
or other reasons for the couplet, I simply gave less importance to it than the
form of the sonnet expects, and much less attention than is demanded by
the title and context given to it in *Songes and Sonettes*.

"Spring" is a title one would expect to find only rarely if at all for poems
of Tottel's period, but much more often beginning in the nineteenth century; Gardner included a sonnet by Hopkins that he titled "Spring." That is
an anachronistic title for a sixteenth-century poem because it avoids stating
the poem's form, or naming the occasion that determines its narrative
shape. And it avoids these features in the interest of promoting spontaneity
or immediacy; that is, mistakenly, in the interest of noninterference between the reader and the text of the poem.

POLISHING, IMPROVING, MODERNIZING

Until the recent past, anthologists made changes great and small in the texts of their chosen entries. Yet the marks of their presence in the internal space of the poem tended to go unnoticed by readers, most of whom had not seen the poem before it was retouched or remade. Now Tottel's liberties with poems in *Songes and Sonettes* are notorious, subjected to the contempt lavished these days on any tamperer with a poet's text.

In the different literary situation of his own time, the many changes he made in poems, if they were noticed, which is doubtful, would hardly have raised objections. He was doing nothing more than following the tradition-ally accepted practices of professional scribes and owners of private manu-scripts, who had the authority of possession over the poems they tran-scribed. Besides, it is unlikely that any manuscript coming into Tottel's hands would have passed to him directly from the author or even at second hand, or with his knowledge and approval (unless from Grimald, who was still living in 1557).

When the prefatory paragraph to Tottel's anthology offered readers a gathering of poems rivaling Latin and Italian work in short forms, it flat-tered them that they would appreciate the "eloquence" of "learned" authors in "the Englishe tong" for their "stateliness of stile" beyond the "rude skill of common eares." The writer of this advertisement might have been remem-bering conventional tributes like Skelton's in a poem of 1523 to "Noble Chaucer, whos pullisshyd eloquence / Oure Englysshe rude so fresshely hath set out."[6]

By *polished* sixteenth-century writers meant elegant and refined in dic-tion, smooth in meter, regular in form—the qualities that came to be asso-ciated with Wyatt and Surrey as they were widely known in Tottel's pres-entation of them. In 1589, in *The Arte of English Poesie,* George Puttenham praised these early Tudor "courtly makers" who, "hauing trauailed into Italie, and there tasted the sweete and stately measures and stile of the Italian Poesie," then "greatly pollished our rude & homely maner of vulgar [mean-ing vernacular] Poesie, from that it had bene before."[7]

This critical commonplace was testimony to the skill of whoever pol-ished the entries in *Songes and Sonettes,* Tottel or someone acting for him in the anthologist's role. He aimed to make them attractive to readers who could not have known the poems had been altered; who would not have been surprised or troubled had they known, since questions of authenticity were of as little interest to readers as to most publishers in the mid-sixteenth century.

There is no way to know the state of the manuscripts that were put together to make Tottel's book, but it is clear that those prepared for printing in the first edition were, as its modern editor Hyder Rollins concluded, "thoroughly" edited by some one person whose "methods are plainly visible."[8] They are specially so in the entries by Wyatt, the earliest in date of the three named authors (though preceded in the anthology by Surrey, who took first place by social rank). Since by rare good fortune we now have access to the Egerton manuscript where the texts of many poems by Wyatt are authenticated in his handwriting, entries by him in *Songes and Sonettes* are the most helpful measure of the reviser's methods.

Among the forms of polishing in Tottel's book, some would now be described as *modernizing*, a verb that did not come into English until the eighteenth century. This practice is still so fully accepted for verse anthologies that readers whose experiences of poems take place almost entirely in those specially prepared situations would be surprised to be told that they are given sixteenth-century and even later poems in a much altered state.

It is also surprising to modern readers that, even from the perspective of the mid-sixteenth century, Wyatt's poems written only about twenty years earlier would already have seemed to need polishing in such fundamental features as grammar, spelling, and punctuation, as well as in the more literary dimensions of meter and verse form. This was so because English of the period was changing much more rapidly than has been true since the last quarter of the seventeenth century, by which time linguistic standards were largely in place.

In the lifetime of Tottel's first generation of readers, many Old English grammatical constructions had virtually disappeared, but some were still in transition, so that Wyatt's verbs, for instance, were often in what must have seemed old-fashioned or rustic, awkward or incorrect forms. Three lines transcribed by Richard Harrier from the Egerton original of the sonnet beginning "The longe loue" (37), placed first among Wyatt's entries by Tottel, illustrate grammatical shifts, and changes in habits of spelling and punctuation:

> She that me lerneth to love & suffre
> and will that my trust & lust negligence
> be rayned by reason shame & reverence[9]

In Tottel's version, "lerneth" became "learns" and "suffre" is lengthened as "to suffer" to fill out the metrical line by replacing the syllable cropped from the first verb; in the next line "will" is corrected as "willes" and "lust" is put in the possessive form "lustes." Spellings are also brought up to date— "rayned" in the third line is modernized "reined"—to suit what had become standard forms more or less fixed by printing, which were at least supposed to mirror pronunciations spoken in London and for a radius of some miles from it.

Periods or full stops, colons, and commas began to be used more often especially in printing (handwritten texts like Wyatt's went on being more casual in their use of such markings). Tottel's punctuation shows that signaling the lengths of pauses or stops in reading aloud (still the common practice even in private) was not the only purpose of punctuation marks. They were also beginning to be placed, though with nothing like agreed-upon consistency, to separate semantic units, as these lines and the two poems to be quoted in full illustrate.

The practice of modernizing entries in anthologies is so pervasive still that in this century most readers of poetry in English have probably never seen a poem of Tottel's period, or even a sonnet by Shakespeare, in its original language. The reason for modern modernizing is at least purported to be that it removes misunderstandings between the reader and the poet's words. Its professed aim is no longer to elevate the style of the poem as a way to please or educate its readers, or to raise its value as a national treasure, what Tottel's preface implies were the aims of the extensive revisions in his anthology.

Somewhat similar intentions were shared by the equally famous— meaning both successful and influential—eighteenth-century anthologist Thomas Percy, in *Reliques of Ancient English Poetry: Consisting of Old Heroic Ballads, Songs, and Other Pieces of our earlier Poets (chiefly of the Lyric Kind.) Together with some few of later Date.* Hyder Rollins compared the revising practices of the two historically distant anthologists in a generalization that has long been a commonplace of literary history:

Both editors, judged by the standards of their times, were justified in 'improving' their texts, and beyond question the improvements thus introduced helped both the *Songs and Sonnets* and the *Reliques* to attain their remarkable popularity.[10]

Of course the standards of their times were dissimilar, and, as Percy's title carefully announced to prospective buyers, his was a much more mixed retrospective than Tottel's collection of only short poems looking back (with a few undated exceptions) over roughly half a century. The chronologically extended and formally mixed contents of the *Reliques*, and the association of that term with antiquarian discoveries, ensured an audience with varied expectations and judgments that Percy's presentations of poems tried to mediate among. In the preface to the fourth edition (dated 1794) he gave an explanation, or perhaps an apology, for this effort, using the conventional, self-effacing editorial third person: "His object was to please both the judicious Antiquary, and the Reader of Taste; and he hath endeavoured to gratify both without offending either."[11]

What prompted this decorous self-defense is that Percy had given offense, above all by his treatment of the old ballads, to a small number of readers with antiquarian interests who had already absorbed some knowledge of the genre and of proper editorial methods from earlier collections, such as Edward Capell's of 1760: *Prolusions, or Select Pieces of Antient Poetry, compil'd with great care from their several Originals, and offer'd to the Publick as Specimens of the Integrity that should be found in the Editions of Worthy Authors*.

Attacks from antiquarians began as early as 1783 in Joseph Ritson's *A Select Collection of English Songs*, and reached a high pitch in 1867 when John Hales and Frederick Furnivall denounced Percy's revisions of ballads which "puffed," "powdered," "pomatumed" them to make them fit for "Polite Society."[12] Meanwhile Percy's contemporary "reader of taste," undisturbed by questions of authenticity or editorial integrity, welcomed the elegantly Gothic-flavored ballads. Thomas Warton wrote to Percy as soon as his *Reliques* first appeared: "At Oxford it is a favourite Work; and I doubt not, but it is equally popular in Town."[13] A later admirer predicted in *The Gentleman's Magazine* in 1793 that "Dr. Percy's elegant Collection . . . will remain a standard book, while the *more strictly accurate* compilations of a *peevish* antiquarian or two are forgotten."[14]

Scarcely any members of Percy's audience seemed to notice or argue with his revisions of poems by what his title called *our earlier Poets*—seventeenth-century authors and a few Elizabethans—(*chiefly of the Lyric Kind*). While the ballads, both for their popularity and their notoriety, established Percy's later reputation, the poems in short forms more often than the ballads found spaces in later anthologies. Percy's selection contributed, with *Songes and Sonettes* and *The Golden Treasury*, to the steady rise in status of the lyric kind or genre, and probably to the modern use of the term *lyric*, ever widening in meaning at least since the publication of the *Lyrical Ballads*.

Percy's presentations of the shorter poems were designed to satisfy antiquarian interests by surrounding the entries with commentary while producing them in a form suited to "a polished age, like the present."[15] In each volume he intermingled "the rudeness of more obsolete poems" (meaning the old, long ballads) with what he called "little elegant pieces of the lyric kind."[16] To enhance their elegance, he continued polishing his shorter selections by treating them with *corrections* and *improvements*. These widely current critical terms could be interpreted to mean conforming their texts more closely to the most authoritative versions or modernizing them according to present standards, depending on the different understandings of antiquarians and readers not so specialized.

In the second book of Volume I "(Containing Ballads that illustrate Shakespeare)" Percy included the Elizabethan song "The Passionate Shepherd to His Love." He introduced it in his commentary as a "beautiful sonnet" attributed to Shakespeare in *The Passionate Pilgrim* of 1599, but reassigned a year later to Christopher Marlowe by his signature in "the old poetical miscellany, intitled *Englands Helicon*"; then again in 1651 in *The Compleat Angler* by Isaac Walton, who quoted it "under the character of 'that smooth song, which was made by Kit. Marlow, now at least fifty years ago. . . . Old-fashioned poetry, but choicely good.'"[17]

Here is the text of Marlowe's poem as it was printed in 1600 in *Englands Helicon* (now considered the authoritative version):

> *The passionate Sheepheard to his loue.*
>
> Come liue with mee, and be my loue,
> And we will all the pleasures proue,
> That Vallies, groues, hills and fieldes,
> Woods, or steepie mountaine yeeldes.

And wee will sit vpon the Rocks,
Seeing the Sheepheards feede theyr flocks,
By shallow Riuers, to whose falls,
Melodious byrds sings Madrigalls.

And I will make thee beds of Roses,
And a thousand fragrant poesies,
A cap of flowers, and a kirtle,
Imbroydred all with leaues of Mirtle.

A gowne made of the finest wooll,
Which from our pretty Lambes we pull,
Fayre lined slippers for the cold:
With buckles of the purest gold.

A belt of straw, and Iuie buds,
With Corall clasps and Amber studs,
And if these pleasures may thee moue,
Come liue with mee, and be my loue.

The Sheepheards Swaines shall daunce & sing,
For thy delight each May-morning,
If these delights thy minde may moue;
Then liue with mee, and be my loue.[18]

Percy's text of Marlowe's song in the fourth edition differs in only one detail from the version he had prepared for the first: there the opening line is printed "Live with me, and be my love." This closeness in the texts makes the much greater difference between the two introductory commentaries to the poem puzzling. In the first edition the corroboration of Marlowe's authorship in *Englands Helicon* is brought in only indirectly, at two removes: "for the editor of the 'Muses Library,' has reprinted a poem from *Englands Helicon*, 1600, subscribed *Ignoto*, and thus intitled 'In Imitation of C. Marlow, beginning thus,

'Come live with me, and be my dear,
And we will revel all the year,
In plains and groves, &c.'

whereas the note in the later edition quoted above sounds as if Percy had seen the older miscellany.[19] If so, there is no sign that he used it to make corrections and improvements in his later text of the poem. Either the note to it is misleading, or he chose to ignore the Elizabethan version, choosing details from Walton's printed half a century closer to his own time, and using his own judgment of what would please.

Here is Percy's last version of the poem for comparison with the text in *Englands Helicon*:

Come live with me, and be my love,
And we wil all the pleasures prove
That hils and vallies, dale and field,
And all the craggy mountains yield.

There will we sit upon the rocks,
And see the shepherds feed their flocks,
By shallow rivers, to whose falls
Melodious birds sing madrigals.

There will I make thee beds of roses
With a thousand fragrant posies,
A cap of flowers, and a kirtle
Imbrodered all with leaves of mirtle;

A gown made of the finest wool,
Which from our pretty lambs we pull;
Slippers lin'd choicely for the cold;
With buckles of the purest gold;

A belt of straw, and ivie buds,
With coral clasps, and amber studs:
And if these pleasures may thee move,
Then live with me, and be my love.

The shepherd swains shall dance and sing
For thy delight each May morning:
If these delights thy mind may move,
Then live with me, and be my love.[20]

Some of the variants from the text of 1600 already existed in Walton's: the verbs "yeeldes" in the first stanza and "sings" in the second were corrected in both Walton's and Percy's versions; the archaic *es* plurals were dropped from "Lambes" and "swaines"; "daunce" was conformed to the modern spelling "dance," "Sheepheards" to "shepherds"; capital letters were taken from "Vallies," "Corall," "Iuie." Percy also copied Walton's substitution for the simple, unmistakably Elizabethan line "Fayre lined slippers for the cold" the mid-seventeenth century, fashion-conscious sophistication of "Slippers lin'd choicely for the cold." In many other details, Percy went further than Walton from the linguistic practices of 1600 by changing virtually all spellings, capitalizations, and punctuation marks that might have seemed old-fashioned in 1651 but were obsolete by the later eighteenth century.

Beyond even this thorough linguistic modernizing, Percy transformed the Elizabethan song stylistically into one that would not have seemed out of place in Dodsley's miscellany. He accomplished this mainly by disguising its seemingly naive line of persuasion: "Come liue with mee, and be my loue, / And we will all the pleasures proue," "And we wil sit vpon the Rocks," "And I will make thee beds of Roses, / And a thousand fragrant posies," "And if these pleasures may thee moue, / Come liue with mee, and be my loue."

Percy erased this artful imitation of simple rustic speech by substituting connectives "There," "There," "With," "Then" to make a more logical than merely additive sequence, and by using the literary inversions in "There will I," "There will we" to replace the direct, spoken order of "And we will," "And I will." He made a skillful attempt to render the poem agreeable to modern taste with the least damage to its interest as a specimen of earlier English verse.

Percy's interests in polishing, or improving and correcting the poems in his anthology were closer to the social and patriotic intentions Tottel announced in his preface than to the assumption of anthology makers now: that the purpose of modernizing is simply to make poems more understandable. Somehow, though that view is generally held, it has not brought a common agreement about how it should be put into practice.

At one end of the spectrum are the few anthologists who try to respect the variousness of English in periods before their own. A remarkably early instance is *The Principles and Progress of English Poetry* of 1904, principally edited by Charles Gayley, a professor of English at the University of California. Though the anthology was designed for "the general reader" as well as for students, the preface argues against modernizing on the grounds that to make an earlier poet "look like one of to-day" misleads readers to "expect of this modernly apparelled gentleman the sentiments of our modern age," and obscures the historical "flavor" and "development of the language."[21]

This position was scarcely taken again until the publication in 1950 of the multivolume *Poets of the English Language* edited by W. H. Auden and Norman Holmes Pearson, which includes authors from Langland to Yeats. The anthologists made what was in 1950 and is still (except in special period anthologies) the unusual decision not to make revisions in the grammar or spelling of the earlier entries. In their preface they protested that modernizing by anthologists "does violence to both the meaning and the poetic effect" of the poems in their charge, while they themselves changed or added punctuation in the early poems.[22]

The happy event of Christopher Ricks's decision to break with the convention of Oxford anthologies by leaving the poems in his edition of *The Oxford Book of English Verse* unmodernized should set a compellingly respected example. Beyond that, Ricks's prefatory explanation of the decision should have educational effects on the presentation of poems in retrospective anthologies. His main argument against the common practice is that while modernizing may make the poems more immediately accessible, that is, easier to read, not modernizing encourages another sort of accessibility. His reasoning is that "a duller page—and modernizing does have a dulling effect, a bland levelling—has its own quietly powerful way of being inaccessible."[23]

At the other end of the spectrum is the first edition of *The Norton Anthology of Poetry*, published twenty years after the Auden/Pearson volumes. Its preface says that the texts "derive from authoritative editions but have been normalized in spelling and capitalization according to modern American usage" (except where such changes would "significantly obscure meter or meaning").[24] The term *normalizing* as it seems to be used here has even more radical implications of uniformity than would *modernizing*. Besides removing some obstacles to the reader's understanding, the process of normalizing goes farther, setting new standards of regularity and familiarity for the presentation of poems in an anthology. It makes them all seem to have been treated by the same, and for that reason mechanical, process, and to come from the same impersonal source: the anthology itself or its committee of five compilers. The regularizing of texts intensifies the effect that all anthologies have to some degree: of making the poems in it contemporaneous or out of time, so that the sequential order of pages substitutes for and blots out the participations of poems in any kind of history.

RESTRUCTURING AND REINTERPRETING

For English poets the earlier sixteenth century was a period of learning and experimenting with meters and short forms being imported from modern literatures, mainly Italian and French. The sonnet, in particular, was beginning to grow in prestige, a movement Tottel apparently recognized and followed where he could, promoting the form by his choices, placing, and recastings of poems.

Of Surrey's thirty-six entries, fifteen are sonnets; among Wyatt's ninety-some, almost a third. By contrast, among about the same number of unassigned poems, there are nine sonnets (two of them tributes to Petrarch's, whose name was better known in England than his poems), and Grimald contributed three. These proportions suggest that the sonnet still had more reputation than practitioners, and that it was still mainly associated with courtly makers like Surrey and Wyatt.

Tottel, in turn, associated his anthology especially with their work in sonnets, both original and translated from Italian models. He promoted their sonnets not just by the number of them, but by their arrangement. For example, the pages given to Wyatt open with fifteen sonnets in a row, a preference hardly to be missed by readers to whom sonnets in English were still something of a novelty.

Possibly in the interest of strengthening this association with the more learned kind of poetry promised in the preface to the reader, Tottel included three poems restructured as sonnets that the Egerton manuscript shows Wyatt wrote in the different form of the rondeau. Tottel probably recognized this fixed form—Chaucer worked in it once—of three stanzas, two with a refrain, but for his readers it would have been easy to confuse with songs in the native tradition.

Tottel tried consistently to exclude or disguise that kind of poem along with others too readily mistakable for popular verse. Of the sixty-odd songs by Wyatt surviving wholly or partly in his handwriting or attributed to him in the sixteenth century, only three were published in Tottel's anthology.

He printed them and all other stanzaic poems in his book without spaces marking divisions between stanzas, with the effect of weakening the prominence of the refrain and the likeness to popular songs.

Wyatt structured his rondeaux, with some allowed variations, according to the fixed features of the form. It has only two rhymes distributed in thirteen rhymed lines of eight or ten syllables separated into three stanzas. The second and third stanzas end in an unrhymed refrain of only three or four syllables repeating the opening words of line 1. The order of rhymes is typically aabba/aab refrain/aabba refrain. In *Songes and Sonettes* the restructuring of Wyatt's rondeaux suited them to the book's preferred "stateliness of stile," polishing and promoting them to the more learned—more courtly, sophisticated, Italianate—sonnet form.

The rondeau quoted here is mainly as it was printed in *Collected Poems of Sir Thomas Wyatt*, edited by Kenneth Muir and Patricia Thomson. Their version follows wording of the Egerton manuscript, with punctuation added (while the indentation used here follows the indentation in Harrier's transcription):

> What vaileth trouth? or, by it, to take payn?
>> To stryve, by stedfastnes, for to attayne,
>> To be iuste and true: and fle from dowblenes:
>> Sythens all alike, where rueleth craftines
>> Rewarded is boeth fals, and plain.
>> Sonest he spedeth, that moost can fain;
>> True meanyng hert is had in disdayn.
>> Against deceipte and dowblenes
>>> What vaileth trouth?
>
>> Decyved is he by crafty trayn
>> That meaneth no gile and doeth remayn
>> Within the trappe, withoute redresse,
>> But, for to love, lo, suche a maisteres,
>> Whose crueltie nothing can refrayn,
>>> What vaileth trouth?[25]

The version in *Songes and Sonettes* suggests that whoever restructured the rondeau was working from a manuscript copy quite faithful to the Egerton model.

The changes made in Tottel's version, besides the modernizing of spelling and punctuation found throughout the anthology, are all consistent with the reviser's aim of transforming Wyatt's rondeau into a sonnet. His logistic problem was to recast a poem of thirteen rhymed lines (only the first three countable as iambic pentameter) and two unrhymed refrains as a poem of fourteen iambic pentameter lines with interlocking rhymes:

> Complaint for true loue
> vnrequited.

> What vaileth troth? or by it, to take payn?
> To striue by stedfastnesse, for to attayn
> How to be iust: and flee from doublenesse?
> Since all alyke, where ruleth craftinesse,
> Rewarded is both crafty false, and plain.
> Soonest he spedes, that most can lye and fayne.
> True meaning hart is had in hye disdain.
> Against deceyt, and cloked doubleness,
> What vaileth troth, or parfit stedfastnesse.
> Deceaud is he, by false and crafty trayn,
> That meanes no gyle, and faithfull doth remayn
> Within the trap, without help or redresse.
> But for to loue (lo) such a sterne maistresse,
> Where cruelty dwelles, alas it were in vain. (70)

Working close to the given structure, the reviser turned the first eight lines more consistently into five stresses, and repeated the first refrain as the opening of line nine, perhaps to keep going the original effect of forward-moving argument in stanzas frustrated by repetition in refrains. He kept equally close to the lines of the third stanza, while regularizing their stress pattern, until the end when, forced by his chosen verse form to drop the refrain, he rewrote the line before it to end the sonnet with a restatement of the lover's bitter sense of helplessness.

Readers now who know Wyatt's work would miss in this recasting his characteristic energy and immediacy. In the Egerton original these qualities depend in some large measure on the uneven lines, the abrupt questions (perhaps over-emphasized in modernized versions by inserted question marks), and the pointing of the short refrains. If we can forgive what would now be considered the anthologist's unacceptable enterprise of transforming a poem from its author's chosen form to another, we can see that the revised version in *Songes and Sonettes* is a quite sophisticated recasting that shows considerable sense of what Wyatt's rondeau used its shape to express, and awareness of the demands made by different verse forms.

The reviser of this poem deserves a more respectful judgment than Rollins's, that "his chief qualification was the ability to count syllables and accents on his fingers, and thus to make the verses regular."[26] In this revision he produced a poem polished in all the senses that made the adjective a favorite term of praise in Tottel's period for the kinds of poems promised to readers in his preface. Rollins explained Tottel's restructurings like this one as expressions of personal prejudices in taste: that "he disliked refrains and needlessly omitted" them from poems of Wyatt's.[27] What we can see instead is that the revisions are the anthologist's responses to the literary expectations of the readers he aimed to please, and to the poem's situation in the kind of book he designed.

By setting another entry of Wyatt's from *Songes and Sonettes* against the wording of its authorial text in the Egerton manuscript, we can watch the ways many small revisions of the poem's linguistic and formal dimensions working together can create a sense of the reviser's presence as it were beneath his polishing of the poem's surface.

Muir and Thomson's printing of the poem reproduces Wyatt's wording with punctuation added (but I have again followed the pattern of indentations in Harrier's transcript):

> They fle from me that sometyme did me seke
>   With naked fote stalking in my chambre.
>   I have sene theim gentill tame and meke
>   That nowe are wyld and do not remembre
>   That sometyme they put theimself in daunger
>   To take bred at my hand; and nowe they raunge
>   Besely seking with a continuell chaunge.
> Thancked be fortune, it hath ben othrewise
>   Twenty tymes better; but ons in speciall,
>   In thyn arraye after a pleasaunt gyse
>   When her lose gowne from her shoulders did fall,
>   And she me caught in her armes long and small;

Therewithall swetely did me kysse,
And softely said, 'dere hert, howe like you this?'
It was no dreme: I lay brode waking.
But all is torned thorough my gentilnes
Into a straunge fasshion of forsaking;
And I have leve to goo of her goodeness,
And she also to vse new fangilnes.
But syns that I so kyndely ame serued,
I would fain knowe what she hath deserued.[28]

Tottel's printed version shows that the copy that came into his hands must again have been quite faithful to the Egerton model. Indentations parallel the lineation in Wyatt's text because they divide the poem into three seven-line stanzas. Nine of the original lines are unchanged (except for the reviser's habitual modernizing of grammar, spelling, and punctuation), and the rest—until the last line—are modified only in a single detail:

The louer sheweth how he is
forsaken of such as he somtime enioyed.

They flee from me, that somtime did me seke
With naked fote stalkyng within my chamber.
Once haue I seen them gentle, tame, and meke,
That now are wild, and do not once remember
That sometyme they haue put them selues in danger,
To take bread at my hand, and now they range,
Busily sekyng in continuall change.
Thanked be fortune, it hath bene otherwise
Twenty tymes better: but once especiall,
In thinne aray, after a pleasant gyse,
When her loose gowne did from her shoulders fall,
And she me caught in her armes long and small,
And therwithall, so swetely did me kysse,
And softly sayd: deare hart, how like you this?
It was no dreame: for I lay broade awakyng.
But all is turnde now through my gentlenesse.
Into a bitter fashion of forsakyng:
And I haue leaue to go of her goodnesse,
And she also to vse newfanglenesse.

> But, sins that I vnkyndly so am serued:
> How like you this, what hath she now deserued? (52)

Apart from the modernizing, all the changes in words and word order point to the reviser's aim of making the other lines in the poem conform to the metrical pattern set up in the first: ten syllables, in an arrangement of stresses that could be and probably was counted as iambic pentameter. The other lines of Wyatt's that had ten syllables—6, 8, 9, 10, 12, 14, 18, 19—were left undisturbed, having evidently passed the reviser's test. How clearly he made a distinction between decasyllabic and iambic pentameter lines is hard to tell; certainly he did not understand what or if principles guided Wyatt's metrical stresses, a question discussed in all its complexity by John Thompson.[29] Even so, what the maker of this revised poem was doing is clear; almost all of his changes were additions or substitutions of a word that would bring the number of syllables in each line up to the requisite ten.

If stretching lines into decasyllables were all that the revisions accomplished, they would support Rollins's view that they required nothing of the reviser but fingers to count syllables and stresses. Instead, the particular choices of added or substituted words suggest that the process of making the metrical changes led their author, inadvertently perhaps, to possibilities of interpretation interestingly tilted in a new direction from Wyatt's poem, and predicted in the specially crafted title added to the anthology's version.

The title of this poem in *Songes and Sonettes*, "The louer sheweth how he is forsaken of such as he somtime enioyed," fits it more particularly than would some general formula like one used for another entry by Wyatt, "The louer complaineth himself forsaken" (66), which could have more loosely described "They flee from me." The precise fit of its title also shows sharply in contrast with the one given by the editor G. F. Nott in 1814 to his presentation of Wyatt's poem: "The Lover sheweth how he is forsaken of Fortune who sometime favoured him."[30] Nott's title points the reader to a general truth more than to the particular occasion that prompted the resentful boasting compressed in the reviser's telling choice of "enioyed."

The formula "The louer sheweth" in Tottel's title fits it to his preferred type by presenting the poem as a performance in a stylized form: in this instance not a complaint or a description, but more exactly a demonstration or proof. Although any performance implies an audience, the act of showing is different from complaining or describing because it suggests that this performer has an interest in persuading his listeners by his argument, en-listing them on his side. He is making a case to an audience who will be asked to pronounce the justness of his cause, which is what happens in the last line of the revised poem: "How like you this, what hath she now dese-rued?"

The small revisions leading up to this one radically rewritten line pre-pare for it in more than metrical ways. The particular words added have a combined effect that other words the reviser could easily have chosen to fill out the metrical line would not. Building on the contrast Wyatt made of "ons" in line 9 with "nowe" in line 4, the reviser left these two words in place and repeated them in two other places: "Once haue I seen," "do not once remember"; "But all is turnde now," "what hath she now deserued?" This pattern suggests that design, not just luck, went into the reviser's choices. To the particular point here, they give the lover a more calculating manner, as if he had carefully shaped his proof in advance to convince his audience that his settled anger and resentment are justified.

The much reviled revision of Wyatt's line (in manuscript unpunctu-ated) "It was no dreme I lay brode waking" by the intrusion of the logical connective "for" (to add a syllable) is the clearest instance of this expressive pattern of revisions. The line loses its powerful immediacy: the sense of the lover reliving the beauty and wonder of that "ons in speciall," while at the same time feeling "nowe" a bewildering mixture of resentment, pain, anger, and bereavement. Instead, the revised line strengthens the sense that the lover is in control of his memory, using it to support his grievance. The sub-stitution in line 17 of "bitter" for Wyatt's more subtle "straunge"—foreign, unfamiliar, unaccountable, astonishing—reflects the lover's narrowed, hardened feelings. So does the change of Wyatt's richly contradictory "Kyndly"—according to nature, graciously—to the simply reviling "vn-kindly"—unnaturally, cruelly. The revised last line is a fully prepared cul-mination of this series of choices, but still powerful in the shocking naked-ness of the lover's appeal to his audience to approve his vindictiveness, and by their approval to soothe his injured vanity at being now deprived of what he once rightly "enioyed."

This poem has often been the chosen example in discussions of Wyatt's expressively effective use of metrically irregular lines: their special immedi-acy, their dramatic re-creation of a living voice; their allowance of ambiguities. It is the poem of Wyatt's that readers now are most likely to know, but it got to be an anthology-piece only recently, when *immediate, dramatic, spoken, ambiguous*—a far cry from *polished, corrected, improved*—became preferred terms to describe favorite poems in short forms.

In a representative sample of eight nineteenth-century retrospective anthologies where any poems at all by Wyatt were included, "They flee from me" was never among them, while Surrey's more polished poem "The soote season" was in every one. Even as late as 1900, while Quiller-Couch did make space for "They flee from me" in *The Oxford Book of English Verse*, he chose to print it in Tottel's revised interpretation instead of the more authoritative text that had been easy to come by since it was published by Nott, who gave "the Harington MS" as its source and added the comment: "The Ode is one of no inconsiderable merit: it is original and full of feeling."[31]

The ideals of polished poetry that the revisions in *Songes and Sonettes* were designed to achieve held their high place until well into the twentieth century. Quiller-Couch replaced Tottel's poem with Wyatt's in the 1939 edition of his anthology, though even then could not resist repeating the title he had used in the first edition: a quotation, untranslated and unidentified, from one of Horace's odes, which could not fail to make Quiller-Couch's Oxonian presence felt.

Like Tottel, Palgrave planned a gathering of poems in short forms defined in the full title of *The Golden Treasury* as *Songs and Lyrical Poems*, terms similar to, and as loose as, Tottel's *Songes and Sonettes*. Palgrave described them in his preface as polished poems having "finish in proportion to brevity," a requirement that dictated not only the choice of entries but also their presentation, that is, their arrangement and Palgrave's revisions of them, structural as well as linguistic:

The poems are printed entire, except in a very few instances (specified in the notes) where a stanza has been omitted. The omissions have been risked only when the piece could be thus brought to a closer lyrical unity: and, as essentially opposed to this unity, extracts, obviously such, are excluded. In regard to the text, the purpose of the book has appeared to justify the choice of the most poetical version, wherever more than one exists: and much labour has been given to present each poem, in disposition, spelling, and punctuation, to the greatest advantage.[32]

This description of textual changes seems to limit Palgrave's structural revisions to "a very few" omissions of a stanza or several lines, when in fact there are instances where his cuts were extensive. In the first edition he admitted to having left out two "intermediate stanzas" from a poem by Thomas Hood, but did not report some more serious extractions.[33] By acknowledging a few, he encouraged whether deliberately or not the impression that other poems were printed in their entirety. In later editions he was more consistent in response to criticisms in acknowledging his changes.

Palgrave's recastings in the interest of "closer lyrical unity" sometimes transformed the poem from one kind or genre to another that would better suit the design of the anthology, as Wyatt's rondeau was recast in the preferred sonnet form for *Songes and Sonettes*. The following entry perfectly illustrates, as Palgrave intended by his revisions that it should, his requirement for its admission to *The Golden Treasury*: "finish in proportion to brevity." This is precisely the recommendation of the author of these lines for excellence in the conduct of life and in the "measures" of poetry:

> The Noble Nature
>
> It is not growing like a tree
> In bulk, doth make Man better be;
> Or standing long an oak, three hundred year,
> To fall a log at last, dry, bald, and sere:
> A lily of a day
> Is fairer far in May,
> Although it fall and die that night—
> It was the plant and flower of Light.
> In small proportions we just beauties see;
> And in short measures life may perfect be. (LXXIII)
>
> *B. Jonson*

Nothing in the presentation of the poem or in Palgrave's notes tells readers not familiar with Jonson's poems that these lines are one stanza of twelve from his heroic ode "To the Immortal Memorie, and Friendship of That Noble Paire, Sir Lucius Cary, and Sir H. Morison." By all ways of measuring, one would call this stanza an extract, included by Palgrave in violation of his own requirement of a poem's wholeness, to further the "closer lyrical unity" of the anthology itself.

Another example of Palgrave's ways of refinishing poems is his treatment of some stanzas he assigned by signature to Thomas Carew. He gave no note on this entry, so readers who have never seen the lines elsewhere can have no way of knowing that they are looking at a poem very different from Carew's though in the same song form, its title bearing no resemblance to the original:

The True Beauty

He that loves a rosy cheek
  Or a coral lip admires,
Or from star-like eyes doth seek
  Fuel to maintain his fires;
As old Time makes these decay,
So his flames must waste away.

But a smooth and steadfast mind,
  Gentle thoughts, and calm desires,
Hearts with equal love combined,
  Kindle never-dying fires: -
Where these are not, I despise
Lovely cheeks or lips or eyes. (LXXXVII)
  T. Carew

The title virtually pairs these stanzas with the one of Jonson's given the title "The Noble Nature," and the lines themselves support the likeness. They seem to be almost as "smooth" in their measures and "steadfast"—though perhaps too complacent—in their control of commonplaces that are the traditional matter of the moral epigram.

Here is Carew's poem as it appeared in his *Poems* of 1640:

Disdaine returned

Hee that loves a Rosie cheeke,
  Or a corall lip admires,
Or from star-like eyes doth seeke,
  Fuell to maintaine his fires;
As old *Time* makes these decay,
So his flames must waste away.

But a smooth, and stedfast mind,
  Gentle thoughts, and calme desires,
Hearts, with equall love combind,
  Kindle never dying fires.

Where these are not, I despise
Lovely cheekes, or lips, or eyes.

No teares, *Celia*, now shall win,
    My resolv'd heart, to returne;
I have searcht thy soule within,
    And find nought, but pride, and scorne;
I have learn'd thy arts, and now
    Can disdaine as much as thou.
Some power, in my revenge convay
That love to her, I cast away.[34]

The wittily vindictive turn at the last stanza, wittily predicted by the impersonal title, exposes the "smooth, and stedfast" posture of the vengeful
lover masking himself as an author of Jonsonian moral epigrams. The poem
turns personal, immediate, dramatic, giving new force to the shift in grammatical persons from "his fires," "his flames" to "I despise" in the second
stanza. The reader of the poem in Palgrave's version can easily ignore these
early signals. In Carew's, the third stanza brings them to life, and makes the
reader a knowing participant in the poet-lover's game.

This is a different experience from the one encouraged by a poem like
"The True Beauty," which offers the pleasure of recognition as the reader
appreciates the fitting of commonplaces to perfectly finished form. Witty
and dramatic qualities are subordinated to what Palgrave in his preface
called "that loftier and finer excellence here required."

To harmonize the poem with this ideal for his anthology, Palgrave, acting something like Percy in his borrowings from Walton to refashion Marlowe's song, felt justified in preferring "the most poetical version, wherever
more than one exists." In this instance, the version of Carew's song that he
picked was one that Percy revised for his *Reliques*, although Palgrave certainly had seen the poem in its entirety, with the title given it in its first
printing, in Allingham's *Nightingale Valley*. Palgrave modernized the obsolete spellings preserved in the two stanzas of Carew's included in the *Reliques*, substituted his own title for Percy's "Unfading Beauty," and left out
Percy's note that introduced them:

This little beautiful sonnet is reprinted from a small volume of 'Poems by Thomas Carew, Esq. . .1640.' This elegant, and almost-forgotten writer, whose po-

ems have been deservedly revived, died in the prime of his age, in 1639. In the original follows a third stanza; which, not being of general application, nor of equal merit, I have ventured to omit.[35]

The similar but also different practices of the two anthologists point to several simultaneously possible conclusions. One is that the relatively unmixed character of Palgrave's selections gave him more freedom than Percy was allowed, because it simplified the expectations of his readers. Another is that Palgrave's passionate assurance about the truth and beauty of his symphonic design for *The Golden Treasury* gave him a stronger sense of proprietary rights over his chosen poems as author of the book in which he had disposed them.

Still another possible conclusion of a more general sort is that during the hundred years between the publications of the *Reliques* and *The Golden Treasury*, retrospective anthologies intended for the more educated among the steadily growing numbers of readers had made further gains in respectability, had found their way more as a matter of course into those readers' libraries, and were more often and more seriously reviewed along with other established kinds of poetry books. Once recognized as a genre, anthologies in this class might be allowed to follow their own conventions. Even those designed for less educated readers than Palgrave's could imitate his freedoms with poems, often simply reprinting his radically revised texts. Agnes Repplier copied "The True Beauty" without noting Palgrave's changes in *A Book of Famous Verse* of 1892; Burton Stevenson reprinted "The Noble Nature" (identified as an extract from the ode) in 1918 in *The Home Book of Verse*.[36]

Percy, unlike Tottel and Palgrave, did not escape criticism in his own time for his treatment of entries in his anthology, largely because, unlike them, he made some antiquarian claims for his work. Still, a hundred years later his reception among poets and large numbers of poetry readers was so admiring that even the antiquarian scholars who were his most ferocious attackers, Hales and Furnivall, acknowledged the value of his anthology: "But though, as between Ritson and Percy, I hope we are all now on Ritson's side, we must not let this blind us to the great debt we allow to Percy," who led the vanguard of the army later commanded by Wordsworth, "which has won us back to nature and truth."[37] These severe critics paid Percy the sort of tribute that has been given, among anthologists otherwise, only to Tottel and Palgrave:

> The publication of the *Reliques*, then, constitutes an epoch in the history of
> the great revival of taste, in whose blessings we now participate. . . . The noble
> reformation, that received so great an impulse in 1765, advanced thenceforward
> steadily. The taste that was awakened never slumbered again.[38]

Paradoxically, the entries in his anthology that Percy revised most radically
were the ones that spread the widest influence through reprintings, and
earned the most praise.

Given modern standards of integrity in the presentation of the poem's
text, it is unsettling to recognize that anthologists who were among those
showing least respect for that principle, and who set the most influential examples for ignoring it, should be the three who had the most creative effects
on the history of poetry in English. This odd juxtaposition could be only
historical coincidence. Or it could have come about because Tottel, Percy,
and Palgrave were specially aware of what might be the experience for readers of meeting poems they did not know, often from periods not their own,
and were specially attentive to how the anthologist's presence might enhance the experience. They showed that quality of attention by their skills in
exercising what in their periods were recognized to be the prerogatives of
anthology makers: to rewrite, recast, revise, and give titles to poems so that
they could take their places in the enhancing design of the anthology, and
could please its readers.

PART II

WHAT MAKES AN ANTHOLOGY-PIECE

CHAPTER FOUR

"ECHOING SONG"

ELIZABETHAN AND SEVENTEENTH-
CENTURY POEMS

No generation of English poets before the early nineteenth century has been uninterruptedly represented in collections of poets put together after their own time. And no one poem has been a continuous presence in printed anthologies from their beginnings through the twentieth century. These discontinuities in time are not surprising when we consider that the history of anthologies participates in the history of poetry and in the history of criticism, re-enacting or representing their shifts in direction; sometimes, in some measure, shaping them.

We can trace this pattern most faithfully by following the fortunes of sixteenth- and earlier seventeenth-century poems, since they have a longer presence in verse collections than poems written later, while paradoxically they also have a longer history in anthologies than poems that preceded them in the chronology of poetry writing. This paradox neatly diagrams the curious situation of poems in an anthology: that the history they are located in there is the history of anthologies. One of the ways this book charts that history is by tracing the discontinuities and the persistence of the poems that do and do not appear in them.

DISCONTINUITIES

To start, then, where printed poetry anthologies in English began, which quite uncoincidentally coincided with a surge of interest in shorter lyric forms (encouraged by Italian and French models), we look back again to the sixteenth-century. Anthologies that imitated Tottel's *Songes and Sonettes* included poems—even some of the same ones—by some of the same poets, but gave bigger and better spaces to the work of more recent or even living authors. Prestigious favorites were Spenser, and above all Sir Philip Sidney, whose poems were still being given pride of place (befitting his high social rank, it was stated or implied) some fifteen years after his death as the opening entries in *Englands Helicon* of 1600 and *A Poetical Rapsody* of 1602.

Englands Helicon was reprinted in 1614 and *A Poetical Rapsody* went on being published in revised editions up to 1621, but interest in new printed miscellanies seems to have dwindled or to have been thwarted by political circumstances until after the Restoration. In those that were printed, sixteenth-century poems were virtually ignored. *Witts Recreation* (1640), where all entries were unassigned according to common practice in this period, included only a small number of very short poems by Marlowe, Shakespeare, and a few now no longer anthologized Elizabethan writers, among quantities of more recent verses mostly by these days little-known poets and translators with university connections. *Parnassus Biceps* (1656) is a retrospective collection of nearly a hundred poems going only as far back as early Stuart verse. *The Academy of Compliments* (1663) has one poem by Sir Walter Ralegh in among its small selection of earlier seventeenth-century poems, and the same is true of *Le Prince d'Amour* (1660).

Contrary to what we might expect, sixteenth-century poems were not pushed aside to make room for the work of the next generations of poets that readers now are used to seeing on the pages of anthologies after the Elizabethans. Among the vast quantities of *ignotos* and the many unfamiliar names in these later seventeenth-century collections, there are only scattered poems by those authors no retrospective anthology now would be without. The combined list is short: Jonson represented by a few poems and Donne by even fewer; Abraham Cowley, Sir John Suckling, and Herrick present in single entries; Henry King and Richard Corbett given more space than is now allotted for their one or two poems usually found in modern anthologies; Carew most often and most generously included.

The same earlier seventeenth-century poets appeared again in 1716 and 1727 in the last editions of the Dryden/Tonson miscellanies, unexpectedly since the series had been originally designed, as Dryden had written to Tonson in 1684, "to have nothing but new."[1] It seems likely that the addition of earlier poets was meant to persuade potential buyers that the later sets of volumes were worth adding to their libraries.

The Jacobean and Caroline poets were displayed in these two last editions in fuller selections than they had been allowed in any of the seventeenth-century collections, with the added presence of Michael Drayton, Edmund Waller and Sir John Denham, Andrew Marvell and Milton. After these editions of the miscellanies, eighteenth-century anthologies up to about 1790 (excepting *The Muses Library*) encouraged the vague impression that there were no shorter poems before the Restoration worth preserving. They mapped English poetry the way it came to be defined within the bounds of the series associated with Johnson's *Lives of the English Poets*, as if its history began with Cowley.

Still, an audience was preparing or being prepared to receive anthologies that would look further into the literary past than the list of poets the publishers of Johnson's *Lives* had dictated to him as the only names likely to sell the series. Johnson himself contributed to this stirring of interest by encouraging his friend Percy to publish his *Reliques of Ancient English Poetry*. Johnson's support, strategically mentioned in Percy's preface, probably helped to make the elegantly printed anthology an acceptable addition to a gentleman's library (aided by the careful choice of dedication to the "Countess of Northumberland: In Her Own Right Baroness Percy").[2]

Percy's *Reliques* was best known in its own time, as it still is, for its success in making a respected place in literary tradition for what its full title calls *Old Heroic Ballads*, [and] *Songs*, but the anthology also helped toward the acceptance of earlier lyric poems as well. Listed among the contents in the title are *other Pieces of our earlier Poets, (Chiefly of the Lyric Kind.)*, among them some by the same seventeenth-century authors preferred in earlier anthologies—Jonson, Carew, Suckling—along with Richard Lovelace and Sir Henry Wotton.

More unpredictably, readers of the *Reliques* also came on sixteenth-century poems that had sunk almost out of sight by the 1620s with the Elizabethan miscellanies where Percy dug to find his choices: verses by Thomas Lord Vaux, Gascoigne, Marlowe, Ralegh, Samuel Daniel, John Lyly, and some unidentified authors. It could be said, with some exaggeration and simplification, that the revival of Elizabethan lyric poetry had its beginnings in the pages of Percy's *Reliques*. Robert Southey suggested almost as much in his preface to *Specimens of the Later English Poets* (companion to Ellis's early *Specimens*) published in 1807. It was his opinion that the growing interest in Shakespeare had brought "our old writers" to public attention, that "Warton aided in this good work," but that it "was forwarded more effectually by the publication of the Reliques of Ancient Poetry."[3]

Though Percy's selection of earlier lyric poems was slim and unobtrusively scattered among many more prominently displayed entries, the prestige of his anthology seems to have promoted certain of his chosen poems to their positions ever since as anthology-pieces. Percy was cited in the prefaces to Henry Headley's *Select Beauties of Ancient English Poetry* of 1787, and Ellis's *Specimens*. Both collections, in keeping with their specialized focus, enlarged the space given to *ancient*—meaning sixteenth- and seventeenth-century—poems.

Their common aim was, as Headley stated in his preface, "to strengthen and co-operate with the taste for poetical antiquities which for some time past has been considerably advancing." They addressed their collections to the audience *The Muses Library* had hoped to create in 1737: not antiquarian scholars and book collectors, but readers of anthologies, who "through the medium of compilation . . . are generally made acquainted with the obscurer poets of their country."[4]

The interest in earlier verse—soon ceasing to be categorized by the fossilizing term *antiquities*—went on growing in the nineteenth century. In 1805, Sir Egerton Brydges wrote in *Censura Literaria*, his annotated catalogue of "*Old English Books*," that a complete collection of sixteenth- and seventeenth-century poetry "would be an invaluable treasure," not only to satisfy antiquarians but for readers generally, because we "have seen the fashion for black letter reading increase in the last ten years with wonderful celerity."[5] In response, anthologies going as far back as Chaucer with spaces given to both sixteenth- and seventeenth-century poems multiplied in the nineteenth.

In this period anthologists engaged in retrospection of another kind as well, in that they positioned their collections by looking back at earlier anthologies to find ways of distinguishing their own. Such generic citations show up first in prefaces beginning at the very end of the eighteenth century, which when put together with those that follow read like a sort of chain-letter: Headley's prefatory remarks mention Percy; Ellis's refer to Percy and Headley; Chalmers's to Ellis; Palgrave's to Chalmers; Trench's to Palgrave; Thomas Ward's to Chalmers, Palgrave, and Campbell; John

Churton Collins's to Palgrave, Trench, Frederick Locker-Lampson, and Ward. Quiller-Couch in 1900 included in his longer list of debts the anthologies made by Palgrave, Trench, Locker-Lampson, and Churton Collins. American anthologists of the same period followed the same practice: Ralph Waldo Emerson situated his *Parnassus* (1874) in relation to Dana, Chalmers, and Palgrave; John Greenleaf Whittier in *Songs of Three Centuries* (1877) cited Dana and Emerson.

Inevitably, as the roll-call grew longer anthologists felt more uneasily the possibility Trench feared when he asked himself whether Palgrave might have already "occupied the ground." This expression—drawn from the vocabulary of war—exposes the sources of uneasiness expressed by anthologists about securing a space for their books, because *ground* revealingly stands for both the marketplace and the territory spanned by poetry in English. What succeeded best in the marketplace was the poetry that readers had come to expect in anthologies.

Already in 1868 Trench deplored the fact that most anthologists chose their entries from "what has already been offered by others"—his example was "doubtless a very graceful lyric," Jonson's "Queen and huntress"—while his own aim was to make "new treasures" available to those who are "little able," or "little likely, to go and discover such for themselves."[6] By 1900, Quiller-Couch showed with special intensity the anthologist's fear of redundancy by the efforts he made to dismiss it.

It lurks unacknowledged behind his refusal to make the expected prefatory claims to difference for *The Oxford Book of English Verse*:

Having set my heart on choosing the best, I resolved not to be dissuaded by common objections against anthologies—that they repeat one another . . . or perturbed if my judgement should often agree with that of good critics. The best is the best, though a hundred judges have declared it so; nor had it been any feat to search out and insert the second-rate merely because it happened to be recondite.[7]

His complacent-sounding self-justification here is exposed in his next paragraph as anxiety about his own replication of other anthologies, especially Palgrave's (whose selection and arrangement of entries he had already lavishly borrowed from only five years earlier in an anthology with the unmistakably imitative title *The Golden Pomp*):

Few of my contemporaries can erase—or would wish to erase—the dye their minds took from the late Mr. Palgrave's *Golden Treasury*: and he who has returned to it again and again with an affection born of companionship on many journeys must remember not only what the *Golden Treasury* includes, but the moment when this or that poem appealed to him, and even how it lies on the page.[8]

The "common objections" to repetitiousness that Quiller-Couch tried to brush off were rarely made by anthologists themselves, since most of them including himself were doing what their publishers wanted by gathering poems that readers liked and expected to find in books with titles that promised *Favorite, Famous, Familiar, Popular, Standard* verse. Some prefaces, for instance Walter Learned's for *A Treasury of Favorite Poems* of 1893, even admitted outright (what is implicit but layered over in Quiller-Couch's self-defensive boast), that "this volume is largely collected from collections."[9]

W. J. Linton confronted the accepted practice of copying new anthologies from old by making one in 1882 that announced itself as a sort of appendix to others: *Rare Poems of the Sixteenth and Seventeenth Centuries: A Supplement to the Anthologies*. Another exception was the preface to *A Treasury of Minor British Poetry* of 1896, compiled by the famously contentious reviewer and essayist John Churton Collins. Advertising his *Treasury* as "an experiment" never before attempted, he claimed for it an "independent place" by virtue of its "freedom from indebtedness" to other anthologies: "It is commonly objected to anthologies that they copy each other," and that "this applies not merely to poets who have long been classical and whose names are household words, but to the minor poets also."[10] His own independent aim was "to introduce the general reader" to poems not "in popular anthologies," purposefully avoiding what were commonly called "'gems' with which everyone is familiar."[11]

Churton Collins's chosen examples of what he preferred to call "stock pieces" rather than "gems" shows that he found this pattern of repetition most apparent—he would more likely have said most egregious—in the selection of poems from the early period:

Thus, assuredly as Ben Jonson, Herrick, and Waller are presented, so surely is the one the herald of *Drink to me only with thine eyes*, and *Queen and huntress*, the other of *Gather ye rosebuds* and *Faire Daffodils*, and the third of *Go, lovely rose*.[12]

The same objection was again raised to selections of earlier poems by H. J. Massingham in 1919 in his introduction to *A Treasury of Seventeenth Century English Verse*, also dedicated to avoiding poems "sufficiently before the public notice" in "numerous anthologies." All five poems listed as "stock pieces" by Churton Collins were excluded by explicitly stated choice from Massingham's *Treasury* along with others equally "familiar in anthologies," that had come to be inevitable presences in the course of anthology-making over centuries.[13]

CONTINUITIES

One explanation of what makes an anthology-poem is suggested, then, by the simple fact that it has been passed from one collection to another, a process quickly illustrated by James Shirley's very fine lyric, "The glories of our blood and state." This is a poem almost all readers who know it have met exclusively but regularly in anthologies. It is also likely to be the only example they know of its author's poems, a circumstance qualifying it for inclusion in 1877 in an anthology of anthology-pieces called *Single Famous Poems*.

It had entered the tradition, it seems, in Percy's *Reliques*, and passed from there into Ellis's *Specimens*. Then it rated inclusion in S. C. Hall's *The Book of Gems* of 1836; was reprinted in 1854 in Robert Bell's *Songs from the Dramatists*; was taken up in turn by Mackay, Trench, Bryant, Emerson (who printed only the last stanza), Whittier, Ward, Quiller-Couch, and countless lesser known compilers. In an anthology of *Fifty Perfect Poems* edited by Dana with Rossiter Johnson in 1883, it was included among only three other early selections: Spenser's "Prothalamion," Milton's "Lycidas," and Henry Vaughan's most often anthologized poem, "They are all gone into the world of light."

Though the fineness of Shirley's poem earns its fame, there still seems to be something almost accidental in its recovery. It might easily have been overlooked in the forming of anthological tradition because it did not appear among Shirley's *Poems* published in 1646, but as a song in one of his less well known dramatic works printed in 1659. Though there is some evidence of its having been set to music, there is little to show that this circumstance encouraged further appearances. The only instance I have found of a re-printing, other than Percy's and Ellis's, before the nineteenth century is its inclusion in *The New Academy of Complements* of 1671.

Even so, the history of Shirley's poem once it was to be found in Percy's *Reliques* can be read not as accidental but predictable. It supports the point that the process of making an anthology-piece originates in the peculiar di-mensions that make an anthology: that the authors of such books are at least as conscious of working in a tradition fashioned by their predecessors as are the makers of other kinds of poetry books. The difference is that the anxiety of precedence felt by anthologists is more acutely focused because they are constrained by conventions of the genre that call in question the reason for being of more such collections.

This results from an implicit if not an openly advertised feature of most retrospective anthologies since the early nineteenth century: that they are useful to readers because they have culled the best poems of the periods within their scope. This claim, flattering because we want to be thought to want the best, has naturally encouraged readers to equate the best with those very poems and, since successive anthologists have apparently agreed on their superior value, to expect them in any later gathering. Since quite early in the nineteenth century, the retrospective anthologies that have attracted many buyers have largely been shaped to meet those expectations.

Other forces that go into the making of an anthology-piece are sug-gested by the history of the single poem in English with the longest and most nearly continuous presence in printed anthologies, Christopher Mar-lowe's "The Passionate Shepherd to His Love." It was already becoming well known by the late 1580s, having been set to music that made it one of the most popular airs in the later years of the century.[14] It was first printed— untitled—in 1599, six years after Marlowe's death, in *The Passionate Pilgrim*, where it was passed off as Shakespeare's. The next year in *Englands Helicon* it was presented in what is now its accepted form, titled as we know it, and signed "Chr. Marlowe," which did not prevent it from being included in 1640 with other miscellaneous verses in *Poems, written by Wil. Shakespeare* (a mutilated edition of his sonnets masquerading as the first).

All through the earlier half of the seventeenth century, Marlowe's stan-zas—sometimes with deletions, additions, modifications, and different titles—kept their favored place as the lyric most often reprinted, quoted, imitated, answered, or parodied by unknown and lesser known authors, and by Ralegh, Donne, Herrick, and Milton. There are references to it in works by Robert Greene, Thomas Lodge, and Shakespeare; in 1604 Nicholas Breton gave his collection of pastoral verse the title *The Passionate Shepherd*.[15]

Then, along with almost all Elizabethan poems, it virtually disappeared from printed collections for more than a century, although *The Muses Library* mentioned—but did not print—"some Stanzas of Marlows, Beginning come live with me &c." Percy rescued it in 1765, gaining a place for it in the hall of fame constituted of retrospective anthologies gathered in the late eighteenth century and all through the nineteenth by such respected compilers as Headley, Ellis, Campbell, Dana, Palgrave, Whittier, Ward, and Quiller-Couch. (Churton Collins, although he consulted *Englands Helicon*, left out Marlowe's poem along with other conspicuous "gems.") The song was also a favorite in less prestigious popular anthologies such as Knox's *Elegant Extracts*, Mackay's *A Thousand and One Gems*, and *Beeton's Great Book of Poetry*. Its presence in retrospective anthologies since has been virtually guaranteed.

Englands Helicon was, according to Rollins, the most beautifully presented of the early miscellanies, giving it special appeal to its first buyers.[16] It also had the most distinguished selection of poems, which attracted the attention of later compilers, so that it was an advantageous volume for Marlowe's song to have its place. Its familiarity was prolonged after its appearances in the first half of the seventeenth century because it was printed (with the startlingly inappropriate title "The Milkmaid's Song") in Izaac Walton's *The Compleat Angler*, which went through at least nine editions between 1653 and 1770. The poem's revived presence in Percy's *Reliques* among only a handful of other sixteenth-century poems, and Percy's note that it "appears to have been (as it deserved) a great favorite with our early poets," elevated it (as it deserved) to the place it seems to have filled in the revival of Elizabethan poetry as the quintessential lyric of its time.[17]

That is how Sir Egerton Brydges positioned it, using it to illustrate an opinion generally shared by critics and their readers in the later eighteenth and earlier nineteenth centuries. Their view was, as Brydges stated it in 1805, that the "pure and unsophisticated poetry" of Marlowe's generation "has

never since been equalled" for its "grace of expression," "happiness of sentiment," "attractive simplicity"; least of all by Donne and his followers:
"After the exquisite song of Marlow, 'Come live with me, and be my love,'
who could have supposed that a nation could have suddenly relapsed into
such barbarism?"[18]

Brydges's vocabulary for praising the qualities epitomized by Marlowe's
stanzas is of course in the currency of his own period in the history of criticism; he could have found most of his terms, along with Marlowe's poem,
among Percy's commentaries in his anthology. There Elizabethan and earlier seventeenth-century verses are set apart from the poetry of "a polished
age, like the present" by "pleasing simplicity" and "artless graces," and from
the "rudeness of the more obsolete poems."[19] These qualities Percy believed
he had found in virtually every line of every poem "in the *Paradise of Dainty
Devises*, (the Dodsley's miscellany of those times)." He also saw them epitomized in an unassigned entry preserved in Tottel's *Songes and Sonettes*,
which Percy chose to illustrate the "natural, unaffected sentiments," the
"simplicity of style," the "easy flow of versification, and all other beauties of
pastoral poetry."[20]

In its own time Marlowe's poem would not have been appreciated in
these terms. Brydges's most heavily loaded interpretive word "unsophisticated" had not yet entered English in the sixteenth century, a small sign of
large conceptual differences. For it is altogether unlikely that the compiler
or first readers of *Englands Helicon* would have recognized the appropriateness of describing Marlowe's poem by a term suggesting unpolished or artless simplicity, a naturalness distinguished by lack of artifice.

The maker of the anthology presented his book for his readers' approval
with the enticing claim that "Many honoured names haue heretofor (in
their particuler interest,) patronized some part of these inuentions."[21] He
put forward the most honored name of "S. Phil. Sidney" as the signature for
the opening poem, and used Sidney's famous literary name, "Astrophel," in
the titles he gave not only to five other poems by Sidney, but to one assigned
to "N[icholas]. Breton," whose courtly credentials were the patronage of the
Countess of Pembroke and the style of his verses.

These presentational devices, supported by the handsome appearance of
the book itself, made appeals to the desires of readers for a share in the entertainments of courtly society: one entry is located in Sidney's private cir-

cle, where his poems first circulated, by its title "The Countesse of Pem-
brookes Pastorali" (signed with the coterie pseudonym "Shep. Tonie"). The
pastoralizing of *Englands Helicon* beginning with its title was designed to
give the impression of easy elegance or elegant ease defined by Sidney in *An
Apologie for Poetrie* as the courtier's "practise"—"fittest to nature"—of "Art
. . . to hide Art."[22] His own poems were thought to be the model for this art.

A century after Percy, Palgrave anthologized Marlowe's poem with a
note intended to correct earlier wrong readings of it. He argued that it
should not be read as an unsophisticated song, and not as an instance of the
seemingly effortless elegance of courtly poetry in the late sixteenth century,
but as a "fine example of the highwrought and conventional Elizabethan
Pastoralism." Correcting a third wrong reading (probably with Johnson's
strictures against pastoral as his target, and certainly with Tennyson as his
ally), Palgrave added severely that it would be "ludicrous" to criticize "The
Passionate Shepherd to His Love" for "the unshepherdlike or unreal character of some images suggested."[23]

A phrase in William Empson's *Some Versions of Pastoral,* first published
in 1935, negotiated for twentieth-century criticism a way to read poems like
Marlowe's that mediates between Percy's discovery of "pleasing simplicity,"
of "artless graces" in the lyrics he gathered of the early period, and Palgrave's
defense of their "highwrought" conventionality. Empson's rebalancing act
is his definition of "the pastoral process" as "putting the complex into the
simple (in itself a great help to the concentration needed for poetry)," which
is a version in a modern critical vocabulary of what Sidney may have meant
by "art . . . to hide art."[24]

Paul Alpers put Empson's formula in a still more recent idiom in *What Is
Pastoral?* There among other anthology-pieces classified as "definitive" examples of English Renaissance verse, Marlowe's is praised for its "pellucid
sophistication."[25] As we use it, *pellucid* (introduced into English as a scientific term in the sixteenth century) names a defining quality of this verse described metaphorically in the poems themselves by one of their favorite adjectives, *crystal.*

THE PARADIGM

These instances of critical revaluation have not been included here to
show what is too obvious to need demonstrating, that they happen even to

the best—or best-known—poems. It may even be that because of their status as *definitive* period pieces, anthology favorites are particularly the focus for revisions of judgment and fancy in changing cultural situations. The point to be illustrated is that Marlowe's "Come live with me and be my love" can be a useful paradigm of what makes a certain kind of lyric susceptible to becoming an anthology-piece. The song can work this way not only because it has the longest and least interrupted history in poetry anthologies, but also by virtue of effects it has in common with other poems of the early period that have themselves become inevitable presences since they began to be reprinted in eighteenth-century anthologies.

These shared effects seem to be ones that are specially recognizable and acceptable in different cultural situations. This is to say, they are specially accessible to readings that can adjust them to those changing situations in changing and even contradictory critical vocabularies. The other early poems, chosen because they have been most often cited for being most often anthologized, are: Jonson's "Hymn" ("Queen and huntress"); Herbert's "Virtue"; Carew's "Song" ("Ask me no more"); Waller's "Song" ("Go, lovely rose"); Herrick's "To Daffodils." A composite portrait drawn from their shared features shows what qualities have so long and so continuously (more than poems of any other period or kind) made them, and others with family resemblances, into anthology-pieces.

Their similarity in length is the most immediately obvious common feature of these poems, visible at once in the space they take up on the page. They are all what Tottel's preface calls "small parcelles." Sixty years later Drayton described the contributions of "that Princely *Surrey*" and of Wyatt as "those small poems, which the title beare, Of songs and sonnets."[26] These spatial terms seem to have been used to classify the verses not only or mainly by the numbers of lines that measure their spatial dimensions, but generically. They fit poems into their conceptual space in the rhetorical hierarchy of "greate, small, meane" forms and styles, assigning them to what Sidney called "that Lyricall kind of Songs and Sonnets" as distinct from poems belonging to *greater* kinds like the epic and the ode.[27] Now (since the loosening of generic distinctions that began in the nineteenth century) the same poems are measured as *short* to contrast them with that generically blurred, elusive entity *the long poem*.

The similar length of these early lyrics is also the most obvious common feature to qualify them as anthology-pieces: obvious because the conventions of the retrospective anthology encourage readers to expect that it will include few if any whole poems much longer than, say, "Lycidas" or "Elegy Written in a Country Church Yard," "Lines Written . . . above Tintern Abbey" or "The Love Song of J. Alfred Prufrock." Still, as is true of all literary conventions, the short number of lines in most of the poems in anthologies has significations that are not entirely obvious.

Irresistibly and increasingly, the spatial dimensions of the anthology have been translated into, or conflated with, temporal measurements, which have both conceptual and practical implications. As early as 1655, John Cotgrave suggested the beneficial saving of time that the spatial dimensions of anthologies insured. In the preface to *The English Treasury of Wit and Language* he answered the question, "if Salomon could say, That the reading of many Bookes is weariness to the flesh":

How much is that wearinesse increased since the Art of Printing has so infinitely multiplyed large and vast volums in every place, that the longest life of a man is not sufficient to explore so much as the substance of them, which (in many) is but slender? Extractions therefore are the best conservers of knowledge, if not the readiest way to it.[28]

By the eighteenth century the advantage of short poems that they take less time to read had become a common assumption in support of anthology reading. In an essay of 1731 giving directions for collecting a library, John Clarke spelled out who might appropriately spend leisure time for such reading: "Gentlemen"; "Persons of Genteel Professions or Trades" with "a pretty good deal of empty Time upon their Hands"; "Clergy-Men"; and "Ladys of Fortune" (presumed to have nothing but empty time on their hands). Among the few books of poetry he recommended for "their Leisure-Hours" are Dryden's and Pope's miscellanies.[29]

Vicesimus Knox also recommended "miscellanies" as "the proper amusement of a vacant hour" in an essay of 1778 about the kinds of books suited to "Small Portions of Leisure." It was directed to the "common reader," generations of whom were brought up on his series of *Elegant Extracts*.[30] Imitating that kind of collection, an anthology of 1827 advertised the time-saving value of its own extracts in its inelegant title *Much Instruction From Little Reading*, with the last two words—suggesting both temporal and spatial dimensions—in larger and bolder letters to speed their message.

As the anthology went on being promoted to all sorts of readers in the nineteenth century for its benefits as a special kind of book, its dimensions in time and space began to be more explicitly combined. Whittier offered his "comparatively small volume" to "the great mass of readers to whose 'snatched leasure' my brief lyrical selection would seem to have a special adaptation."[31] Robert Bell in *Art and Song* of 1868, a lavishly illustrated gathering of short poems, appealed to its leisured readers on the grounds of the short time it takes to read short poems—to "dip hastily into their dainty leaves"—and in books of a size to fit conveniently accessible places:

A book that never fatigues the attention . . . and that may be opened anywhere for five minutes with the certainty of lighting on something worth retaining for life, ought to be one of the most popular books for the luxurious table of a town mansion, or the liberal window-seat of a country house.[32]

Elsewhere anthologies are recommended for being portable, adaptable to spaces like *the trunk, the knapsack*, and most often *the pocket*. Again their economy of space is a metonym for the conveniently short time any one entry takes to read (discrete pieces being suited to disconnected intervals of reading).

Palgrave himself claimed that his "little collection" contained matter of "better worth" than "much of what fills the scanty hours that most men spare" for reading, but he was precluded from more overtly advertising either the practicality of size or time-saving economy of his carefully selected gathering of short poems by his more elevated sense of poetry's power of "leading us in higher and healthier ways than those of the world."[33] Still, the precise vocabulary he used to describe his aesthetic "principles" for choosing only "Lyrical pieces and Songs" makes connections between this literary preference and the temporal and spatial dimensions of the short poem.

His decision excluded "narrative, descriptive, and didactic poems," all tending to more lines than his preferred forms, unless accompanied by "rapidity of movement, brevity, and the colouring of human passion" which were his requisites for "lyric unity." This ideal suggests some version, perhaps, of what Empson may have meant by "the concentration needed for poetry," but Palgrave's preferred critical terms—"rapidity," "brevity," "unity"—are more suggestive of the special ways the short poem occupies time and space.[34] Palgrave's raising of these practical considerations to higher aesthetic ideals, along with the stunning influence of *The Golden Treasury* as their embodiment, have in turn been a powerful force in elevating the lyric to the high rank it now holds among forms of poetry, and to making the term *lyric* nearly synonymous with *the short poem*.

The spatial figures the six early poems for discussion make are like one another in their total number of lines: the shortest, Herbert's, is sixteen lines; Marlowe's, the longest, is twenty-four. More particularly they resemble one another in the arrangement of their lines: they are all stanzaic poems, which seems to have bearing on the question of what has made them anthology-pieces. That is to say by way of contrast, no one sonnet achieved the status of an anthology-piece in that time or until much later, even after sonnets emerged in the Elizabethan revival following an eclipse of more than a hundred years. An inference to be explored, then, is that the stanzaic nature of the poems in question makes an essential contribution toward their special appropriateness for anthologies.

Stanzaic poems, even ones like Herbert's "Virtue" with only two more lines than a sonnet, make very different shapes on the page. Sonnets have lines looking more or less the same length because they must have the same number of metrical units. Tottel printed sonnets in blocks with no indentations; during the rest of the sixteenth century they were usually printed, as they have been typically since, with the closing couplet only set apart by indentation.

A poem in stanzas makes a much more detailed diagram of its structure visually (even more than sonnets untypically printed like Spenser's in *Amoretti* where the divisions into quatrains as well as the couplet are marked by indentations). A stanzaic poem uses blank spaces to separate the stanzas, and within them there are commonly indentations making patterns when lines have different numbers of feet, patterns corresponding in successive stanzas.

These visual effects are specially clear because the poems under discussion are short and so are the stanzas. Each poem except one consists of between three and six stanzas of either four, five, or six lines, predominantly four-foot but with some two-foot lines. The one exception, which was the last of these poems to be published, Herrick's "To Daffodils," is divided into two stanzas each of ten lines varying in length from four iambs to one.

The linear patterns of these short stanzas are also reinforced by the close proximity of the end-rhymes, all adjacent or alternating, which often look alike in spelling (poets and printers could adjust the spelling to make these likenesses still more visible before English orthography was regularized by the late seventeenth century). Visual designs support sound patterns even more strikingly in repeated lines opening or closing stanzas in all of these poems. The visible pattern of each stanza can be read at a glance, and so can the repetition of it through all the stanzas.

The heard patterns of short stanzaic groupings (four being the preferred length) in predominantly four-stressed lines with closely rhymed end-words, usually monosyllabic, are easily recognizable in these visual designs. That is, the spatial diagram made by the lineation is a guide to the stress pattern, which tends to regular iambics or iambics with a variant foot regularly placed (actually enhancing the sense of regularity).

All these features make the poems specially easy to set to music and to memorize, by contrast with sonnets where visual and heard patterns are less clearly discernible. The reasons are that the stresses in the sonnet's five-foot iambic line tend to be less strongly marked, especially where the lines are enjambed as they are more often in sonnets than in songs, while the arrangement of end-rhymes in a sonnet is often more intricate, and there are more changes in rhymed sounds.

These differences in patterning that set the song form apart may have had a lot to do with the early and widespread appearances of Marlowe's song, often in slightly or more radically variant forms, since in their own time these poems seem to have been transmitted orally and then copied down from memory. Once they were given space in printed anthologies, their designs diagrammed spatially in easily heard patterns allowed large numbers of readers to memorize them almost without trying. This made the songs affectionately familiar and satisfying in the special way suggested in the very old expression *to get by heart*. Their pleasing familiarity in turn made them welcome and expected in poetry collections.

Marlowe's poem is paradigmatic because it represents this kind of short stanzaic poem in its purest or clearest form. Besides the dimensions just given in the composite description, this song shows the additive structure that short stanzas lend themselves to, clearly marked here by stanzas and lines beginning with "And," along with "and" used repeatedly some place within a line to link nouns in a catalogue.

At the same time, the song shows how the spatial separation into groups of four end-stopped lines allows each stanza to complete itself with a partial closure after the first two lines, fulfilled by the full stop after the second pair. Line terminations are marked by punctuation pointing to the closely matching curves of line and syntax; paired rhymes articulate the balanced divisions into two-line units within the groupings of four lines. Then just as clearly, Marlowe's song illustrates how such stanzaic poems give a still fuller and more complete sense of closure to their essentially *and . . . and* structure by their use and placing of repeated whole lines; in this instance the opening line is repeated in the last lines of the two final stanzas. The poem as it appeared in *Englands Helicon* is given in Chapter 3 on pages 81–82.

Even at first reading this poem is capable of giving the special pleasure of recognition because its particular stanzaic groupings are in an arrangement deeply familiar to readers in every period. In the expert view of Derek Attridge, the "*underlying rhythmic structure*: four lines of four beats each"—"a pair of pairs of pairs of beats"—"is by far the commonest rhythmic structure in popular song (as well as . . . in more elaborate musical works) and . . . it occurs in, or underlies, nearly all popular verse in English."[35]

Following his observation that it "is also common in the literary tradition," Attridge's predictable choice to illustrate this most familiar of all rhythmic structures in poetry is Marlowe's song.[36] His broader conclusion, supported by the findings of other scholars, is that the "four-beat rhythm" of this stanzaic pattern has been "a recurrent feature in the rhythmic arts of Western Europe; and it seems likely that this is a reflection of something fundamental in the faculty of rhythmic production and perception itself."[37] The same basic structure underlies the variations on Marlowe's four-line stanza form in the earlier seventeenth-century lyrics.

Although the editor of *Englands Helicon* did not use the term *song* in the title he gave to Marlowe's stanzas, his readers would not have needed to be told that the poem is in the form of a popular song worked on by courtly art. As such, it realizes what Empson called the "pastoral process" of "putting the complex into the simple" figured by the singer of the song, transparently disguised as a rustic shepherd who transplants "Roses" into garden "beds" (also couches to recline on), or gathers and arranges them into "poesies" (a commonplace word-play on the double meanings of *bouquet* and *poesy*). Familiarity would also have taught Elizabethan readers how to decode the trope of "Rivers, to whose falls,/Melodious byrds sings Madrigalls" as the signature of such a pastoral song.[38] Its music partakes in the harmony made by the "falls" (in musical terminology the drop to a lower note) of waters cascading in counterpoint with the birds singing in woodnotes artfully arranged in the complex polyphonic form of "Madrigalls" (a noun made to stand out by being the one trisyllabic end-word paired with a single syllable, among almost exclusively monosyllabic rhymed pairs).

The gifts the passionate shepherd promises his beloved match the amplitude and generosity of yielding nature (another classical trope favored by Renaissance poets). His ornamenting of each natural gift with gems or embroidery to adorn the lady shows the art of the courtly maker. The "delights" that will "moue" his lady's "minde" find their full embodiment in his song, as he says in the last pair of lines of the last stanza. There the first line of the first stanza is repeated but with a variant first word that effects the poem's closure—"Then liue with mee, and be my loue"—and in doing so deepens the echoing song: "delight to moue" Sidney called the "noblest scope" of poetry.[39]

The imagined pastoral garden yielding "purest gold" figures what Sidney, the star of *Englands Helicon*, envisioned in *An Apologie for Poetry* to be the prefallen world remade by the poet's art: "Nature neuer set forth the earth in so rich tapistry as diuers Poets haue done. . . . Her world is brasen, the Poets only deliuer a golden."[40] And it figures Palgrave's lyric ideal in *The Golden Treasury*: "Poetry gives treasures 'more golden than gold,' leading us in higher and healthier ways than those of the world, and interpreting to us the lessons of Nature."[41]

Carew's "Ask me no more" and Waller's "Go, lovely rose" when first printed in collections of their verse, and later in anthologies, were classified in their titles as songs, and Jonson's "Queen and huntress" was called a hymn, one of the types of short poem (along with the song, the ballad, and the nursery rhyme) traditionally practicing the most common four-beat rhythm defined by Attridge. Herbert never named secular verse forms in the titles he gave to his poems, but "Virtue" is recognizably a song in four-line stanzas described by its singer as "My Musick," and sounding the note struck by the repeated sound of *sweet,* so that the poem itself is a figure for a music "box where sweets compacted lie."[42]

Each of these seventeenth-century lyrics repeats with variations the simple metrical line and stanzaic pattern exemplified by Marlowe's song, so that rhythm and structure themselves create echoes that become part of the matter of the song. This process realizes what John Hollander has speculated may be true of all poems, but must be specially true of poems that are internally repetitive and also reiterative of similar poems in so many of their dimensions:

They are more like each other than they are like reality, and it may even be true that they are more *about* each other in this way as well. A full reading of a poem will depend upon recognition of its genre, and its version of that genre.[43]

Most obviously these poems are about the pastoral language that reverberates among them in radiant evocations of spring, flowers, birds' songs, gold, pearls, crystal: the sweets yielded by willing nature and the adornments of art. This vocabulary both describes and stands for the golden world fashioned by poets from the brazen natural world where spring is "short" and "each May-morning" is quickly "past," the rose is "fading," the dew "shall weep" for it, the hart must fly the arrow and the nightingale must haste before the winter comes.

The glimpses in each of these poems of this darker knowledge are— equally with the "bright" celebratory images—built into their shared pastoral language in a variety of ways: in the delicate suggestion of Marlowe's "Fayre lined slippers for the cold"; Waller's comparison of the young woman to a "lovely Rose"; Jonson's disruption of his masculine rhymes in the second of the lines "Give unto the flying hart / Space to breathe, how short soeuer"; Carew's closing word-play on the meanings of "dyes."

All of these poems verge on or come to full recognition that the vision of a timeless golden world is a beautiful fiction. Even so, the pastoral balance is preserved by the poets' many ways of echoing the conventions of form, language, and matter of other poems. These echoes are an assurance of continuity that is an expression of poetic tradition, and is felt with special force in the conscious art of putting the complex into the simple, which marks the short stanzaic pastoral lyric.

It may be this pastoral balance that constitutes the appeal of these poems in successive periods, and their adaptability to changing critical values and vocabularies. Renato Poggioli, in words that many writers for centuries before him would have found sympathetic, said, "there is a pastoral cluster in any form of poetry. . . . In a certain sense, and in its purest form, the pastoral represents ideally the Golden Age of poetry."[44]

There may be another reason as well why these poems have been particularly welcomed by anthologies: that books of this kind have claimed for themselves some of the qualities of the pastoral lyric by figuring themselves as gardens of immortal flowers, sequestered holdings of golden treasures.

RESPACINGS

These Elizabethan and earlier seventeenth-century stanzaic poems have taken their places in twentieth-century retrospective collections made by both English and American anthologists, and not only in such massively inclusive gatherings as *The New Oxford Book of English Verse* or *The Norton Anthology of Poetry*, first published in 1970 and on up to 1996 with all six poems still in their places. All six have also been included through the twentieth century in smaller collections, for instance: *The English Galaxy of Shorter Poems* (1933); *The Viking Book of Poetry of the English-Speaking World* (1941); *Six Centuries of Great Poetry* (1955); *The London Book of English Verse* (1977); *The Top 500 Poems* (1992).

Meanwhile poems of the same period by the same poets, ones that had scarcely ever before appeared in anthologies, began by the 1920s to be given spaces along with these long established anthology-pieces, with the result that the first occupants have been made to move over. The process can be seen if we look at the recent history of one earlier favorite, "Virtue."

According to Massingham in the notes to his *Treasury* of 1919, it was still Herbert's "best known poem," as it had been all through the nineteenth century (on which grounds Massingham excluded it); but about "The Collar," which filled the first space in the pages he allowed to Herbert, he wrote: "It is surprising that this noble and spirited poem with its deep feeling and fine dramatic change of mood at the close appears rarely, if at all, in anthologies."[45] Since then it has come to be expected in any selection of Herbert.

It is generally true of such late arrivals that they take their place at first beside rather than instead of firmly ensconced anthology-pieces, as "The

Collar" joined "Virtue" in 1941 in Richard Aldington's *The Viking Book of Poetry of the English-Speaking World*. In 1950 in *Poems in English 1530–1940*, compiled by David Daiches and William Charvat, both poems appeared again. Here, some thirty years after Massingham excluded "Virtue" for its familiarity while claiming to have rescued "The Collar" from obscurity, the notes to this mid-century anthology tell us that "Virtue" was still, perhaps, "the best known of Herbert's poems," but do not say that "The Collar" had been overlooked. On the contrary, it is praised again for the "dramatic" power Massingham saw as its special quality, but in 1950 that term is used to place the poem in what the editors assumed to be its familiar context: "The dramatic opening here is somewhat reminiscent of Donne."[46] "The Collar" continued to share with "Virtue" the space given to Herbert by anthologists. In addition to the anthologies listed above, both poems are included, for example, in: *The Atlantic Book of British and American Poetry* (1958); *The Harper Anthology of English Poetry* (1981); *British and American Poets: Chaucer to the Present* (1986); *Poetry in English* (1987).

As the process of introducing changes in the choices of anthology-pieces unfolds, the new arrivals sometimes do displace the old. Again to follow the same recent history, "The Collar" among other poems by Herbert but not including "Virtue" appeared in *Poets of the English Language II: Marlowe to Marvell* (1950); *Memorable Poetry from All Periods* (1965); *The English Poets from Chaucer to Edward Thomas* (1974); *The Columbia Anthology of British Poetry* (1995). Oscar Williams, for a gathering of what the title calls *Master Poems of the English Language* (1966), chose "The Collar" as the one entry to represent Herbert. It has a commentary by Dudley Fitts that opens by appreciating the poem for the same quality seen by Massingham: "'The Collar' is a miniature drama."[47]

This minihistory of two poems by Herbert—and one could trace the same pattern for other pairs of poems such as Jonson's "Queen and huntress" and "On My First Son"—is a very small manifestation of a larger movement in critical history discussed in more detail in the Coda: the twentieth-century rereading of sixteenth- and seventeenth-century poetry, which valued the dramatic lyric above pastoral songs and elevated Donne and Marvell as its masters.

Before this century, Donne had consistently been given far less attention than Herrick, and "To His Coy Mistress" had been as nearly absent from

anthologies as "The Collar," arrangements represented in—and also prom-
ulgated by—Palgrave's choices. The first edition of *The Golden Treasury* ignored Donne altogether while making space for seven of Herrick's poems,
and the selection of Marvell's was typically slim: "Horatian Ode Upon
Cromwell's Return from Ireland"; "The Garden" (titled "Thoughts in a
Garden"); and "Bermudas" ("Song of the Emigrants in Bermuda"), the one
poem of Marvell's on Massingham's list of "stock pieces" he chose to exclude. A few other poems by Marvell were occasionally printed in nineteenth-century anthologies, almost all of them pastoral lyrics in stanzas of
four four-foot lines.

Anthologists during the first third of the twentieth century played a direct part in reordering the centuries-old hierarchy: Massingham brought
"Donne into the fold" as an "overmastering influence" on seventeenth-
century poetry, and Sir Herbert Grierson in the introduction to *Metaphysical Lyrics and Poems of the Seventeenth Century* praised "To His Coy Mistress" as the "very crown and roof of the metaphysical love lyric."[48] Less than
twenty years later, Cleanth Brooks and Robert Penn Warren published *Understanding Poetry*, which though not a retrospective anthology, used its
different design with extraordinary effectiveness (Karl Shapiro described it
as "almost biblical" in its influence) to promote the same cause: the eleva-
tion of the "dramatic" lyric as the ideal of the new aesthetic.[49] The means to
this end are visible in the anthologists' treatment of the pastoral lyrics already discussed, and of "To His Coy Mistress."

Understanding Poetry includes entries from almost the whole time-span
of shorter poems in English, grouped by types (such as narratives or descriptions), by formal dimensions (for instance metrics, tone, images), or by
theme, with no clues to their chronological sequence or their connections in
literary history. The first edition of 1938 gives space to "The Passionate Shepherd to His Love" and "Virtue," but to none of the other most often anthologized seventeenth-century lyrics. In the editions of 1950 and 1960, those two
poems are dropped while Waller's "Go, lovely rose" is added, the one of the six
most often anthologized pastoral songs that might come closest to following
the rubric urged in all three editions (1938, 1950, 1960) for the reader to remember: that "all poetry, including even short lyrics . . . involves a dramatic
organization," to which the introduction of 1960 added that "every poem can
be—and in fact must be—regarded as a little drama."[50]

Unsurprisingly, "To His Coy Mistress" was included from the start. It is followed in editions after the first by expanded study questions that point to its most admired features: shifts in the "tone of each division"; the "range" of effects created by its images—from "playful, conversational, and absurd" to "grand" and then "exciting"—and the "interpenetration among them."[51] In these directives Brooks and Warren sound very like Grierson praising "To His Coy Mistress" for the "sudden soar of passion in bold and felicitous image, in clangorous lines," "at once fantastic and passionate," all qualities contributing to its Donne-like "dramatic expression."[52]

Six Centuries of Great Poetry, edited by Robert Penn Warren with Albert Erskine, was published in 1955 midway between the second and third editions of *Understanding Poetry*. In it "To His Coy Mistress" is among ten poems by Marvell located in the space nearly at the end of well over 150 pages occupied by Elizabethan and earlier seventeenth-century poems, including all the pastoral stanzaic lyrics discussed earlier.

Just before "To His Coy Mistress," the reader is met by "Bermudas," a poem in the form of four-foot, predominantly iambic lines, the lineation mainly coinciding with the syntax and marked by paired end-rhymes mostly made of simple, monosyllabic sounds. These evocatively familiar visual and heard patterns of pastoral lyric represent the rhythms of the "song" made by the emigrants in their precarious little boat, as "With falling oars they kept the time."[53] What they sing of is a prefallen garden world where "eternal spring / . . . enamels everything," where willing nature "hangs in shades the orange bright, / Like golden lamps in a green night," and in ripe fruits encloses "Jewels more rich than Ormus shows."

These immediate and larger situations of "To His Coy Mistress" in the arrangement of *Six Centuries of Great Poetry* encourage somewhat different responses to the poem than are evoked by the treatment of it in *Understanding Poetry*. Certainly the poem again demands our attention by all the brilliant devices that catch us up in the dramatic situation. At the same time, we respond also to other dimensions of the poem, because we hear the sounds echoing from "Bermudas" and other pastoral lyrics and songs of the period on nearby pages.

In "To His Coy Mistress," the imagined "world" the lover conjures up by echoing the familiar rhythms and diction of pastoral song is another unfallen garden: recognizable in its freely yielded "rubies," its "long loves day," the renewals of "morning dew" and the revolving "sun," and recognizable even in its conditional or perilously threatened state, acknowledged from its opening line: "Had we but world enough, and time."[54] We see again the shadow of change and loss that to some degree darkens every pastoral poem, but at the same time we again hear in multitudinous allusions the preserving continuity that makes poetic tradition. The interchanges of the lover's "ecchoing Song" with other poems of its kind are, to repeat Hollander's point, importantly a part of what "To His Coy Mistress" is "about."

Together the different responses to it evokes by its different settings in these two anthologies suggest a way of thinking about Marvell's dramatic lyric as an anthology-piece that shares essential features with the earlier pastoral songs excluded from *Understanding Poetry*. Rather than displacing them, in *Six Centuries of Great Poetry* "To His Coy Mistress" takes up its position in line with them, giving support to the speculation that their common features are specially adaptable to changing situations of poetry and criticism, even in the twentieth century.

CHAPTER FIVE

"A DARKLING PLAIN"

PUBLIC POEMS OF 1770, 1867, 1955

Of course any writing in print is a form of social expression, even if it pretends not to be, or if nobody reads it. Any printed book of poems put together by its author hopes for an audience. Even if the poems are antisocial, seeming to ignore or exclude the possibility of readers, that rudeness acknowledges them. An edited collection of a poet's work, though the presentation of it is typically impersonal, is social in its expectation of a sympathetic class of readers who have an interest in common with one another and with the editor. Anthologies of poetry are much more explicitly sociable, and in more of their dimensions than are these other kinds of poetry collections. Their sociable character is not in contradiction of their claims to be sequestered pastoral spaces; the coexistence of the two modes represents the complex nature of this kind of book as well as of pastoral itself.

As earlier chapters have shown, anthologists—in many ways and by a variety of presentational means—make their presence continuously felt, so that reading an anthology is harder to experience as an act of private absorption. Discontinuity, a distinguishing feature of this kind of poetry book, is itself an ever-present reminder that someone along with the reader, or rather just ahead of the reader, is as it were turning the pages, pointing out poems and directing attention to how they act toward one another.

PUBLIC SPACES

The first premise of the anthology, that it exists to offer its audience a preselected assortment of entries, makes readers aware not only of the anthologist, but in curious ways of one another. The book is by self-definition not designed for private discoveries, but to build a community of shared experiences, which are then passed on in succeeding anthologies. This is one of the reasons—along with many obviously practical and economic advantages—why anthologies have been used in classrooms at least since the late eighteenth-century, when Vicesimus Knox began producing his series of *Elegant Extracts*, a title so widely known that it became generic.

To the same end of drawing social groups together, the titles of many anthologies beginning in the nineteenth century promoted their use in the *Home*, *Family*, or *Household* for reading aloud in domestic gatherings. When the preface to an anthology locates it on a parlor table or by the fireside, it is placing the book in a domestic space where the social life of a family—and its guests and servants—goes on. By implication, of course, the same scene is acted out in any family, widening the social circle of readers.

Titles that describe the poems inside the space of the book itself as *Famous*, *Familiar*, *Best Loved* stretch the community even to previous readers whose experiences have been handed down. Because this kind of collection offers poems already woven into the cultural fabric, readers come on snatches of language they have heard repeated around them, often not knowing what poems they come from. This feature contributes to making the anthology a public meeting ground.

Many anthology titles have invoked the presence of a large gathering of readers by explicitly associating the book with public spaces. Titles going as far back as 1600 to *Englands Helicon* and *Englands Parnassus* dress up the practical work of telling potential buyers about the contents of the anthology—in these instances verse in English by English authors—in an appeal to feelings of national identity. Still earlier, Tottel's prefatory letter to his readers had attached to his anthology the patriotic motive of publishing poems that would prove English verse to be equal in short forms to ancient and modern literatures. Two centuries later Percy presented his anthology as an offering to English readers of hitherto buried relics, their national and ancestral treasures.

At least through the nineteenth and earlier twentieth centuries, those appeals to readers' sense of national interest were effectively built into titles that identified the contents of the book as *English*, *British*, *American*, *Victorian*, or as belonging to *This England*, *This Nation*.[1] An anthology with a title more subtly making this kind of association is *The Golden Treasury*, which Palgrave's dedication ("To Alfred Tennyson Poet Laureate") says he hoped would "make a true national Anthology." More often since the end of the nineteenth century than before, titles of anthologies have responded to, and helped to fashion, people's sense of belonging to a particular time— a generation or decade or cultural moment—by descriptive words like *Georgian, the Thirties, Post-War.*

The wide social audiences more explicitly drawn into anthologies as distinct from other books of poetry, along with the anthology reader's awareness of the company of other readers—past, present, or to come— have the effect of making all entries in anthologies seem in some more special sense than other printed poems to be public, like works of art displayed in a museum. Pound compared his ideal of an anthology to the National Gallery; other anthologists liken their books to *museums,* to an *annual exhibition* or *salon,* to a *gallery,* a *laboratory,* a *monument.* This sense of publicity holds true even though we would not use the term *public poem* as we typically understand it to describe "Come live with me and be my love," or "Virtue," or the other early anthology-pieces looked at in the preceding chapter.

The poems we would include in the category of public poetry make up a rather loose assemblage. The class or mode—it is certainly not a genre— includes Spenser's "Epithalamion," Milton's "Lycidas," Dryden's "A Song for St. Cecilia's Day," Collins's "Ode Written in the Beginning of the Year 1746," Emerson's "Concord Hymn," Yeats's "The Second Coming," Auden's "September, 1939," Robert Lowell's "For the Union Dead," although they are in very different forms on many sorts of subjects. These have in common that they all write about an actual or mythical public happening, or about an occasion made into a public event like Spenser's celebration of his own marriage (at least as imagined in the poem), or Milton's elegy on the drowning of a fellow student at Cambridge. The term *public* is often used about poetry as if it were synonymous with *occasional,* but not every occasional poem is public: for instance, Jonson's "On My First Daughter" is not.

Nor is every public poem occasional. The category of public poetry also includes Addison's psalmic "Ode" ("The spacious firmament on high") because the grandeur of its language "publishes to every land" what the firmament declares in "glorious voice," invoking a vast audience in a "spacious" setting. At the same time the category is loose enough to let in Wordsworth's sonnet "The world is too much with us," which is quietly spoken, almost privately meditative if it were not for the plural pronouns that implicate all of "us" in the too pressingly present world of "ours." Allen Ginsberg's "Howl" begins with "I" who speaks for "My generation."

The examples just given in these two lists of public poems are all anthology-pieces, and there are very many other poems we would say belong in both these categories. This chapter is predicated on the notion that their coinciding is not coincidental. That is, what classifies these very different poems as public makes them specially welcome and appropriate choices for anthologies by reason of the anthology's status as a public space.

The poems to be explored here were written within the period from the later 1700s to the middle of the twentieth century, during which time the number of readers grew much larger and their educational preparation more various; the body of poems had vastly increased and was coming within reach of more readers; and anthologies began to be the places where the majority of those who read poetry (still as always a small segment of the total population) looked to find it.

The three poems—Oliver Goldsmith's "The Deserted Village," Matthew Arnold's "Dover Beach," Philip Larkin's "Church Going"—have all won status as anthology-pieces. Goldsmith's and Larkin's arrived at that rank very soon after they appeared, Arnold's only after more than half a century. Because each of the three poems writes about cultural losses which for the author defined the period of history he was living in, they are presented by their makers, and then implicitly or overtly by anthologists, as representative. It is in this sense that they belong to a type of public poetry, and are suited to the anthology as cultural meeting ground.

GOLDSMITH: "THE DESERTED VILLAGE"

The historical topic of Goldsmith's poem is the phase of the enclosure movement in England when the open land in some country villages was being transferred to wealthy landowners for their private use, forcing the rural inhabitants to leave their homes for the city or to emigrate; when (according to Goldsmith's traditional Tory way of thinking) commerce was threatening ancient forms of country life, and luxury eating away the old moral virtues.

Even when "The Deserted Village" was first received in 1770 with louder applause than any English poem since Gray's "Elegy Written in a Country Church-yard" in 1751, the poem's historical argument was largely set aside by most reviewers, as it continued to be in the period of its greatest popularity through much of the nineteenth century.

In 1804, William Mudford in his *Essays on Men and Matters* wrote about Goldsmith's political message that he "perceived, or thought he perceived, a national calamity; a calamity he would willingly have been instrumental in redressing," but that poetry "never yet redressed a public grievance": "Men in general read poetry for amusement; they do not expect serious argumentation; and if they find it, they regard it only as the sportive sallies of imagination, or the fictitious embellishments of an ardent fancy."[2] Other reviewers, and later Goldsmith's biographers, typically agreed. They dismissed the poem's social theorizing as untenable or uninteresting—some, including Mudford it seems, disbelieved that the social problem even existed in England—while praising other dimensions of "The Deserted Village" that made it "welcome alike where the rich inhabit, and in huts where poor men lie."[3]

Following Joseph Addison's example in the *Spectator*, reviewers writing for the growing number of literary periodicals isolated for quotation and discussion the *beauties* of long poems, which then became popular extracts for display in anthologies. Johnson gave his support to such collections, being known as "a great friend to books like . . . *Beauties of Watts*, &c.,&c.," which he said a reader will often look into "and be tempted to go on, when he would have been frightened at books of a larger size and of a more erudite appearance."[4] The practice of culling prized passages for readers' better enjoyment, and to economize on time, itself became so generally popular that Knox in the preface to the 1805 edition of *Elegant Extracts in Poetry* hoped it would not be cause for complaint that he had included some poems "entire."[5]

The passages from "The Deserted Village" most often extracted—the descriptions of the village preacher, the schoolmaster, and the tavern—allowed readers to ignore the explicitly political argument and social theorizing in the poem. Even so, the poem's concern with public matter, whether or not readers cared about the issue in particular, had something important to do with their feeling that "The Deserted Village" somehow belonged to them, a feeling directly expressed in extraordinary ways.

The public bought up five editions of Goldsmith's poem in the year it was first published, followed shortly by two more, along with four pirated printings. Admirers of the poem by the thousands who visited the village supposed to be the actual setting of the poem expressed their proprietary sense concretely. Over years they stripped a hawthorn tree resembling one described by the poet for souvenirs to take home, until virtually nothing was left of it, not even of its roots.[6] Another striking sign that readers felt they were included in the poem, almost as if they lived in it, is that numerous villages in both England and America began to be named *Auburn* after Goldsmith's imagined place. Emerson wrote in 1824 of a rural part of Cambridge, Massachusetts, much enjoyed by students, which was known as *Sweet Auburn*, the epithet introducing the village in the first words of the poem.[7]

Though these readers seem not to have shown interest in Goldsmith's historical argument, the ways he created and used that public dimension made it a strand in a design that expands the setting of the poem, the village of the speaker's childhood, into a public space, and in doing so draws readers into it. Who these readers were, or at least who they were conceived to be in the period of the poem's greatest popularity—one biographical account by John Foster in 1848 numbered them in the "hundreds of thousands"—pertains to its means of effectiveness as a public poem.[8]

In the eighteenth century, discussions of poetry, when they brought *the public* into the argument, meant that part of it—always a small proportion in every generation in every century—who read poetry, and only a segment of those. In the decade when Gray's "Elegy" first appeared, the more educated audience for poetry was fairly represented by the readers of Dodsley's *Collection*. Dodsley himself, equating his readers with "the Public" in the postscript to the last volume of his collection, implied what the term encoded by the way he phrased his valedictory claim as anthologist: of "having furnish'd to the Public an elegant and polite Amusement."[9] When the poet William Shenstone in 1753 wrote on Dodsley's behalf to a friend asking for poems to give Dodsley for his collection, he used the persuasion that, if published there, "they will be read by the polite World."[10] In a letter of 1760 advising Percy how best to alter or correct the entries to be published in *Reliques*, Shenstone referred to its future readers as "the Class that will be your principal Readers."[11] Writing again a month later, he described those readers more specifically in his prediction that "All People of taste thro'out the Kingdom, will rejoice to see a judicious, a correct & elegant collection of such Pieces."[12]

The habit that shows up in these quotations of using the same vocabulary to apply to poems chosen for Dodsley's or Percy's anthology and to the "polite World" of poetry readers shows a degree of like-mindedness among writers, readers, and what might be called literary entrepreneurs like Dodsley, publisher as well as anthologist and author, that would be unimaginable in later situations of poetry. This agreement of interest began to unravel in the second half of the eighteenth century for no doubt many complex reasons, at least one reflected in Goldsmith's critical writings, which show an emerging sense of the audience for poetry somewhat different from Dodsley's. This way of thinking helped to shape "The Deserted Village" as a public poem that quickly became an anthology-piece.

In 1757, Goldsmith wrote a review of Gray's *Odes*, a Dodsley publication, for the *Monthly Review*. Choosing not to mention Gray's already famously famous "Elegy," published only six years before, Goldsmith concentrated his ironies on the seemingly deliberate inaccessibility to the public of Gray's two forbiddingly difficult new odes, "The Bard" and "The Progress of Poetry." While other critics made aesthetic objections to the obscurity or pedantry which they considered to be violations of politeness and elegance, the stated grounds of Goldsmith's criticism were social. They were predicated on a conception of an expanded and more varied body of readers for poetry whose judgment on the merits of poems were not based on an education shared with members of polite society:

As this publication seems designed for those who have formed their taste by the models of antiquity, the generality of Readers cannot be supposed adequate Judges of its merit. . . . We cannot, however, without some regret behold . . . this rising Poet seeking fame among the learned, without hinting to him the same advice that Isocrates used to give his Scholars, *Study the People*. This study it is that has conducted the great Masters of antiquity up to immortality.[13]

Goldsmith argued more broadly in an essay "Upon Criticism" of 1759 the view that only authors who designed their poems to be appreciated by "the public in general" were worthy of immortality. There he extended to the current generation of poets essentially the same objection he had made specifically to Gray's odes: their appeal to "the tribunal of criticism" rather than to "that of the people."[14] By contrast, gaining the approval of "the public in general" brings lasting fame. The reason given is not that they shared with poets and other members of polite society the taste formed at the grammar schools and two universities, but by virtue of "common sense." That by definition belongs to the general reader and not to the specialist.

Goldsmith gave a more specific description of the social class being steadily added to what he called "the generality of Readers" in the preface to an anthology he made in 1767, which contained almost exclusively poems by the same eighteenth-century authors who had appeared in Dodsley's collection, but was nevertheless titled *The Beauties of English Poesy*: "Compilations of this kind are chiefly designed for such as either want leisure, skill, or fortune to choose for themselves"; for those "persons whose professions turn them to different pursuits," different presumably from the pursuits of better educated members of the public with whom they could nevertheless enjoy the poems that common sense had already granted fame. "The best productions are most easily found," Goldsmith argued, to support his boast that every poem in the anthology "is well known."[15]

As historians such as Richard Altick have long been teaching, the literary situation was changing in this period from what it "had been ever since Caxton's time, a dialogue of equals" among readers, writers, and anthology makers, who shared the same education.[16] The change accelerated when, four years after the publication of "The Deserted Village," the claim of booksellers to perpetual copyright was abolished, legalizing reprints of the English classic poets in cheap editions and encouraging anthologies.

The three-pronged argument in Goldsmith's preface reflects his awareness of new configurations among the reading population (which his own relatively humble background may have helped him to recognize). His premises were that the category of the common reader had expanded socially as well as by number; that common sense was a defining possession of this general public; and that it was the faculty most capable of making the best judgments of poetic merit. This composite argument had obvious entrepreneurial value for those makers of anthologies like Goldsmith who wanted to appeal to the larger public.

Knox, one of the most influential, used it in the same way to promote his *Elegant Extracts* beginning to appear in the 1780s and continued, along with

countless imitations, well into the nineteenth century. His selections from
English poetry in the 1805 edition included "The Deserted Village" entire,
along with most of the anthology-pieces already included in Goldsmith's
Beauties for their very familiarity. Knox was guided by the same conviction
that the "best pieces are usually the most popular," that "public opinion . . .
when general and long continued, is the best criterion of merit in the fine
arts, and particularly in Poetry."[17] He justified his selections of poems "*publicly known and universally celebrated*" on the grounds that his anthology
was intended for "the well educated gentleman," "the man of liberal profes-
sion," "the mercantile classes," but not for "*virtuoso readers*" who value
"scarce and curious works . . . chiefly for *their rarity*."[18]

This line of argument, though of particular practical use to anthologists,
was not invented by them, but expressed attitudes shared by other members
of literary society in this period, who considered Johnson to be their principal setter of standards. To the point here are two passages in Johnson's *Life
of Gray*: the first about the popular reception of the two odes Goldsmith had
lavished his ironies on; the second about the fame of the "Elegy," a passage
which itself achieved a fame that suggests its fidelity to deeply felt attitudes
widely shared by Johnson's readers.

His ironies about the "*Wonderful Wonder of Wonders*, the two Sister
Odes," though more playful than Goldsmith's, imply the same serious
point that the difficulty of the poems was a sign that they courted a special
audience while ignoring the generality of readers who, due either to "vulgar
ignorance or common sense at first universally rejected them," though
"many have been since persuaded to think themselves delighted."[19] Slyly
allying himself with those "willing to be pleased," Johnson confessed that he
"would gladly find the meaning of the first stanza of *The Progress of Poetry*."

The attitudes embedded in these back-handed sentences are recast in the
high praises of the "Elegy" which close the *Life of Gray*:

In the character of his *Elegy* I rejoice to concur with the common reader; for by
the common sense of readers uncorrupted with literary prejudices, after all the
refinements of subtilty and the dogmatism of learning, must be finally decided
all claim to poetical honours. The *Church-yard* abounds with images which find
a mirrour in every mind, and with sentiments to which every bosom returns an
echo. The four stanzas beginning *Yet even these bones*, are to me original: I have
never seen the notions in any other place; yet he that reads them here, persuades

himself that he has always felt them. Had Gray written often thus, it had been vain to blame, and useless to praise him.[20]

These attitudes seem to have contributed to the promotion of public poetry as a specially valued mode because of its inclusiveness, making it specially appropriate for anthologies which, being public spaces, serve as common meeting ground.

What qualities qualify a poem as public, and why those qualities have public appeal, must change with the changing situations of poetry. In this period of the later eighteenth century, "The Deserted Village" is the ideal site where these questions can be looked at, the more so because it is relatively untrodden ground for such an exploration. Although the poem has an overt political and social message, it has not been studied as it might have been as a repository of the "bourgeois ideology" so described by William Empson in his discussion of Gray's "Elegy," or as an example of what has since been called "cultural capital."[21] It may be that it has not attracted this line of criticism because later as well as earlier readers have sensed that its argument is more important, or more interesting, as an element in the poem's design than as an ideology or social instrument.

Lesser writers of the period, who were quite likely to know Johnson's famous sentences about Gray's "Elegy," translated his metaphors of the "mirrour" and the "echo" into terms like *the recognizable, the familiar,* by which they summed up the qualities that, in their view, made "The Deserted Village" a public favorite: "Its sentiments speak to the heart; and I know of no author more capable of seizing upon the feelings of his reader as Goldsmith"; his reader "feels the throbbing of assent beat in his bosom"; "almost all the imagery is familiar to our eyes, and all the sentiments to our hearts"; its "scenes and incidents . . . such as almost all men have participated in"; its "characters of that familiar description that they came therefore before us with all the claims of old friends"; to the "matter and the harmonious numbers in which it is conveyed, there exists something responsive in every bosom"; the "sentiments expressed, are the feelings and language most naturally suggested by the objects which were presented to the poet's view"; the reader "recognises, with a mixture of wonder and delight, the scenes of reality moulded into the cadences of poetry."[22]

We can infer from the passages of critical prose by Goldsmith that he quite deliberately set himself to follow the advice he quoted to Gray, to

"Study the People": to write a poem that would be accessible to their good judgment, the only guarantee of lasting fame (and that as such would fetch a high price from the publisher, which "The Deserted Village" in fact did).[23] To that end, Goldsmith created and put to use the public dimension of the poem in ways that invited readers to feel—as one biographer said they did—that they "participated" in its space.[24] Watching how he made that happen, we can infer what were in this period qualities that made a kind of public poem.

The opening fourteen-line sentence of "The Deserted Village," although the verbs are all in the past tense, does not seem to look back at the history that prompted the title:[25]

> Sweet Auburn, lovliest village of the plain,
> Where health and plenty cheared the labouring swain,
> Where smiling spring its earliest visit paid,
> And parting summer's lingering blooms delayed,
> Dear lovely bowers of innocence and ease,
> Seats of my youth, when every sport could please,
> How often have I loitered o'er thy green,
> Where humble happiness endeared each scene;
> How often have I paused on every charm,
> The sheltered cot, the cultivated farm,
> The never failing brook, the busy mill,
> The decent church that topt the neighbouring hill,
> The hawthorn bush, with seats beneath the shade,
> For talking age and whispering lovers made. (1–14)

The verbs are generalized into composite memories by the repetition of "How often have I"—the phrase comes again in the same opening position in line 15—but the memories belong only to "I," the poet: they are attached to "my youth." Even so, Auburn's seats do have a certain kind of familiarity for the reader, though not as personal recollections but as literary conventions. We recognize the setting of "Sweet Auburn"—not yet become "The Deserted Village"—as a composite pastoral and therefore timeless image such as eighteenth-century readers met in the poems that fill Dodsley's and Goldsmith's anthologies, so we can agree with the rightness of its "bowers," "green," "cot," "brook," "shade" without the particular sense of having "loitered" there among them ourselves except on the page.

Then time, history, break in on this opening verse paragraph in the middle of the last line: "These were thy charms—But all these charms are fled" (34). The grammar of "are fled" figures history as a past event continuing to be experienced in the present, while "these charms" repeated (where we might expect *those*) locates what is present as near at hand. Carefully combined, these verbal details make the suggestion that the desecration of the village leaves nothing but the description of it, placing the reader, who never knew "Sweet Auburn" except in the poem, at a distance from it. At the same time—and temporality is at issue here—because the loss is historical, it is everyone's past, so that Goldsmith's use of the poem's historical dimension begins here to include us not only as readers of it.

The effects of these subtle adjustments of grammatical time and other details—and there are many like them in "The Deserted Village"—are easier to respond to than to explain, but accounts by contemporaries of Goldsmith describing his almost obsessively slow and careful line-by-line revising of his poems give some support to the internal signs that these refinements of detail were fashioned to work together expressively.[26] Unobtrusively they expand the setting of the poet's native village, so that it belongs as well to the public of readers for whom he designed the poem. This is an instance of the process Edward Casey's theory clarifies: that "places not only *are*, they *happen*. (And it is because they happen that they lend themselves so well to narration, whether as history or as story)."[27]

After the opening verse paragraph comes a description of the desolation dealt by "the tyrant's hand" (37), the first overtly political language in the poem; next several sections where the desecration of the village is mythologized to stand for "the land, to hastening ills a prey" (51), and its unspoiled past to represent a time "ere England's griefs began" (57). The setting—"Sweet smiling village, loveliest of the lawn" (35)—expands into a wider landscape—"Along the lawn, where scattered hamlets rose, / Unwieldy wealth, and cumbrous pomp repose" (65–66). The scene is viewed as if by some traveler surveying it in passing along the public way.

Then, seeming to solace himself, the poet revisits "Sweet Auburn" undesecrated in memory, returning to the past tense of the opening paragraph: "Sweet was the sound when oft at evening's close, / Up yonder hill the village murmur rose" (113–14). This time he does not go back alone: the reader, directed where to look "yonder," goes with him, and eleven lines later when "now" the present breaks in on the poet's memory, we are with him still:

> But now the sounds of population fail,
> No chearful murmurs fluctuate in the gale,
> No busy steps the grass-grown foot-way tread,
> For all the bloomy flush of life is fled.
> All but yon widowed, solitary thing
> That feebly bends beside the plashy spring. . . . (125–30)

We are drawn into both the past and present descriptions of the village by locating phrases in these quoted lines that here direct us to look at something near enough for us to see—"Up yonder hill," "All but yon widowed, solitary thing"—and the same formula works the same way in later descriptive passages: "Near yonder copse" (137), "Beside yon straggling fence" (193), "Near yonder thorn" (219). "Sweet Auburn" now includes us because it has been made to stand for "England's" past as well as the poet's, and the "The Deserted Village" is a representation of the present ills of "the land" that belongs to all.

As the setting expands in the poem, the distance between author and reader narrows from what it was for more than the first hundred lines. In them, a series of apostrophes invoke the village as sole listener, lightly personified as muse, maiden, mother: "Sweet Auburn," "Sweet smiling village," "Sweet Auburn! parent of the blissful hour" (75).

By its form, apostrophe pretends to ignore the reader. In contrast, the verse paragraph beginning "Sweet was the sound when oft at evening's close, / Up yonder hill the village murmur rose" (113–14) drops apostrophe and personification ("Sweet" is not an epithet here), the lines sound less distanced, and the reader's presence is suggested in the pointing word "yonder." Plural pronouns also creep in that include poet and reader in "us" and "our" (89, 274).

As we are gradually being gathered into the setting, the language describing it begins to mix in with the generalized categories of pastoral some more particular, everyday details: "noisy geese," "playful children just let loose from school," "The watch-dog's voice" and "the loud laugh that spoke the vacant mind" (117–22). This kind of detail is piled on in the extended descriptions of the village preacher, the schoolmaster, and the alehouse much favored in anthologies, and sketched in even where the "I" speaks about himself, so that he seems to step out of the traditional, formal role of poet:

> I still had hopes, for pride attends us still,
> Amidst the swains to shew my book-learned skill,
> Around my fire an evening groupe to draw,
> And tell of all I felt, and all I saw. . . . (89–92)

Even in the last part of the poem, where the author invokes "sweet Poetry, thou loveliest maid" in an apostrophe, it does not sound like the formal opening addresses to "Sweet Auburn." Now he speaks to his muse unceremoniously, with teasing affection, as if she were a lovable and not quite respectable mistress:

> Dear charming nymph, neglected and decried,
> My shame in crowds, my solitary pride.
> Thou source of all my bliss, and all my woe,
> That found'st me poor at first, and keep'st me so. . . .
>   (411–14)

This kind of writing, while in fact belonging to a different poetic tradition than the pastoral passages, *seems* to be less literary, to make the poet seem more the reader's contemporary, a member of the same society, using something more like the same language. Again the poem moves in the direction of drawing poet and reader into the same public space rather than toward didactic generality (though that phrase would describe the last four lines of the poem, which were written by Johnson, a master of didactic generalizing).

Goldsmith's more social language in this passage helped to give the impression "The Deserted Village" made on its readers, as Goldsmith's nineteenth-century biographers described it: that the poem is "wholly concerned with common life"; that "everything in it is English"; that "no English poet of equal education has so few obligations to the ancients as Goldsmith"; that he "treats no subject in common with them"; "his topics, descriptions, and incidents are modern, domestic, and almost wholly applicable to English life, manners, and characters."[28]

Ordinary life and Englishness are inherently accessible to the judgment of the common reader. Goldsmith's handling of traditional pastoral brought it too within reach of the mixed audience that made up his generality of readers: by avoiding classical names and mythological allusions; borrowing only images and incidents that could be transported to an English village; and using diction so deeply embedded in familiar English poems—from "Come live with me and be my love" to "Elegy Written in a Country-churchyard"—that it could seem to belong to the common language.

By these adjustments, Goldsmith made the pastoral tradition contribute to the poem's appeal to readers who had not formed their taste by the models of antiquity, as well as to others with a more formal classical education, who would appreciate Goldsmith's assimilations of ancient models such as Virgil's eclogues, his echoes of "Lycidas" (the paradigm of the classical elegy in English). They could also appreciate his style, which Percy claimed to be exemplary of the "height of elegance the English language" may achieve.[29] This class of readers included Johnson, who said that whatever Goldsmith wrote he "did it better than any other man could do," that he "deserved a place in Westminster Abbey"; and it included Gray, who, after hearing "The Deserted Village" read aloud, said "*That man is a poet.*"[30]

The poem, like Gray's "Elegy," was quickly followed by too many imitations, for instance "The Frequented Village" and "The Village Oppressed," and contributed to *The Beauties of Goldsmith; or, the moral and sentimental treasury of genius* in 1782. It began to appear regularly in anthologies published in England and America at least by the 1790s, when collections of familiar favorites were beginning to multiply. It was printed whole by Thomas Janes in *The Beauties of the Poets* and in extracts in William Enfield's *The Speaker*, a gathering of passages suitable for elocution lessons.

All through the nineteenth century Goldsmith's poem could be found in almost any kind of anthology; in the 1850s the famous collection of extracts still known as "Bartlett's *Familiar Quotations*" included twenty-two entries from "The Deserted Village." As late as 1944 an anthology inspired by war-time patriotism called *England* included a passage from "The Deserted Village" under the heading "Countryside."

What most ensured the poem's absorption into the common culture and language was the custom until the late nineteenth-century in England and America of assigning "The Deserted Village"—the same was true of Gray's "Elegy"—to be read and memorized as a school lesson, even for elementary pupils. Matthew Arnold condemned this practice, writing in 1880: "Nothing could be more completely unsuitable. . . . Some of the short pieces by Mrs. Hemans, such as *The Graves of a Household, The Homes of England, The Better Land* are to be recommended."[31] While Goldsmith's poem gradually disappeared from the obligatory school curriculum, it kept its place in anthologies where it can still be found regularly wherever eighteenth-century poems are included.

ARNOLD: "DOVER BEACH"

When Arnold in an essay of 1865 asked "what in literature we mean, by *famous*," his clear intention was to give an answer that would sever poetic immortality from contemporary reputation. To do this was to argue in very different terms from Johnson's in his famous judgment that the "common sense" of the "common reader" must be the final arbiter of "all claim to poetical honours." Arnold's counterargument begins by distinguishing "famous men of genius in literature," whose "praise is for ever and ever," from "famous men of ability in literature," whose "praise is in their own generation," and therefore tenuous because "many once popular reputations" fall on hard times:

Only two kinds of authors are safe. . . . The first kind are the great abounding fountains of truth, whose criticism of life is a source of illumination and joy to the whole human race for ever,—the Homers, the Shakespeares. . . . The second are those . . . of the same family and character with the sacred personages, exercising like them an immortal function, and like them inspiring a permanent interest. . . . They will never, like the Shakespeares, command the homage of the multitude; but they are safe; the multitude will not trample them down.[32]

The differences between Johnson's vocabulary and Arnold's here reflect large social changes in what constituted the reading public for poetry. What later eighteenth-century discussions about literature called *the public* was understood to be a body of readers whose *common sense*—taking the words at their most literal meaning of general understanding—the writers themselves mainly shared. In the changed situation of poetry in the early nineteenth century, *the public* in such discussions became synonymous with the noisy, unconsidering *crowd* which by 1865 had swelled to the *multitude* that Arnold's language in this passage shows he was afraid of.[33] After the publication of *New Poems* gained him some attention from reviewers he wrote scarcely any more poetry, but his retreat to safe refuge was still threatened by the continuing critical discussion of his poetry.

The focus of writers about Arnold during his life and for at least half of the twentieth century was on his own distinction between popular reputation and lasting literary fame, translated into debate about how many of his contemporaries read him, how they read him, and who they were. The social divisions among the readers of poetry were of course the driving issue in this discussion; the possibility of using a phrase like *the public* to hold these disparate groups together seems to have been lost.

In 1868, the year *New Poems* was published, one critic announced that, as the "good judgment of the public" has decided once for all, "Mr. Arnold is a prose writer, not a poet"; another in 1875 that "Mr. Arnold is not a popular poet"; and an obituary writer after Arnold's death in 1888 wrote that he "will never be more than 'the poet of the few.'"[34]

Even among Arnold's admirers, only Swinburne was confident that Arnold's "best poems cannot but live as long as any, of their time" and that his "high and distinct seat is assured to him among English poets."[35] The others could say at most that Arnold's later poems were being "received with a degree of favour which almost amounts to 'popularity'" (1872); that every year "widens the circle" of what began as a "small band" of appreciative readers (1877).[36] In 1886, one writer thought that while Arnold's poetry was reaching a "slowly increasing number of thoughtful readers," at the same time "in the judgment of a smaller circle, he has already won no mean place among the masters of immortal song, and a first place among contemporary poets."[37] Unexpectedly, the author of one obituary wondered "whether Mr. Arnold ever realised the devotedness his verse inspired in the minds of thousands of his countrymen and countrywomen, both in the old world and the new."[38]

His death did not end the troubled debate about the accessibility of Arnold's poems to all classes of readers. Though one notice in 1890 used the fact of a forthcoming "Popular Edition" as proof that "no sooner was he dead" than "the tide of his reputation has steadily risen," there were dissenters.[39] Margaret Oliphant, in *The Victorian Age of English Literature* of 1892, judged Arnold "the poet of the Universities,—of the intellectual classes" who cannot "conciliate that inner circle with the wider one of the general world" or reach "the common heart."[40] Hugh Walker wrote more sympathetically three years later in *The Greater Victorian Poets* that "of all Englishmen Arnold is the one who is farthest from the place he ought to hold in the hearts of his countrymen."[41] Quiller-Couch, in his introduction to the Oxford edition of Arnold's poems first published in 1909 and nine more times by 1945, made the official-sounding pronouncement that Arnold "was never popular, and never will be."[42]

Anthologies of the period reflected something like the same uncertainties about the reception of Arnold's poetry among different groups of readers. Anthologists in England and America showed little if any interest in Arnold's verse until ten or so years after *New Poems* had brought him attention (about the same time lag was true for "The Deserted Village," but in that period many fewer anthologies were being produced than in the late nineteenth century). For two more decades the assortment of Arnold's poems thinly scattered among anthologies shows no emerging popular favorites. Instead, the titles of the poems chosen even as much as a handful of times—"Thyrsis," "Philomela," "Urania," "Euphrosene," "Requiescat"—suggest that makers of anthologies were reflecting the views of readers whose taste in poetry was formed by classical, meaning largely university, education. Around the turn of the century there was a cult of admirers of "Thyrsis" and "The Scholar-Gypsy" at Oxford.[43]

Beginning about that time, there were signs in anthologies of some widening interest in Arnold as a poet, partly promoted by Edmund Stedman, who claimed in the introduction to *A Victorian Anthology* to be as it were the inventor of "Victorian" poetry: "Even the adjective 'Victorian' was unfamiliar, if it had been employed at all, when I used it in the title of a magazine essay . . . in January, 1873. It is now as well in use as 'Elizabethan' or 'Georgian.'"[44] His large, up-to-date, and widely read anthology was ordered by chronological divisions with canonizing headings: "Period of Tennyson, Arnold, Browning, Rossetti, and Swinburne." Arnold was represented by eleven entries (only "Philomela" with a classical title), and among them was "Dover Beach."

From that time forth, the poem ensconced itself more and more firmly in its place as an anthology-piece in collections that suit an academic curriculum, such as *An Oxford Anthology of English Poetry* (1935) and *The Norton Anthology of Poetry* (in all its editions since 1970). In 1972 Helen Gardner said in her preface to *The New Oxford Book of English Literature* that "nobody today would not include such poems as 'Ulysses,' 'My Last Duchess,' and 'Dover Beach' as being finely characteristic of their authors' best work.'"[45]

"Dover Beach" was also regularly included in anthologies designed for a more general public, for instance in *The Home Book of Verse* (1918), and in Untermeyer's *The Book of Living Verse* (1932), a selection said by its editor to consist only of poems that "have persisted in spite of changing times and shifting tastes."[46] In Max Eastman's *Anthology for the Enjoyment of Poetry* of 1939, which he boasted had no poems of the "unintelligible" cult, "Dover Beach" was saved for the last place because the editor believed it "might ultimately rise above everything else that has been written representative of this era."[47] Bartlett's *Familiar Quotations* testified that the poem had become known by the 1950s, and it duly appeared in 1952 in Stephen Graham's *100 Best Poems in the English Language*. In 1966 it was chosen to be the only entry by Arnold in Oscar Williams's selection of then undisputed anthology-pieces, *Master Poems of the English Language*. The next year, exactly a century after *New Poems* was published, Lionel Trilling in his anthology *The Experience of Language* noted about "Dover Beach" that for "many readers it is the single most memorable poem of the Victorian Age."[48]

Reviews of Arnold's poems during his lifetime suggest a reason why he eventually won fame in this century from a wider audience than the intellectual class, and why it took time for that fame to mature. Predictors that Arnold would never find favor with the wider public as well as those who believed, or hoped, that he would, essentially agreed with what Stedman wrote in 1876 in *Victorian Poetry* (his critical companion to *A Victorian Anthology*): that Arnold's poems were a "reflection of the unrest and bewilderment of our time," that he was "the pensive doubting Hamlet of modern verse."[49] Even so, such agreement did not prevent critics from putting different values on this dimension of his poetry, as we can judge from a few quotations chosen from a surprisingly large number of comments on his poems, above all on "Dover Beach," calling them representative of "the tendencies of the day."[50]

A reviewer in 1869 praising *New Poems* described what he thought were its best entries as "the strong words of a strong poet who is himself affected—depressed and oppressed—by the malaria taint that is all about him in the air—the subtle disease which paralyses our energies, and mars our work."[51] In 1884, Henry James admired Arnold as "the poet of his age, of the moment in which we live, of our 'modernity,' as the new school of criticism in France gives us perhaps license to say."[52] Charles Eliot Norton in 1888 made a pronouncement that sounds almost as if it were fashioned as the poet's epitaph: "Arnold's poetry was the poetry of a scholar, but a scholar in closest sympathy with the sentiment and emotions of his own generation."[53]

Meanwhile a hostile review in 1869 defined the "consciousness" that informed Arnold's poems as the sense "of his own comparative powerlessness, and that of his poetical contemporaries," a feeling that the "age" has "benumbed him far more than it has benumbed all save the chosen few whom he resembles."[54] This straight-faced mocking scorns Arnold as an elitist unaware that his appropriation of the age to conform it to the mood of its poetry was self-dramatizing.

Another unsympathetic review of 1872 turned the representative dimension of Arnold's poetry against him by giving a slightly different twist to its mocking:

When I come to ask what Mr. Arnold's poetry has done for this generation, the answer must be that no one has expressed more powerfully and poetically its spiritual weaknesses, its craving for a passion that it cannot feel, its admiration for a self-mastery that it cannot achieve, its desire for a creed that it fails to accept, its sympathy with a faith that it will not share, its aspiration for a peace that it does not know.[55]

Both these comments, sarcastic while grudgingly acknowledging Arnold's power, give some idea of why the reflection of the age in his poems did not at once appeal to the sense of recognition among the general public of readers, who were brought up on the poems collected in anthologies like *Popular Poetic Pearls* of 1887. Among its entries readers could find: Gray's "Elegy"; "The Deserted Village"; such favorites by Tennyson as "Break, break, break," "The Old Home," "Ring Out Wild Bells," an extract from "The Princess"; other anthology-pieces by Wordsworth, Robert Burns, Southey, Hood, Scott, Leigh Hunt, Elizabeth Browning, Whittier, Longfellow, Lowell; and many entries by authors we have never heard of, but none by Arnold.

If these poems, many of them patriotic and religious in spirit, had shaped what most readers would have called their natural sentiments rather than what critics called their generation's consciousness, Arnold's despairing sense of isolation, his troubled doubting would not have found an echo in their collective bosom. The poetry they preferred had not taught them to recognize the feelings expressed in Arnold's *modern* poems as their own.

Stedman's claim to have invented the adjective *Victorian* points to another reason why the generality of readers were not immediately responsive to the representative voice reviewers heard in Arnold's poetry. The very idea of belonging to a generation was itself not yet strongly entrenched, it seems, and certainly not the sense of belonging to a generation with a distinctive, common *consciousness* (1837 is the earliest date given in the *OED* for the use of the word to mean a collective faculty of an aggregate of people who think or feel alike). This recently invented notion was the product of innumerable cultural changes that altered ways of thinking about even the most elemental temporal experiences, as recent studies such as Stephen Kern's *The Culture of Time and Space* have shown.[56]

It follows, then, that a large portion of the reading public had not been prepared to accept, even to comprehend, the concept of a poem's power to express a complex of commonly held contemporary attitudes and moods. When Johnson praised Gray's "Elegy" for its abundance of "images which find a mirrour in every mind" and "sentiments to which every bosom returns an echo," we can be sure his contemporaries did not understand him to mean those minds and hearts cast in a mold peculiar to their moment in history. When admirers of "The Deserted Village" praised it for its power to express sentiments any reader could feel to be *natural*, that meant they were recognized as timeless and universal rather than specially if not uniquely characteristic of a particular age. For these deeply rooted ways of thinking in the minds of the majority of readers to change took time.

Those writers of Arnold's period who had begun to conceive of a consciousness or spirit of the age—Hazlitt and Mill were not the only ones to title a piece of writing *The Spirit of the Age*—were in some large part responding to Wordsworth, as one retrospective notice written in 1888 suggested was Arnold's experience. The critic found that Wordsworthian connection concentrated in "Dover Beach":

This note of unrest, confusion, powerlessness—'the eternal note of sadness' which Sophocles 'heard long ago on the Ægean'—runs through nearly all his poetry. . . . All his most characteristic and finished work is, in a word, but an amplification of Wordsworth's famous couplet:—

> The world is too much with us; late and soon,
> Getting and spending, we lay waste our powers. . . .[57]

Even earlier, critics without the advantage of a retrospective view chose "Dover Beach" as the fullest expression of Arnold's power to represent the contemporary mood. One, reviewing *New Poems*, wrote in 1869: "We suffer from weariness not merely of the flesh but of the spirit. 'Dover Beach,' which gives expression to this complaint, is at once the finest and the most despondent of these poems."[58] Another in 1878 found that the "poet's own uneasiness," the discontent of the "soul" that cannot "find any satisfactory substitute for the faith it has rejected," most powerfully "breaks forth in a lyrical burst unsurpassed in modern poetry for grandeur and breadth": the passage in "Dover Beach" comparing "The Sea of Faith" to "this distant northern sea."[59]

The anthology-reading public had not yet caught up with this judgment, and nineteenth-century anthologists reflected their indifference, if not resistance, by largely ignoring Arnold's distinctively modern poems, including "Dover Beach." It was the work of poets after Arnold who had learned from him that prepared readers to recognize the modern attitudes and mood, for which "Dover Beach" was seen to be the quintessential expression.

Eliot preferred Arnold to Browning and Tennyson for being "more intimate with us," for writing his best poems entirely out of "his genuine feelings of unrest, loneliness and dissatisfaction."[60] Poems that had become anthology-pieces themselves—"The Lake Isle of Innisfree," "The Darkling Thrush," "The Love Song of J. Alfred Prufrock" come to mind—have entered deeply into what Richard Poirier has called "the vernacular and the assumptions" that have governed "the consciousness of a generation or two" since Arnold's.[61] The effect of such poems, having themselves become cultural events, has been to make what in "Dover Beach" is presented as a reflection of the mental and emotional state of Arnold's contemporaries seem a continuing condition, the legacy of historical forces that brought about the sense of cultural loss we seem to have always, or still, with us.

In this way readers of poets following Arnold have been prepared, as many of his contemporaries were not, to respond to his means of making us feel that we can recognize the consciousness of his generation as like our own. This public state of mind and feeling is ultimately the conceptual space "Dover Beach" draws readers into, by means very different from those Goldsmith used in "The Deserted Village." They make Arnold's a distinctively modern form of public poem.

The title of "Dover Beach" names an actual place as the setting of the poem, a feature emphasized in *New Poems* because it is shared by the titles of entries positioned just before, "Calais Sands," and after, "The Terrace at Berne" and "Stanzas Composed at Carnac." By contrast, the title "The Deserted Village" describes a figuratively suggestive category that then becomes an imaginatively realized particular place with a name in the poem.

In the context created in *New Poems*, Arnold's grouped place-names in titles imply that the specific places were sites of the poet's personal experiences; that he had made the journey between Calais and Dover (scholars agree that Arnold wrote much of "Dover Beach" in 1851, the year of his marriage and honeymoon at Dover).[62] The title "Dover Beach" names a place specific to the poet's experience that is also a public space with a national and literary history, woven together in poems Arnold and many readers, through the nineteenth century at least, are likely to have known. Dover was a common point of departure and return for English travelers and soldiers sailing to and from the continent, and as such was celebrated as an emotionally weighted space: border, brink, fortress, haven, sanctuary, the threshold of home and freedom.

William Lisle Bowles, in a sonnet of 1787 with Dover as its setting, imagined a "lonely wanderer" standing "On these white cliffs, that calm above the flood, / / Hear not the surge that has for ages beat." Though torn by regrets at leaving home and England, he heroically commits himself to "the wild winds and unhearing tide—/ The World his country, and his God his side."[63] Probably more for its popular sentiments than for its literary virtues, the sonnet kept its place in anthologies spanning the nineteenth and continuing in the twentieth century, for instance in William Hazlitt's *Select British Poets* (1824), J. C. M. Bellew's *Poets' Corner* (1868), Stevenson's *The Home Book of Verse* (1918).

Drawing on much the same associations, Wordsworth wrote four sonnets set near the shore at Dover. One of a pair composed in 1802 describes how, seeing through the "clear" air "the coast of France how near!/Drawn almost into frightful neighborhood," the poet recognized in the "barrier" of "calm" sea a promise that "Even so doth God protect us if we be/Virtuous and wise." In the companion sonnet—Keats blasted it with the rhyme "viler Wordsworth's sonnet/On Dover: Dover! who could write upon it?"—the returning traveler rejoices that "Thou art free,/My Country!" and revels in the "bliss, to tread the grass/Of England once again."[64] By 1837, the place "Under the white cliff's battlemented crown" had for Wordsworth come to be a sanctuary from "social noise," where he could hear "the dread Voice that speaks from out the sea/Of God's eternal word."[65]

A literary source known more widely at least to the English public for its connection with Dover was the scene in *King Lear* when Edgar, having led his father, blind Gloucester, to safe haven at Dover, describes the place imagined as from the brink of the "chalky cliffs" (IV,iv,11–24). In the nineteenth century, when Shakespeare climbed to the pinnacle of his fame as a figure in England's national and literary history, the cliffs at Dover were popularly known as "Shakespeare's cliffs," an expression Arnold referred to in a letter in 1859.[66]

In anthologies both English and American, these lines by Shakespeare have become something of an anthology-piece: in Emerson's *Parnassus* of 1874 they are printed as a separate poem with the title "Dover Cliffs"; most recently they are extracted in *The Oxford Book of English Verse* of 1999, where they suit the character of anthologies in this series as a public repository of England's heritage.

The actual place named in the title and described as the setting in the first five lines of "Dover Beach" lives up to its historical and literary past:

> The sea is calm to-night.
> The tide is full, the moon lies fair
> Upon the straits; on the French coast the light
> Gleams and is gone; the cliffs of England stand,
> Glimmering and vast, out in the tranquil bay.[67]

The pause marked by punctuation and line-ending after "the cliffs of England stand," likens them here to traditional figurings of them as a national fortress unshakable by time, the forces of nature, or human enemies (who often came from "the French coast"). The famous cliffs are most of all felt to be a protection of the "calm" and "tranquil" scene with its unmistakable echoes of Wordsworth's much anthologized sonnet (Palgrave titled it "By the Sea"): "It is a beauteous evening, calm and free, / / . . . the broad sun / Is sinking down in its tranquility."

The familiarity of the scene in this description is undisturbed until line six rearranges it: "Come to the window, sweet is the night air!" Though in Wordsworth's sonnet the description of the beach at sundown is interrupted—again in the sixth line—by an invitation to "Listen!" there is here an unWordsworthian suggestion that the companion is a beloved, that this may be a love poem. What is much more surprising is that Arnold's speaker is indoors, enclosed and separated from the place, not experiencing it as Wordsworth's typically do by walking beside the sea or standing on the lea of it. Here Dover becomes a landscape as if in a framed painting; an image of beauty in nature looked at rather than a vital place immediately surrounding the observer and penetrating his being.

"Only," the oddly chosen word set off by a comma at the beginning of the next line, qualifies or even seems to take back what had come before:

> Only, from the long line of spray
> Where the sea meets the moon-blanched land,
> Listen! you hear the grating roar
> Of pebbles which the waves draw back, and fling,
> At their return, up the high strand,
> Begin, and cease, and then again begin,
> With tremulous cadence slow, and bring
> The eternal note of sadness in.

The speaker breathes in the sweetness of the night air for just a moment. Then even what can be seen from the window is displaced by sounds that "bring/ . . . in" to the room and the poem the "tremulous cadence," the "eternal note of sadness." This is what the speaker experiences and what "you hear": *you* the intimate companion; but also the generalizing plural *you* in the collective sense: the readers of the poem, who do hear in these lines the cadence and note of the waves.

The actual place is gradually being dissolved, and traditional descriptions of it disappear. Line six makes a moment's gesture toward earlier love poems where one little room becomes a metaphor for the passionate intimacy of lovers that crowds out the public world, but the generalizing power of "you" breaks in, allowing the next two groups of lines to blot out the love poem with generalized philosophical statement.

The stanza space that follows the sentence spoken to "you" marks off these first fourteen lines as a sonnet disturbed in rhyme scheme and in line lengths—varying from iambic pentameter to tetrameter, trimeter, even dimeter—but thick with allusions both generic and particular to the matter and form of traditional sonnets. The stanza space disconnects the poem from these antecedents:

> Sophocles long ago
> Heard it on the Ægean, and it brought
> Into his mind the turbid ebb and flow
> Of human misery; we
> Find also in the sound a thought,
> Hearing it by this distant northern sea.

In the "sound" of the waves "we" discover our own state of mind, so that the actual place named in the title is close to being wholly conceptualized. The spatial range from the "Ægean" to "this distant northern sea" (geographically distant from Greece but also distant—cut-off, utterly remote—from the human observer) cannot be seen from the window, but only in the collective mind of whoever "we" are (the new pronoun strongly stressed by its suspended position and its adjacent internal rhyme with "misery"). Surely, in these philosophically generalizing lines, the poet and his readers are more present than the two lovers looking out from their little room.

The formal extended metaphor that constructs the next group of lines is a figurative expounding of the thought "we" were said to discover in the sound of the sea. It completes the transfiguration of the beach at Dover into a conceptual space, which is paradoxically both internalized and made public as *the consciousness of the age* "now." This paradox is concentrated in the paradoxical line "But now I only hear":

> The Sea of Faith
> Was once, too, at the full, and round earth's shore
> Lay like the folds of a bright girdle furled.
> But now I only hear
> Its melancholy, long, withdrawing roar,

Retreating, to the breath
Of the night-wind, down the vast edges drear
And naked shingles of the world.

"But now I only hear" in one of its senses—*I alone hear*—only seems to deny the sense of commonality with a collective public *we* expressed just before in "we / Find also in the sound a thought." Actually, *I alone hear* is a more bitter restatement of the thought "we" discover: that the common consciousness of this generation is the recognition that "we" are each "I only," alone, alienated, in the same distress as every isolated one.

"But now I only hear" in its other sense—*I hear nothing except*—is also an expression of modern collective consciousness. What the speaker cannot hear is the actual movement of the waves as they "draw back, and . . . / . . . return," their "ebb and flow," because he is enclosed, separated from the natural world. He can hear only their "withdrawing," a deliberately broken metaphor—actual tides always return—which in its failure expresses the modern condition it figures.[68]

That is, the withdrawal of "The Sea of Faith" has emptied nature of divinely implanted meanings which minds of earlier ages could find in it, so that it is "now" no longer the living source poets could once draw on for figures true to the human condition, not even to "human misery." Figures from nature made by the poet of the present must either falsify or collapse. It follows that "I" by now representing "we" cannot trust the traditional readings of nature in earlier poems alluded to in the opening lines, some so closely echoed they could be said to be quoted.

To have continued the poem in the manner and mood of those five opening lines, drawing on the rich historical and literary associations suggested by the title, would have been to lie. To complete the love poem suggested only for the length of line six—"Come to the window, sweet is the night air!"—proves also unsustainable. Though the impulse recurs, it lasts no longer than what amounts again to a single line, this one a broken iambic pentameter: "Ah, love, let us be true / To one another!" The line break makes sadder the juxtaposition of the pronouns "us" to "one another," a reminder of the shift from "we" to "I only." Even lovers are separated islands.

In spite of the exclamation point, this modern version of a traditional persuasion to love—compare Marvell's "Let us roll all our strength and

all / Our sweetness up into one ball"—is too troubled, doubtful, frightened
to be sustained:

> Ah, love, let us be true
> To one another! for the world, which seems
> To lie before us like a land of dreams,
> So various, so beautiful, so new,
> Hath really neither joy, nor love, nor light,
> Nor certitude, nor peace, nor help for pain;
> And we are here as on a darkling plain
> Swept with confused alarms of struggle and flight,
> Where ignorant armies clash by night.

The setting of Dover beach at evening—"The tide is full, the moon lies
fair / Upon the straits"—returns here as a simile "like a land of dreams," only
a simile, only fairy-"land." It only "seems / To lie before us," a compound of
words suggesting deception: "seems" rhyming with "dreams" coupled with
"lie" here recalling with a difference "lies fair" in the second line of the
poem. The two lovers disappear into the general "we," and "here" is located
only in another simile, so that it is dislocated from space and outside time
"as on a darkling plain." Dwight Culler called this the "most famous
phrase" of the "most famous of Arnold's poems," the "central statement
which Arnold makes about the human condition."[69]

The disconnection between the calm, moonlit sea—in retrospect a de-
ceptive description—and "a darkling plain / . . . of struggle and flight" is so
extreme and abrupt that some critics have felt the need to explain it by the
fact that Arnold wrote these last nine lines earlier than the rest, intending
them for another poem.[70] The reading of "Dover Beach" here proposes that
the discontinuity is significantly there, as an expressive feature of the poem's
final design: a series of displacements in its diction, address, form, as one
after another the traditional sources and strengths of poetry fail "now."
"Dover Beach" must be among the earliest poems in English to make its
own failure of language an effectively expressive device, one that Eliot rein-
vented (using it in "Preludes," "The Love Song of J. Alfred Prufrock," "The
Hollow Men," and as we shall see, in "Whispers of Immortality"), if he did
not learn it from Arnold.

Another way to describe the design of "Dover Beach" in the context of
the wider discussion here is that it effects a transformation of a kind of tra-

ditional public poem, a kind illustrated in this discussion by the Dover sonnets of Bowles and Wordsworth. They draw on the rich historical and literary associations attached to a specific place, which by the presence of those associations is made a public space.

"Dover Beach" internalizes the place that begins as its setting, a process that it seems Arnold meant to point to by his change in the context he made for the poem in his final arrangement of his work. In the last edition of his poetry before he died, instead of surrounding "Dover Beach" with other poems naming actual places in their titles, he placed it right after "Despondency" and "Self-Deception" and just before "Growing Old." He followed that sequence with "The Progress of Poetry," a title taken from Gray's ode announcing the diminishment of poetic inspiration generation by generation as a historical decline and as a personal loss. The setting that "Dover Beach" begins by describing in traditional ways is transfigured as the consciousness shared among a generation of people who feel themselves to be alone.

Arnold seems to have foreseen that this distinctively modern paradox of collective separateness called for a kind of public poem that has redefined what readers by now have been persuaded that they have in common. In 1856, he wrote to his sister that "my poems are making their way, I think, though slowly. . . . The fact is however that the state of mind expressed in many of the poems is becoming more common."[71] In 1869, the year after "Dover Beach" was published, he expanded this point in a letter to his mother:

My poems represent, on the whole, the main movement of mind of the last quarter of a century, and thus they will probably have their day as people become conscious to themselves of what that movement of mind is, and interested in the literary productions which reflect it. It might fairly be urged that I have less poetical sentiment than Tennyson and less intellectual vigour and abundance than Browning; yet because I have perhaps more of a fusion of the two than either of them, and have more regularly applied that fusion to the main line of modern development, I am likely enough to have my turn as they have had theirs.[72]

The editors of *Victorian and Later English Poetry*, an anthology reprinted several times in the 1930s, quoted this uneasy statement of Arnold's hope for immortality in defiance of his apparent failure to win popular approval from his contemporaries. The editors used it as an opportunity to raise this question for their own time. In the introduction to their large selection of Arnold's poems, including "Dover Beach," they asked: "What will the future write of Matthew Arnold the poet? It is a question that cannot be surely answered now."[73] By the 1990s, Cecil Lang, the editor of Arnold's letters, felt sure he could answer it when he wrote that Arnold remains "visible because of one poem, 'Dover Beach,' honored wherever English literature is honored."[74] The testimonial to the poem is borne out by its status as an anthology-piece for more than the past half-century; in that position it has been described as the poem most fully representative of the Victorian age.

The question still needing some sort of answer is why "Dover Beach" was the one among what even some of Arnold's contemporaries called his *modern* poems to secure this honor. He seems to have left no evidence that he deliberated about how to adapt his poems to make them accessible to readers unfamiliar with his advanced line of thinking, who had not had the suggestion made to them by their poets that they shared an ethos particular to their generation. Still, in "Dover Beach" more than in any other of his poems, there are signs of such shaping. They can be seen in allusions to popular mythologies about the cliffs of Dover rather than to classical myths; in unmistakable echoes of anthology-pieces by Wordsworth; and in evocations of patterns of feeling that Wordsworth's writings have imprinted so deeply in the minds of a great many readers that they have wielded unmeasurable influence since the mid-nineteenth century.

Arnold's shaping of "Dover Beach" into an accessible public poem also shows in its explicit inclusion of the poet with the readers in "We" and "us," fellow inhabitants of the modern "world" conceptualized as "a darkling plain." These distinctive internal features of "Dover Beach" suggest why, in due season, it became the poem of Arnold's most known and most highly valued by the large, mixed public of readers he hoped to reach.

LARKIN: "CHURCH GOING"

Philip Larkin's "Church Going," the centerpiece—literally—of his volume *The Less Deceived* of 1955, was quickly and continuously praised as the "most significant" poem in the book; the one most representative of Larkin's "prevalent tone"; his "public, representative statement"; the "most important English poem of the 1950s"; the "show-piece" of the "New

Movement" in poetry that he was associated with; "one of the type-poems of the century . . . much discussed in every sixth-form English class and literary extension course, anthologized and duplicated" until it sometimes seemed almost "too thoroughly institutionalized."[75] It was recognized not only to be "a central poem in Larkin's work," but to be "as important a statement of the mid-twentieth century consciousness as Arnold's 'Dover Beach' was of the mid-nineteenth."[76]

What the two poems were found to have in common, what also makes them alike in being representative, is the "consciousness" they express, which writers about Larkin's work have described in phrases very close to those used about "Dover Beach": a sense of "apartness," of "the isolation, the loneliness that is part of the condition of us all"; an awareness of "man as a creature isolated in a universe from which God seems to have withdrawn."[77]

Even so, there is no suggestion in the writings of Larkin's many admirers or fewer detractors that "Church Going" is anachronistic, a nostalgic leftover from a literary period that much of earlier twentieth-century poetry had tried to distance itself from. They described Larkin as introducing an "individual, contemporary voice," a "new poetic voice," the "authentic voice of our troubled day," much as Stedman called Arnold the "voice of the age."[78] The critic A. Alvarez, reviewing *The Less Deceived*, fine-tuned that phrase by crediting Larkin with having created "a tone of voice for the time."[79] In this discussion the distinction will be a useful measure of the poetic distance between Arnold's Victorian and Larkin's mid-twentieth-century public poems.

"Church Going" creates "a tone of voice for the age" even in its title (a trick Larkin learned most probably from Auden, who probably learned it from Frost). It sounds like ordinary speech because it is close in form to common idioms: one of the first to come to mind is *movie going* because we use it often—John Hollander made it the title for a poem—when we talk about one of our most popular, distinctively present-day communal pastimes. The closeness to it of "Church Going" makes the title sound like just another casual bit of speech, emptied of what going to church used to mean (like the current slang phrase *see you in church*, which means anything but what it says). The idiom is new but too much like existing ones to have the energy or freshness of an idiosyncratic turn of speech—compare Frost's "Mending Wall."

Larkin's title prepares for the flat, tired, skeptical, self-mocking tone of voice in the opening lines, which belongs to a solitary figure who has no apparent attachments. "Another church" with "nothing going on" sounds bored, unsurprised because already disappointed, without illusions, though like the title phrase which it echoes, the tired cliché "nothing going on" means more (or in another sense less) than it says: that *there isn't anything happening* and that *nothing is, as usual, what is happening.*[80] Repeated, repetitive acts of church going go on leaving the speaker "at a loss," another idiom representing the sense of diminishment, of emptying in the language of the title and the poem, which is itself a representation of the way we speak now. So are other colloquial phrases the church goer says habitually: "God knows," not meaning that any more than we usually do; or "Wondering," "wondering," "I wonder," which means something very much closer to *I can only try to guess* than to *I am struck with awe by wonders.*

Colloquialism is itself a defining feature of much poetry in this century, one of its escape routes from Victorian poetic diction. Larkin made his a colloquial language for his generation by loading it with current slang and stock phrases—"brass and stuff," "on show," "rent-free"—and in some poems with brasher vulgarities. His colloquial idiom is deliberately restricted in the tones of voice it is capable of—unrhetorical, unsentimental, unsurprised (to borrow his habit of negatives)—expressing a less than tragic sense of being let down: "Another church," "not worth stopping for," "And what remains, when disbelief has gone?" As much in character are expressions of self-doubt and of unwillingness to be convinced: "From where I stand," "Someone would know; I don't," "my representative,/ Bored, uninformed."

This manner of speaking is largely suited to settings in what one critic called "the urban, industrialized Britain that most of us now inhabit," a 1950s version of Yeats's late-nineteenth-century city with its "pavements grey," and specially of Auden's dreary England in the 1930s.[81]

The setting of "Church Going" is typical in the opportunities it offered Larkin: an empty church surrounded by "suburb scrub." The speaker "inside" is more radically separated from nature than Arnold's, who can look out at, though he cannot feel about, the Wordsworthian setting framed by the window. What more the church goer can see of nature once he shuts the door on "scrub" is only "sprawlings of flowers, cut / For Sunday, brownish now."

The descriptions are in an unpoetic poetic style appropriate to the setting and the speaker's response to it. Some are like versions of much earlier lines of poetry but brought so up-to-date that their precedents can barely be heard. When the church goer imagines what will in time be left of the building he stands in—"Grass, weedy pavement, brambles, buttress, sky"—the "ghostly silt / Dispersed" includes Wordsworth's mythic vision of London seen from Westminster Bridge, a ruin reabsorbed into nature so that its structures, its "Ships, towers, domes, theatres, and temples lie / Open unto the fields and to the sky." After the speaker in "Church Going," remembering some long ago church going, has pronounced "'Here endeth' much more loudly than I'd meant," there is a faint reverberation in "The echoes snigger briefly" of countless traditional pastoral echoes and some more recent ones: the "echoes mourn" for Lycidas; "a mocking echo" taunts Frost's hermit in "The Most of It." The echoes in Larkin's empty church are mean and perfunctory.

The matter-of-fact ordinariness of the church goer's language, filled with stock phrases so dulled by use that no one ever questions what or if they mean, validates the shifts from "I"—used nine times through the first three stanzas, later only twice—to "we"—spoken three times in the third stanza—to the hypothetical "he" who will perhaps be the church goer's future "representative." We accept the speaker's right to use "we," and in the last stanza "our," because he *speaks our language* both in the lexical and the idiomatic senses of that phrase, making him in turn our representative.

By the end of the poem we are willing to believe in the nearly Romantic elevation that takes place in diction like "robed as destinies," in the syntactical inversion of "A serious house on serious earth it is," in the more sustained regularity of the iambic pentameter lines, precisely because this elevated rhetorical style expresses an uncharacteristic mood. It takes the undeceived, unhopeful speaker by surprise, but not for long. "If only" in the closing line drops into the tone of voice recognizable as an expression of mid-twentieth-century consciousness, somewhat the way repetitions of *only* expose the speaker's late Romantic disillusion in "Dover Beach."

All this is, of course, to say that the creation of what seems to be a familiar idiom and tone describing the empty suburban church is the expressive means of drawing readers into the poem, who can imagine that they use or have heard that tone and idiom. The effect is that the poem's setting becomes a public space "In whose blent air all our compulsions meet," and "Church Going" is made into a distinctively mid-twentieth-century form of public poem representing a generation that sees itself living in a period of cultural loss.

Its essential difference from Arnold's way of representing his generation's consciousness in "Dover Beach" is that Arnold did not find the voice of his age by approximating the idiom and tone of Victorian speech. Instead, he figured its dispirited disillusionment and weary ineffectuality by the breakdown of Wordsworthian poetic language, by his own signifying inability to sustain it through the poem. Larkin's echoes of Wordsworth's and other earlier poems are not failed versions of their language but rephrasings in a vocabulary that changes the tone to empty it of passionate feeling or conviction.

The earlier discussion of Arnold has already suggested in brief an answer to the question why "Dover Beach" had to wait more than half a century to be accepted by a large, mixed public of readers while "Church Going" won that kind of recognition almost immediately. Larkin had "Dover Beach" and more recent poems that were its descendants as precedents, whereas there were few precedents in English poetry for the kind of public poem Arnold invented in "Dover Beach" ("The world is too much with us" being among the exceptions). In that late-Victorian situation most readers were not prepared to respond to Arnold's ways of drawing them into an internalized public space: they had not been taught to believe that they shared in the consciousness of a generation.

The work of persuading readers of the truth of that representation of themselves was accomplished by poets of the next generation: Yeats, Larkin's first master, and Hardy, his second, among the most effective. The persuasion was carried on by Auden, the model for Larkin who found his milieu in the drabness of England in the 1930s much as Larkin himself used the "dullness" of "ordinary life" in the 1950s.

Auden gave the 1930s a common idiom which became so much a part of the cultural fabric that it added the word *Audenesque* to the *OED*. Along with that casual, slangy style, his legacy to Larkin was a tone of weary disillusionment made familiar above all in his much anthologized public poem

"September, 1939." Its tone is appropriate to its setting, "one of the dives / On Fifty-second Street," which reflects in its drabness the "habit-forming" "compulsory" dullness of the "dense commuters," the desperation of the drinkers at the bar who "Cling to their average day."[82]

Auden hinted that his own public poetry might follow the direction of Arnold's when, in lines of his poem "Matthew Arnold" (written close in time to "September, 1939"), he described how his Victorian predecessor suppressed the "dark disordered city" in himself until "all rang hollow but the clear denunciation / Of a gregarious optimistic generation."[83] Larkin in turn hinted at the line of connection between himself and Auden in their public poems when he wrote of his acknowledged model: "Few poets since Pope have been so committed to their period."[84]

When *The Less Deceived* was just published, *The Times Educational Supplement* applauded it as "a poetic monument that marks the triumph of clarity over the formless mystifications of the last twenty years."[85] By clarity the reviewer meant accessibility to what, without embarrassment, he called "the middle-brow public." While unfavorable reviews translated this praise into accusations of philistinism, Larkin himself, in interviews and writings about writing, slyly or by joking openly, tended to assent to or even encourage this double-edged classification of his poetry.

One interviewer asked Larkin why he pointedly avoided mythological and literary allusions to what he liked to call the modernist "myth-kitty," and sophisticated references he said reminded him of "literary understrappers letting you see they know the right people."[86] Larkin gave as his reason that he had not read the poems alluded to, leading him to add that "in fact poets write for people with the same background and experiences as themselves, which might be taken as a compelling argument in support of provincialism."[87] About assimilations of bits from his poems into the common idiom (and into the new edition of *The Oxford Dictionary of Quotations*) he said: "If someone asked me what lines I am known for it would be the one about mum and dad ['They fuck you up'] or 'Books are a lot of crap'— sentiments to which every bosom returns an echo, as Dr. Johnson said."[88]

Most slyly, and revealingly, to a question whether there is a debate in "Church Going" between "poet and persona," Larkin answered in a slangy idiom and throw-away tone the church goer and his other speakers typically would use: "I think one has to dramatize oneself a little. I don't arse about in churches when I am alone. Not much anyway."[89] What this calculated bit of self-dramatizing acts out is the way Larkin in and out of his poems used a tone of voice that, one reviewer wrote, expressed "an ordinary man's view of the ordinary"; that Barbara Everett described more fully as "an easily-recognisable publicly-private personality," whose anecdotes, reflections, and sayings are "'quotable'—splendidly adaptable to or adoptable by the common stock."[90] Since that tone of voice was a sophisticated literary creation informed by traditions of language and form that it did not make any show of, its effects could be appreciated also by readers whose education in poetry was out of the ordinary.

Larkin was able to create the tone of voice for this generation of readers—"I think writing about unhappiness is probably the source of my popularity, if I have any—after all, most people *are* unhappy, don't you think?"—because, for the purposes of his poetry, he was one of them.[91] His self-presentation—reminding us of the way Frost made himself into someone like the speakers in his poems—helped to persuade readers that he was their representative. Identifying himself with the background and experiences of the *ordinary reader*—not, he well knew, what Johnson meant by allying his judgment with the common sense of the common reader—was his way of preparing his public for a distinctively mid-twentieth-century kind of public poem.

CHAPTER SIX

"THE POET OF 'THE FISH'"
THE ANTHOLOGIZING OF
ELIZABETH BISHOP

The two previous chapters explore the double question of what circumstances and literary situations, and what internal features make an anthology-piece, using a group of early pastoral lyrics and three public poems of the past three centuries as their territory. Here the circumstances and situation, and the internal features of Elizabeth Bishop's narrative-descriptive poem "The Fish," together constitute a vivid instance of what makes an anthology-piece in the later twentieth century.

Bishop, alone among poets contemporary with her who were her equals, was known, and from the beginning of her career, as the author of one ubiquitously anthologized poem. Here inquiries into why that particular poem was so singled out for fame necessarily consider the special shape of her much discussed reputation, and its intimate relation to the broader association of her poetry with its anthologized presence: she was characterized as the *ideal poet for anthologies*.

The unusual history of Bishop's reception and the radically original qualities of her work—her poems and her arrangements of them in successive volumes—come together in the retrospective provided by her last book. This in turn points to a revisionary reading of her early and still widely anthologized poem, "The Fish," that shows in compelling terms what makes it a quintessential anthology-piece.

BEGINNINGS

Sometime after 1965, possibly even as late as 1977, *The Boston Globe* ran an announcement of a poetry reading by "the poet of 'The Fish.'"[1] Someone on the staff of the newspaper assumed, it seems, that its readers would respond with more pleased recognition to the title of that particular poem than to the name of the poet by itself; would even, it is possible, need to be reminded of who Elizabeth Bishop was, the author of the poem they knew so well.

This small item in a newspaper, like the ordinary objects held up to contemplation in many of Bishop's poems, can suggest lines to explore that lead, not to answers, but to more suggestive questions. Here they have to do with the ways Bishop's poems reached their readers, and how their presentation helped to shape those readers' experiences of them. Coming full circle, these investigations can then suggest special qualities of Bishop's work that have raised perplexing questions about the shape of her reputation, questions not invited by the reception of poets who were her contemporaries and friends, writing and publishing within the same literary system.

The wording of the newspaper announcement clearly was not meant to be of particular interest to "critics and fellow poets." For among them— according to the obituary of Bishop in the *New York Times* for October 8, 1979—she had from early on "enjoyed extraordinary esteem."[2] Her first book, *North & South*, was discussed in print the year it appeared, 1946, by Marianne Moore in the *Nation*, Lloyd Frankenberg in the *Saturday Review of Literature*, and Randall Jarrell in the *Partisan Review*; the next year by Robert Lowell in the *Sewanee Review*. From the beginning, notices like these reached a special group of readers and alerted them to look for Bishop's poems as they were printed singly in such magazines, and, often years later, in eagerly expected volumes of her work.

To swell the audience beyond poets, critics, and their followers, the only sure attenders of poetry readings, the *Globe* must have meant to appeal to that less easily defined body, the larger "public," to whom Howard Moss (poetry editor of the *New Yorker* where many of Bishop's poems made their first appearance) writing in 1966 said her poems still "are, oddly, unknown."[3] By that date "The Fish" was the one famous exception.

Where members of this potential audience might first have come across her name could have been the *New York Times Book Review* for October 27, 1946. There the critic Selden Rodman chose "The Fish" for discussion to illustrate her most successful work in *North & South*. In the *New York Herald Tribune* the next year, M. L. Rosenthal again chose "The Fish" as exemplary. So did Coleman Rosenberger, also in the *Tribune*, reviewing *Poems* in 1955. He listed "The Fish" first, along with four other poems from *North & South*, as having "already become almost indispensable items in any anthology of modern poetry."[4]

It may be that widely sold newspapers and popular magazines (*Time* wrote about Bishop, but not until 1962) are first to put poets' names in circulation. Even so, it is more often in anthologies that all but the small groups of readers close to or inside poets' circles first meet their work. This is particularly true of poems by living authors, who have not been summed up in obituaries and have not had their writings gathered in a volume not likely, or soon, to be superseded.

"The Fish" was not among the earliest of Bishop's poems to be anthologized because it was not complete until 1940, when it appeared in the *Partisan Review*. Before that date, only two of the poems Bishop later included in her published volumes were anthologized: "The Map" in 1935; "The Monument" in 1939. During the 1940s, by my count at least nine other poems that had first appeared in magazines and were later to be included among the thirty poems in *North & South* were anthologized, none more than twice. The nine were, in order of their first entrance into anthologies: "The Weed," "Love Lies Sleeping," "The Imaginary Iceberg," "Roosters," "Songs for a Colored Singer," "A Miracle for Breakfast," "The Unbeliever," "The Man-Moth," "Cirque d'Hiver."

It is easier to trace how any author's poems got into anthologies—by what circumstances at work in the literary system—than it is to answer why those particular poems and not others. At the very beginning it was Moore's suggestion that Bishop be published with thirty other young writers (among them J. V. Cunningham, Josephine Miles, Theodore Roethke, Muriel Rukeyser).[5] The plan of the anthology, published in 1935 by Ann Winslow (the pseudonym chosen—one can see why—by Verna Grubbs), was for each author to submit three entries—Bishop's choices were "The Reprimand" and "Three Valentines" along with "The Map"—to be introduced by a well-known poet.[6] The format gave Moore a space in the introduction of her protégé where she could inscribe the terms for precisely the qualities in Bishop's work she wanted readers to see and value.

This early sponsorship by Moore identified Bishop as a promising—and well-connected—young writer who should be represented in collections that wanted to be showcases for the best new work. Before the publication of her first book, two more poems later included in it were chosen for such anthologies: James Laughlin's *New Directions in Prose and Poetry* of 1939, which printed "The Monument"; Tom Boggs' *American Arcade: 68 Poems for the First Time in an Anthology*, where "The Weed" appeared in 1943.

Then in 1946, virtually simultaneously with the publication of *North & South* and the earliest reviews of it, poems by Bishop were first included in an anthology devoted to work by established authors selected by an established anthologist. "The Imaginary Iceberg" and "Roosters" were chosen to represent her by Oscar Williams in his immensely popular collection, *A Little Treasury of Modern Poets, English and American*. For this choice he was rewarded by Jarrell, who wrote the most favorable of the early notices of *North & South*, when he reviewed a group of new anthologies including Williams's. Jarrell ranked him sardonically as "one of the best of this crew of professional anthologists," while applauding the space in the *Treasury* given to "seldom-anthologized poems," of which he named four including "Roosters."[7]

NORTH & SOUTH

Until 1950 no one of Bishop's poems was starred as an anthology piece; "The Fish" began its rise to fame about five years after it had been published singly. Then late in 1949 or in 1950, "The Fish" made what was in effect its debut in "An audible anthology of modern poetry read by its creators," resonantly titled *Pleasure Dome*. This Columbia recording, "edited"—the cover says—by Lloyd Frankenberg, another of Bishop's first reviewers, included her with only seven other authors chosen from the most famous names among living American and British poets: Eliot, Moore, e.e. cummings, William Carlos Williams, Ogden Nash, Auden, Dylan Thomas. This was glamorous company for a writer still in her thirties with only one book of poems before the public.

The authors were picked by the editor to make a "representative anthology" that would "reach a wide audience of readers until now unfamiliar with the experience of hearing poetry," in the "hope that they will acquire a taste for some of the great poetry of our time; that, having acquired it, they will want more."[8]

Whether or not Bishop herself decided the poems for that recorded anthology, around the time of its first making she chose it along with eight other poems she was invited to submit for John Ciardi's *Mid-Century American Poets*, timed to appear in 1950. In the same sort of anthology marking the same year, Louis Untermeyer's *Modern American Poetry: Mid-Century*, "The Fish" took its place with three other poems by Bishop, while simultaneously in Untermeyer's more inclusive combined collection, *The New Modern American and British Poetry*, "The Fish" in a space all to itself represented her to its many readers. These endorsements by Untermeyer, Oscar Williams's chief rival among "the crew of professional anthologists," helped to make "The Fish" from that time forth the poem most readers would associate first with Elizabeth Bishop's name.

Up to a point, then, it is possible to trace the routes by which poems gathered in *North & South* made their ways into anthologies before and soon after its publication. After 1946, anthologists not only had more of Bishop's work to choose from: her poems no longer floated lonely as a cloud without visible means of support. By being entries in a collection arranged by their author, they offered new grounds for choice, and could be seen from more angles, inviting comparisons and distinctions among them.

This opportunity allowed anthology makers to look for answers to questions pertinent to their own peculiar work of refitting those pieces into the design of their own book. They could question which poems are the most accessible, not difficult or obscure; which make the most illuminating connections with poems already known to readers of anthologies, giving them the pleasure of recognition; which poems are the most characteristic of this poet; which are most fully representative of her as a member of a generation of writers, or of some other category; which are the best, the most fully achieved of the poems in the book.

Anthologists wanting to base their choice of poems on answers to such questions, particularly about the pieces in an author's first book, are likely to start by looking to see which of them the reviews have held up for attention and appreciation. The precedence anthology makers gave very soon after the publication of *North & South* to "The Fish" before all other poems in the book is a sign of how closely their readings of it accorded with—if they did not simply follow—the directions they could find in reviews of it.

It is a commonplace repeated by writers about Bishop that few first books have been, in David Kalstone's words, "so immediately praised and understood" as *North & South*.[9] Without question, prestigious friends were waiting in the wings to bring it to the attention of readers as soon as it was published; in the two years after its appearance it was given more notice than would have been likely for a first book less powerfully supported. Perhaps for the same reason, it was written about not only in little magazines like *Poetry* and the *Sewanee Review*, which attracted a small, specialized group of readers, but in magazines of more general interest like the *New Yorker*, the *Nation*, the *New Republic*, the *Atlantic*, and in newspapers with still wider and more variegated readership, the *New York Times* and the *Herald Tribune*. The unusually prompt and widespread attention given to *North & South* constituted an acknowledgment that the book was to be taken into account. It did, after all, come into the world trailing the Houghton Mifflin prize.

What still needs to be called in question is the unqualified statement, often repeated even by a critic as knowledgeable as Kalstone, that it was greeted with general applause, and that it was immediately understood. In fact, the critical response to the book was rather more mixed that the impression we get of it from most writing about Bishop's early work, and mixed in more than one way. Critics contradicted each other and sometimes themselves in describing which features or poems best characterize the book. They also differed from one another in how they valued the poems in it, again at times seeming to switch their own judgments in mid-review.

The first notice of *North & South*, in *Kirkus* in 1946, gave it short shrift, saying the poems are "'visual impressions' in the tradition of Amy Lowell and very few readers would find them interesting."[10] Two longer reviews were almost entirely hostile, more at least partly unenthusiastic. Even reviewers usually referred to or selectively quoted to illustrate the vehement endorsements that Bishop's peers gave her work from the start tended to qualify their approvals, the qualifying statements sometimes outnumbering the praises. The mixed reception of *North & South*, once recognized, can be more finely sifted when we focus on the ways in which reviewers weighed "The Fish" on balance with other entries in the book. Their judgment will in turn be reflected in the poem's promotion as an anthology-piece.

Beyond expressing inevitable differences in interpretations, preferences, and allegiances among critics, the variegated reviewing of *North & South* corresponds to the peculiar nature of the book itself, beginning with its title. The effect of its carefully chosen phrasing, weighed in letters between Bishop and Moore, can be measured by setting it beside Frost's *North of Boston* (a convenient contrast, but probably not deliberately invited by Bishop). Frost's title phrase, borrowed from the heading of an advertisement in a newspaper, announces a unified focus: on the *real estate*, that is, on the circumstances of their living day by day of rural New Englanders. Bishop's title suggests variety without specificity, and of a wide-ranging sort: *North & South* are at a distance from each other, opposites on a map, but the ampersand takes them out of a spoken phrase or written sentence so that they seem to be names of directions more than of places people might live in. Oscar Williams commented with what sounds like irritation on the seeming lack of sharp focus in both title and book when he gave the heading "North but South" to his hostile remarks about the poems (unexpected in view of his early anthologizing of Bishop), which he partly took back in the review's grudging conclusion, "All in all, however, this is a good book."

The suggestion in the title of a kind of unsystematized variety is confirmed in the carefully placed opening poem, "The Map," by what seems to be its direct reference to the book title: "North's as near as West."[11] The same suggestion is supported by lines in the poem that grammatically entertain possibilities—"or," "Or," "as if," "or"—and by its many questions that open alternatives—"does the land lean down ... is the land tugging ...?" "Are they assigned, or can the countries pick their colors?" Title and opening poem present the book as a kind of open-ended exploration guided only by curiosity; an embodiment of *serendipity*, a word Horace Walpole fashioned from the tale *The Three Princes of Serendip* about travelers who along their ways were always coming on things they were not looking for.

The uninsistent order of poems in the book matches the hint in its title of its unschematic shape. Some entries are loosely grouped by locale: (places where the air is colder; a city—probably New York; another city identified as Paris; Florida). Some are linked by titles ("Love Lies Sleeping," "Sleeping on the Ceiling," "Sleeping Standing Up"); some make recurrent but interrupted patterns of images (of the sea, dreams, mornings). The effect of the arrangement or arrangements is almost of poems that have simply been put together in the sequence they happened in—and they do to some extent follow the chronology of their composition—rather than according to some preconceived and therefore interpretive design.

This effect owes much to the unemphatic groupings of entries, but much more to the astonishing variety among the poems, each somehow different from all the rest. They range in type from descriptions of scenes and objects ("Florida," "Large Bad Picture") to dream visions and surreal fantasies ("The Weed," "The Gentleman of Shalott"), and in form from a sestina to free verse in irregular lengths of line and paragraph ("A Miracle for Breakfast," "The Monument"). The remarkable variety of metrical, linear, and rhyme patterns in *North & South* may be unmatched in a single poet's collection since Herbert's *The Temple*, certainly a model for Bishop's formal experimentation. In both their volumes, the effect is freeing, allowing an escape from personality that would impose the limits of idiosyncratic habit. It is as if each poem in *North & South* has taken its own form, a process for which "The Man-Moth" is the paradigm: its bizarre stanzas liken themselves to grotesquely stylized paragraphs from the newspaper where Bishop found the misprint for "mammoth," giving her the poem and its title. She hinted at this way of thinking about the poem as something that *happened to be written* by footnoting the source of its title (though as a rule—and she did not admit to making many—she detested explanatory notes). An answer she gave to an irritating questionnaire prepared by John Ciardi for his anthology *Mid-Century American Poets* generalizes the point: "After all, the poet's concern is not consistency."[12]

Such indifference to consistency, liberating as Bishop found it to be, was constraining for her first reviewers. *North & South* is close to being a uniquely hard collection of poems to characterize, with the consequence that in the beginning, the book provoked strangely mixed reviews. They are at issue here as they bear on the decisions of anthologists trying to represent her work to their readers.

The critics disagreed with one another, as usual, but their differences not only about the quality of the poems but first about what sort of poems they are show the difficulty of characterizing the book in their smallest observations and in their sustained arguments. Skimming the reviews for descriptive adjectives, anthologists looking for guidance would have come on troubling disparities even among notices mainly praising the poems: Moore's

preferred "unspectacular," "modest," "accurate," "neat," by contrast with
M. L. Rosenthal's "unexpected or bizarre"; Edward Weeks's "straight descriptive" not easily compatible with Jarrell's "unusually personal"; Lowell's
"large, controlled and elaborate" as against Barbara Gibbs's "small."[13] In
their more sustained arguments, Bishop's depreciators and admirers can-
celed each other's characterizations of the book. Oscar Williams complained that "Miss Bishop does not break away from the purlieus of the
fashionable," and that in her "poems of class consciousness" she "is defend-
ing the oppressed because it is the thing to do."[14] Yet in the same month in
the *New Yorker*, Louise Bogan praised Bishop for making poems that "strike
no attitudes," that express "unmistakenly her own point of view."[15] Edward
Weeks told readers of the *Atlantic* that *North & South* left him dissatisfied,
being "rather shy of ideas," while Arthur Mizener in *Furioso* admired the
poems in it for their combined "toughness and elegance of mind."[16]

Even when critics met head on the challenge of saying what the book is
like by describing the remarkable variety among its entries, their inferences
from that variousness clashed. Rosenthal stated plainly what the title seems
to hint, that "*North & South* contains efforts in many directions."[17] For him
this variegated collection showed Bishop's "daring skill" as "an experi-
menter in poetic perspective. Her verses emphasize the strangeness of common realities when viewed from unexpected or bizarre angles." Using some
of the same terms, Weeks had previously told readers that the poems in
Bishop's book "may be roughly divided into two categories, bizarre fantasies
which can be interpreted pretty much as the reader chooses, and straight descriptive verse . . . to which she has added a moral or emotional fillip."[18] He
judged what Rosenthal meant by bold experimentation as lack of commitment: the root of Bishop's "difficulty in finishing what she begins so well,"
and of her timidity, was in his view "that she is afraid to risk pure lyricism."

PLACING "THE FISH"

Reviewers agreed in paying more attention to "The Fish" than to any
other poem in *North & South*, though they looked at it from different perspectives and with gradations of enthusiasm, as a contrasting pair of quotations illustrates. The earliest mention of it was a guardedly oblique observation by Moore that "as in the subject of the poem, one is not glad of the
creature's every perquisite; but the poem dominates memory."[19] In direct

contrast, for Rosenthal the "bold painting" of the creature in minute detail was what made the poem the "most striking" of Bishop's "huge closeups," stirring him to exclaim "What a Fish! . . . he is everything absurd and beautiful in the world."[20] Still, the sheer amount of space given to "The Fish," in spite of such differences, was the clearest signal to anthologists that among the thirty entries in *North & South*, this poem, at least, should be given room in their collections.

When reviewers tried to place "The Fish" in relation to other entries in the book, they sent anthologists a less intelligible message. "The Fish" was measured against the poems around it, usually to their disadvantage, by the book's admirers as well as its detractors, even as they tried to argue that the preferred entry was somehow representative of Bishop's poetry.

A case in point: Selden Rodman, in the earliest review to single out "The Fish" as the poem most important to talk about, started off with a generalization about *North & South* so strained that it seems an unhelpful way of preparing readers for what sort of poetry they would find in the book:

If the author of the thirty-two remarkable poems in this book used paint, she would undoubtedly paint 'abstractions.' Yet so sure is her feeling for poetry, that in building her over-all water-color arrangements she never strays from the concrete and the particular.[21]

He tried then to clarify this description by example, saying "'The Fish' is a case in point": "There has not been a poem like it, I think, since Richard Eberhart's 'The Groundhog,' but Miss Bishop approaches her symbol more impersonally, and the diction is less mannered." In the rest of the review, until the very end when it takes back what it had been saying ("Why quibble?"), Rodman disparaged other poems in the book in adjectives like "archaic or literary," "quaint," "pert," "sly." Ultimately "The Fish," set beside these unsatisfactory, "more complicated poems," comes out to be a case in point of a kind of poetry most of the book is not.

Reviews of *North & South* by Jarrell and Lowell are the ones most often quoted to illustrate the general praise and understanding that *North & South* is usually said to have received as soon as it came out. Jarrell made the critic's work of giving an inclusive description of the book easier for himself by mentioning nothing in it he could not praise, though he ranked poems by kind implying quality. He began by celebrating "The Fish" and "Roosters" as "two of the most calmly beautiful, deeply sympathetic poems of our time," later enlarging on what makes them "morally so satisfactory." After them he listed "The Monument," "The Man-Moth," "The Weed," the first "Song for a Colored Singer," and "one or two others" unnamed, along with "charming poems on a smaller scale, or beautiful fragments—for instance, the end of 'Love Lies Sleeping.'" Without insisting on the variety among the poems, or making sharper distinctions in their quality, he drew them together in a loose formula since repeated everywhere in discussions of Bishop: "all her poems have written underneath, *I have seen it.*"[22]

Lowell agreed with Jarrell—they probably discussed their choices—in preferring "The Fish" and "Roosters" when he reviewed *North & South*. Beyond that discrimination, he made problems for himself by drawing sharp distinctions between these "best poems" and two-thirds of the entries in the book: "About ten of its thirty poems are failures. Another ten are unsatisfactory as wholes, or very slight," and these he described as "trivial," "pert," "banal," "over-pointed," "blurred," "foggy," "self-indulgent," tending to "whimsical commentary on an almost non-existent subject." Hardly an accolade. "This leaves 'Roosters' and 'The Fish,' large and perfect, and outside of Marianne Moore, the best poems that I know of by a woman in this century" (the last clause the only wording in the review Bishop ever allowed herself to voice her objections to), and in "roughly descending order, 'The Monument,' 'The Man-Moth,' 'The Weed,'" and eight other poems.[23]

To pull together his divisions among the poems in *North & South* into an inclusive account, Lowell composed a vast allegory that "at least nine tenths of them fall into," between "two opposing factors": between "motion, weary but persisting," and "a terminus: rest, sleep, fulfillment or death."[24] He laid this interpretive grid over "The Fish," or rather, he drew the poem into his scheme by rewriting the ending into his allegory. The eleven-line sentence in the poem leading up to the single end-line takes off from the narrator's experience of seeing suddenly the optical illusion, familiar to any reader, made by oil catching light: until everything "was rainbow, rainbow, rainbow!" Lowell translated this radiant moment of seeing into a symbol: the "rainbow of spiritual peace seen as the author decides to let the fish go."

Then apparently without recognizing what he was doing, Lowell gave up his allegorizing to offer another, quite incompatible way to generalize about the poems in *North & South*:

The structure of a Bishop poem is simple and effective. It will usually start as a description or descriptive narrative, then either the poet or one of her characters or objects reflects. The tone of these reflections is pathetic, witty, fantastic, or shrewd. Frequently, it is all these things at once. Its purpose is to heighten and dramatize the description and, at the same time, to unify and universalize it. In this, and in her marvelous command of shifting speech-tones, Bishop resembles Robert Frost.[25]

This paradigm of a Bishop poem fits "The Fish" and, as Lowell was the only one of the early reviewers to point out, it fits many poems of description or descriptive narrative by Frost, whose antipathy to readings of his poems that transform them into allegory is famous.

Anthologists who may have sifted the differing, contradictory, often self-contradictory reviews of *North & South* to find directions about which poems from it to include in their collections could feel on solid ground only when singling out "The Fish." It had been judged among the best, or even to be the very best of the poems in the book, on the largest scale, alone worthy to take its place in a gathering of anthology-pieces from all periods like Untermeyer's *Treasury of Great Poems: English and American* (1955). Among the anthologies consulted for this chapter, of the twenty published between 1950 and 1960 where Bishop was given space, seven displayed only "The Fish," while no other poem was featured by itself except, once, "The Man-Moth."

FROM THE MID-FIFTIES . . .

"The Fish" was the unchallenged favorite of anthologists by the mid-1950s, and kept its status, as anthology-pieces tend to do, without being displaced by the preferences among the new poems in Bishop's next two volumes, "At the Fishhouses" and "The Armadillo." Even as late as 1992, "The Fish" was the choice among all of Bishop's work for the honor of a place in an anthology edited by William Harmon with a title parodically (one hopes) exposing the formulaic likeness of many anthology titles to commercial advertisements: *The Top 500 Poems*. "The Fish" still fills its position in *The Norton Anthology of Modern Poetry* of 1996, and is included in the careful choice of poems by Bishop in the second volume of *American Poetry: The Twentieth Century*, published by The Library of America in 2000.

Because the poem was asked for so often, Bishop eventually granted permission for it only to anthologists who would agree to print three of her other poems beside it; like other authors, she resisted being identified by a single poem.[26] Yeats wrote in a letter to Robert Bridges of 1901, "I confess I grow not a little jealous of 'The Lake Isle' which has put the noses of all my other children out of joint."[27] To Auden, one of a poet's worst fears was of becoming known by only one or two famous poems. Poe was his example, whose "shade must be more disappointed than most" for having his name identified with "The Raven" and "The Bells": "how he must hate these old war horses."[28] In very much the same tone of rueful amusement, Bishop joked to Lowell in a letter of 1970:

I think I'll try to turn that damned 'Fish' into a sonnet, or something very short and quite different. (I seem to get requests for it every day for anthologies with titles like *Reading as Experience* or *Experience as Reading*, each anthologizer insisting that he is doing something completely different from every other anthologizer. But I'm sure this is an old story to you.)[29]

In fact, none of Lowell's best-known poems gained quite the reputation "The Fish" acquired precisely *for being an anthology-piece*, which is how later reviewers of her work regularly categorized it. Almost inevitably they referred to it—"always, 'The Fish'"—as her "widely-anthologized poem," or "most anthologized poem," or "the great poem . . . that has been so frequently anthologized."[30] When these reviewers named other preferences along with "The Fish," these too were called her "anthology-pieces—the ones that have been popping up for years, such as 'The Fish'"; her "generously anthologized" poems; those of her poems that have "won a firm place in current anthologies."[31] Her reputation among critics, as well as among most readers of modern poetry, had by the late 1950s come to be closely associated with the facts of her anthologized presence.

In an early review of her second book, *Poems: North & South and A Cold Spring*, for the *Herald Tribune Book Review* in 1955, Coleman Rosenberg wrote about the first collection: "One or half a dozen poems" ("The Fish" and four others) "have already become almost indispensable items in any anthology of modern poetry."[32] Then about *A Cold Spring*:

"again, along with slighter and more fragmentary poems, there are a handful . . . which will almost inevitably pass into the general poetic currency"—presumably circulated in anthologies—"where they can be expected to become a permanent part of the poetry of our time." William Jay Smith, in a review of *Questions of Travel* in 1966, found "several poems in the Brazilian section of the book that any anthologist would want to include with Miss Bishop's best work."[33] Helen Vendler, writing in 1977 about *Geography III*, praised "Crusoe in England" as a potential anthology-piece: "It is a classic poem, wonderfully sustained, sparely inclusive, fully considered, sad and complete. It belongs in all the anthologies."[34] She acted on this judgment herself by including the poem, with two shorter entries to represent *Geography III*, in her retrospective selection for *The Harvard Book of Contemporary American Poetry*. To say a poem "belongs in all the anthologies" is to make a very special definition of poetic fame, particularly by comparison with the more literarily traditional language the same reviewer used elsewhere to immortalize poems by Lowell as "votive sculpture, bronzed to imperishability."[35]

The specialized vocabulary for judging and ranking Bishop's poems that kept recurring in reviews of her later books must reflect the growing recognition among poets and writers about poetry of the anthologists' role in the making of reputations. Still, there is more to be said about the application of this vocabulary particularly to Bishop; it was not inevitably used by critics about other poets appearing in anthologies at the same time.

How Lowell was treated makes a telling contrast since he and Bishop were both being reviewed in the 1950s and 1960s, sometimes in the same years and often by the same reviewers. The poems by Lowell regularly praised in reviews unsurprisingly also got into anthologies regularly, but the fact of their ubiquitous presence there went unmentioned. One reviewer identified Lowell as "still the wonderful poet of 'The Quaker Graveyard in Nantucket'"; one described that as his "first major poem"; still another— begrudging its fame—called it his "most commonly overpraised work."[36] "Skunk Hour" was seen in retrospect as "almost the finest poem" in *Life Studies*; "For the Union Dead" as "one of the finest poems Lowell has written."[37]

Why, from the mid-1950s on, especially "The Fish" but also others of Bishop's best-known poems were associated with anthologies in a way that

Lowell's were not might be answered partly by their chronologies. Bishop published new poems in separate volumes in 1946, 1955, 1965, and then not again until 1976; Lowell in 1944, 1946, 1951, 1959, 1961, 1964, 1967, 1968, 1973, 1977. Reviews naturally cluster around the publication dates of books, so in the years that stretched between the appearances of Bishop's new collections, she would have been kept before the public largely in anthologies, since only specially interested followers would have found her poems as they were printed singly in magazines.

Lowell, meanwhile, attracted notice almost steadily by his prolific appearances in new volumes and the reviews of them, in interviews—one of them in *Time* magazine with his picture on the cover—and in public performances. Critics understandably wrote about Lowell as a figure the public had reason to know, although as Richard Poirier pointed out in a review of *For the Union Dead* for *Bookman* in 1964, Lowell's audience was in fact "remarkably small" and "quite special" measured against a popular poet's like Frost.[38] Bishop, by contrast with Lowell, gave scarcely any public readings before the late 1960s, and her first substantial interview not until 1969.

There may be another reason, tangled in the situation of poetry in this period. Signs of it began to show in some reviews of *Poems*, for instance Edwin Honig's in 1956: "Fellow poets have found in her limited performance a judiciousness and sympathy of the greatest distinction," an exalted appreciation Honig thought unhelpful to Bishop's reputation. "Such praise is unfortunate—it sets the reader's expectations too high" of poems that deserve no greater recognition than W. S. Graham's or David Ignatow's, "whose work, with all its defects, is a good deal more vital and penetrative than Miss Bishop's."[39] Although it was not Honig's explicit intention, his remarks made a division between "Fellow poets" and "the reader" in their judgments of Bishop that widened in reviews of her successive books.

Howard Moss expanded the division, as is evident in a fuller quotation from his review of *Questions of Travel*, which was enthusiastically or, it may be, defensively headed "All Praise." While enlarging Bishop's group of admirers beyond her fellow poets to include "critics . . . and anyone genuinely interested in writing," he defended their appreciation against the resistance of a body of readers large enough to be lumped together as "the public" and dull enough to be unworthy of joining in the praise:

This new book can only add substance to Miss Bishop's reputation. And that is a strange one. Her work has hardly been ignored; she has won just about every distinction and prize a poet can. But her poems are, oddly, unknown to the public, even that part of it that is supposed to be interested in poetry. And if obscurity is a general issue in the public's ignorance of poetry, it is not an issue here.[40]

The point is repeated in the *New York Times* obituary of Bishop in 1979, that "although less widely known than contemporaries such as Robert Lowell," she "enjoyed extraordinary esteem among critics and fellow poets."[41] As recently as 1994, the separation between literary professionals and the public figured in Peter Prescott's remarks about Bishop's reputation in the *New York Times Book Review*: "Except among her fellow poets and her friends within the narrow literary precincts, Elizabeth Bishop (1911–79) was never famous in her lifetime."[42]

The perceived distance between the intense appreciation of Bishop's work by poets and their followers and the ignorance or limited knowledge of it among unspecialized readers was an issue for discussion among writers about Bishop—John Ashbery made a serious joke about it by calling her a "writer's writer's writer"—from the mid-1950s on, when the vocabulary describing her best-known poems as anthology-pieces also began to appear over and over.[43]

The connection between these two critical clichés is made visible in H. T. Kirby-Smith's review of *Complete Poems* for the specialized readers of *Sewanee Review* in 1972. Among the pleasures of reading this volume, he listed the "discovery that her anthology pieces—the ones that have been popping up for years, such as 'The Fish' . . . are not necessarily her best work."[44] The slight disparagement lurking in his use of the epithet "anthology pieces" is exaggerated here by the description of them "popping up," a phrase we usually use for repetitively unwanted appearances. Although it was quite common for critics to feel superiority to readers who had no other experience of Bishop's poems than those preselected for them by anthologists, they often, and at the same time, named "The Fish," usually first, among the poems they themselves considered her finest work.

A feature more internal to Bishop's work has been proposed to explain why she was cast as "an ideal poet for anthologies." Jerome Mazzaro first suggested this explanation when he reviewed her *Complete Poems* in 1969. His opinion was that the book "does not, as do most volumes of complete poems, bring together the body of her work in a more unified, recognizable, and coherent way."[45] Then he gave as reasons some more detailed comments on the poems: "Foremost is that Miss Bishop is a miniaturist," "she keeps her subjects isolated, small, and circumscribed"; "when she has amassed details . . . she quits"; her "sense of boundaries militates against any cumulative effects and keeps her works discrete." Although he judged that the "bulk of her best poetry is still in her first volume," he was himself still engaged twenty years later than Bishop's first reviewers in the struggle to find in the apparently unplanned variety of her writings a describable shape.

Reviewers of *North & South* had been unprepared for a volume where serendipity was almost a formal as well as a conceptual principle: unprepared both by their critical training and by their familiarity with the quite differently arranged books made by other contemporary poets. Lowell, again, offers a clear contrast, and is likely to have been seen that way when *Lord Weary's Castle* came out in the same year as *North & South*.

It was written about by the same critics, one of them their mutual friend Jarrell. He had no trouble finding order in *Lord Weary's Castle*, and assured readers that they would be able to see it too: "Underneath all these poems 'there is one story and one story only': when this essential theme or subject is understood, the unity of attitudes and judgments underlying the variety of the poems becomes startlingly explicit."[46]

Although Jarrell included "The Quaker Graveyard in Nantucket" in his list of "the best things in the book," he did not predict that its fame would be its inevitable presence in anthologies, or that Lowell's reputation would be as an author of anthology-pieces. Instead Jarrell eternized him by alluding to the last lines of Shakespeare's ubiquitously anthologized Sonnet 18—"So long as men can breathe or eyes can see / So long lives this and this gives life to thee"—in the last sentence of the review: "One or two of these poems, I think, will be read as long as men remember English."[47]

Paradoxically, as reviewers in the 1950s and 1960s went on trying to make an inclusive characterization of Bishop's poems, they seem to have given up the effort to describe "The Fish" as representative of her work. Instead, they sharpened their sense of it as a poem of a kind that included only a handful of others by Bishop. To illustrate, in 1955 in a review of *Poems*, Howard Nemerov singled out "The Fish," along with "Roosters," as "far more explicitly 'moralized'" than the rest of the poems in *North & South*.[48]

Robert Mazzacco made something like the same discrimination in remarks about Bishop's next volume in 1967: "you can count the poems in which the interior or metaphysical mood holds sway, and you don't get beyond one hand," and named only "The Fish," "The Unbeliever," "The Man-Moth," and "At the Fishhouses."[49]

In this period, critics generally agreed in reading "The Fish" as a celebration of moral "victory," whether the fish's, the fisher's, or a shared triumph. Or they interpreted the ending as a vision of peace or mortality; as an epiphanic release from memory or mastery, or from the antithesis of male and female; even as the imperative to distrust rainbows. Still, all these conclusions were based on the same assumptions: that the poem's ending was a moral or philosophical resolution; that it was not impenetrable by interpretation because the descriptive narrative was weighted with meaning that was not ambiguous or obscure. These assumptions were the same as those that guided readings of Frost's most often anthologized poems—for instance "Birches" or "Stopping by Woods on a Snowy Evening," "Mending Wall" or "The Road not Taken"—and that is the comparison Lowell originally made when he described the "simple and effective" paradigm of "a Bishop poem."

Bishop's resistance to the moralizing of "The Fish" or any others of her poems was as strong as Frost's, and she countered it as mischievously, but she hid her brand of mischief behind blandly self-deprecating politeness. She said that her poems were "just descriptions," that "geography comes first in my work."[50] An interviewer who tried to tempt her to make a larger statement by saying "I admire the philosophy in the poems, the morals" was rewarded with the innocent response, "I didn't know there were any."[51] When she made a mock-confession to Lowell of being a "minor female Wordsworth," she cast herself as a stereotype of the "Nature Lover," not as a philosophical poet.[52]

In this useful mode of self-deprecation, she wrote a letter to Moore soon after she finished "The Fish" in 1940, diminishing it as a "trifle." Long before she grew irritated at the too repetitive anthologizing of it, she seems to have been trying to forestall portentous interpretations of the poem by saying that it might seem too much like "if not Robert Frost perhaps like Ernest Hemingway! I left the last line on so it wouldn't be."[53] Of course she was joking—she later headed a letter to Lowell from Key West "the land of big game fish and Hemingway"—but the joke is likely to have had its uses.[54] By suggesting that the closing line was inessential to the poem, that she might even have entertained the possibility of dispensing with it, she disavowed heavy moral or philosophical readings of it. Years later, in a letter to Dennis Donoghue, she said about "The Fish" that it "wasn't intended as a major statement."[55]

IN RETROSPECT: 'GEOGRAPHY III' AND 'NORTH & SOUTH'

Geography III gathered poems in it and Elizabeth Bishop's earlier writings into a unified, recognizable, and coherent shape for her readers as no critic had succeeded in doing before it appeared in 1976, three years before she died. By its own integral wholeness and by its retrospective power it changed the way her work could be perceived. In that newly understood context, even poems of hers that had long seemed entirely accessible could seem different and unfamiliar, and the argument here will be that this is above all true of "The Fish."

The last book made it possible to see that, although paradox was not a mode of language in her poems, there was a great seeming-paradox at the heart of her way of writing, large enough to be describable in broadly simple terms. One important truth about her work that was sensed by some reviewers quite early is that she is among the least schematic of poets, a poet committed to allowing the order and movement of lines in a poem, of poems in a volume the freedom of whatever happens as it happens. Her work could have written underneath what she often said about "The Fish" and others of her writings: "*it really happened.*" Even so, another and only seemingly contradictory truth that her last book made it possible to see is that no poet's work in retrospect shows a more organic or a deeper sense of direction coming from within itself.

Geography III made so powerful an impression as a volume that reviewers did not have to struggle, as they did with *North & South*, to characterize and praise the qualities that gave it wholeness. Alfred Corn in the *Georgia Review* in 1977 summarized them in phrases that other critics would have subscribed to: "a perfected transparence of expression, warmth of tone, and a singular blend of sadness and good humor, of pain and acceptance—a radiant patience . . . few writers ever successfully render."[56] Along with these "special qualities" of Bishop's last book, reviewers included what J. D. McClatchy in the same year in *Canto* called "its distinctly autobiographical cast," which he and others associated with the ways poems in *Geography III* revise earlier ones.[57] The paired instances he listed were: "The Moose" with "The Fish"; "The End of March" with "Jeronimo's House"; "12 O'Clock News" with "A Miracle for Breakfast"; "In the Waiting Room" with "At the Fishhouses." Other pairings such as "Night City" with "The Man-Moth," "Large Bad Picture" with "Poem," and "Five Flights Up" with "Anaphora" seem to belong on the list.

The fact that all but one of the earlier poems on this list are from *North & South* is a sign that Bishop found her directions there; that poems in her first book could empower her last; and that her returns to them could be a context in which readers could re-experience them. In this sense *Geography III* is a lesson in the topography of her earlier books, filling in what was not understood in the presentation of her work by reviewers and makers of anthologies.

These backward looks act out the workings of memory so that personal history turns into poetic continuity between Bishop's earlier and later work. The rewritings are so inwardly generated in the language of each poem that they defy description by the current critical term *strategies*, which Bishop unsurprisingly often said she loathed. Being shaped by the poems themselves, her later returns to earlier poems were unschematized because they respected the variousness of the originals while rewriting them. Or rather, the process can be more precisely described as writing over them, in both senses of revising them and of being superimposed on them, giving a fuller and more precise reading of them and a context for new readings of other poems even as well known as "The Fish." The most thickly layered example acts out this process: the writing over "The Monument" by "The End of March."[58]

In each of the poems, description of an object—"the monument," "my crypto-dream-house"—is fused with a narrative of a walk by the ocean. The walking is only implied in "The Monument" in the dialogue between contrasting voices—the leader of the walk and a friend taken to see the strange structure? two internal voices of the walker who observes it?—but simply told in the conventional past tense by the narrator in "The End of March." Her companions on the walk are identified by name in the dedication under the title as friends of Bishop, one a fellow poet. The dating of an actual, so-cial visit implied by the combined title and dedication suggests this differ-ence in form and emphasis between the two poems, but they explore some questions so nearly identical that phrases asking those questions are in parts of the poems nearly interchangeable.

The "monument"—or is it "piled-up boxes"?—and the "crypto-dream-house"—"that crooked box/set up on pilings"—are objects perceived as artifacts of unknown origins. They are "set" in a natural setting that is strangely "wooden," so that the resemblance of the objects to the landscape suggests that they are natural phenomena. And yet each poem builds up a sense of some more mysterious agent which might or might not be the maker of the wooden structure, by unobtrusively piling up past participles: "built," "made," "set" (each twice), "pierced," "whittled," "set up," "shingled," "protected," "braced," "boarded up," and many more.

The sense of mystery is not dispelled in either poem as it moves inside the central image to describe whatever might be hidden there that could ex-plain what it is or by what agent it might have been made. The imagined interiors are alike in accommodating the object to the observer's imagina-tion while giving up no secrets.

In "The Monument," the "romantic" possibility opens out in a stately line of iambic pentameter—"The bones of the artist-prince may be in-side"—but then is set aside by a flatter kind of poetry. Lines keep qualifying themselves in "or," "or," "or," "But," a parenthesis admitting that "after all" whatever is inside "cannot have been intended to be seen." We are told only that the mysterious object is "the beginning" of a work of art, the descrip-tion of it in this poem the natural unfolding of some thing "having life, and wishing." The closing sentence of the poem—"Watch it closely."—is a di-rection for reading: "it" must be at once the mysterious object and the poem watching it closely, respecting its mystery.

The end of "The End of March" turns from its central image of the un-reached "crypto-dream-house" to follow the direction of the walk, just as it really happened: "On the way back our faces froze on the other side," and then, "For just a minute, set in their bezels of sand,/the drab, damp, scat-tered stones/were multi-colored." The momentary shift in the sun's light has an effect of a kind any reader can recognize; it is as solidly grounded in experience as the walk itself. So is the shiver such a moment can cause, a sense of some tilt in reality that these lines suggest. They seem to do that by bringing back the participle "set," filling the poem again with awareness of some crypto-force working on things. Its power may be dangerous, in having "scattered" the stones, but it is also creative: now they are "set in" a design framed by sand like jewels held in a chiseled frame.

Although this power, like the secret of "The Monument," is outside of and unknowable by the poet's imagination, she can weave a fable about how the shadows cast by the stones in the altered light "could have been teasing the lion sun,/ except that now he was behind them/—a sun who'd walked the beach the last low tide." While the lines themselves are "teasing" in their resistance to allegorizing profundities, they have a certain majesty. The iambic pentameter line set off by a dash imitates the sun's "majestic" stride too simply and naturally to be only playful, as in the archetypically titled "Poem" the substitution of "looks" for "visions"—"too serious a word"— does not take away the seriousness of the vision.[59] It registers the visionary intensity of the unpredictable moment of seeing that conflates the effect of a change in the sun's light with the making of an artifact, or turns the two acts into figures for each other.

REREADING "THE FISH"

David Bromwich, writing in 1983 about *The Complete Poems: 1927–1979* in the *New York Times Book Review*, organized his retrospective view of Bishop's work in two lists of poems delineating what he saw as the two main directions that her earliest work had pointed for her to follow. One list consisted of two poems from *North & South* and one each from *A Cold Spring* and *Geography III*—"The Map," "The Monument," "At the Fishhouses," and "The End of March"—that show Bishop's continuing interest in exploring the nature of her own art, of art itself.

Bromwich made a different list where he put "The Fish" along with "The Weed" and "Roosters" from the first book, and "The Armadillo" from *Questions of Travel*:

Throughout her career Bishop aimed to bring morality and invention together in a single thought. One can feel this especially in 'The Weed,' with its Herbert-like meditation on the birth of a new feeling; in 'The Armadillo,' which shows the complicity of esthetic pleasures in any grand spectacle, even a scene of suffering; in 'Roosters' and 'The Fish,' those guilty and strangely conciliatory professions of human strength.[60]

Here Bromwich's reading of Bishop's work is continuous with Jarrell's as he offered it in his very early review of *North & South*, where he singled out "The Fish" and "Roosters" as best exemplifying why Bishop's poetry "is morally so attractive":

that beneath our lives 'there is inescapable hope, the pivot,' so that in the revolution of things even the heartsick Peter can someday find 'his dreadful rooster come to mean forgiveness'; that when you see the snapped lines trailing, 'a five-haired beard of wisdom,' from the great fish's aching jaw, it is then that victory fills 'the little rented boat,' that the oil on the bilgewater by the rusty engine is 'rainbow, rainbow, rainbow!'—that you let the fish go.[61]

These reviews at the beginning and end of Bishop's career read "The Fish" as a story-telling poem, a kind that traditionally dramatizes a moral or psychological development in the teller, or reflects the learning of a philosophical lesson. Selden Rodman, in his very early review of *North & South*, was also thinking of poems in this traditional shape when he compared "The Fish" to Richard Eberhart's anthology-piece, "The Groundhog," published ten years before. Beginning "In June, amid the golden fields / I saw a groundhog lying dead," it tells a story that ends when three summers later the poet again stood at the place—"My hand capped a withered heart."[62]

"The Fish" tells the kind of story that poems in this tradition are made of: "I caught a tremendous fish"—"And I let the fish go."[63] Like others in this mode, it keeps its focus on the narrator retelling a remembered experience in the first person: "I caught," "I thought of," "I looked into," "I admired," "I stared and stared." This sequence of opening phrases that mark stages in the narrator's study of the fish seems to trace some development of feeling or understanding, especially as it culminates in an echo of "I gazed and gazed" from one of Wordsworth's great story-telling poems, "I wandered lonely as a cloud."

In support of this teleological reading of "The Fish," the lines between the calmly reportorial "I admired" and the resonantly charged expression of wonder or amazement "I stared and stared" constitute the longest passage of description in the poem, and in its last lines the most faithful to literary convention. Having closely observed the fishing paraphernalia of hooks and lines—"Like medals with their ribbons/frayed and wavering"—the poet was reminded of an old soldier decorated for past bravery, his "beard of wisdom/trailing from his aching jaw." Coming after a series of comparisons all describing the fish by its resemblance to nonhuman objects, this simile is the first figure to liken the creature to a human being, and in the conventional guise of the hero made wise by age and suffering, his head bloody, but unbowed.

There is an inevitable connection to be made between this characterization of the old fish that (we were told at the beginning of the poem) "hadn't fought at all" in its battle with the narrator, and the "victory" that "filled up" the following eleven-line sentence. In this reading, "And I let the fish go" becomes what Bromwich called one of "those guilty and strangely conciliatory professions of human strength," the consequence of a moral or psychological growth reflected in the poet's recognition of the fish as a fellow creature whose "aching" she has learned to feel by a newly developed power of imaginative sympathy.

The desire, continuous among writers about Bishop since Jarrell, to read "The Fish" as a poem belonging to a traditional kind with a perceptibly strong and clear moral intention was probably a determining impulse in anthologists' preference for it as well. Many poems that have achieved the status of anthology-pieces have, it seems, been valued specially because they could be read in this way, and more particularly as a story-poem in which the poet learns a lesson from having contemplated a nonhuman creature or phenomenon. Examples that come to mind are Herbert's "Life," Christopher Smart's "On a Bed of Guernsey Lilies," Wordsworth's "Nutting," Frost's "Design," Richard Wilbur's "The Pardon."

The retrospective character of *Geography III* teaches another reading of "The Fish" by the way the last book looks back at poems in *North & South* where the creative powers of observation are associated with what in "Poem" are fleetingly called "visions." It teaches that "The Fish," like "The Monument," is "a beginning" of the movement Bishop's writings followed in this direction that culminates in "The End of March" (and other late poems like "In the Waiting Room" and "The Moose"). In this light, "I caught a tremendous fish"—"And I let the fish go." is the frame for a somewhat different story, or rather it suggests that the same story happened in a different way.

The last line, which Bishop teasingly said was inessential to the poem, does have a certain air of inconsequence. It casually refuses to imply causality by a connective like *then*, *so*, or *as*, or by some other grammatical link. Bishop's closing sentence fragment is set off as if it were a separate sentence by a capital letter and a period, and distanced also by its simple story-telling style from the preceding eleven intertwined and exclamatory lines of description. True to Bishop's preferred ways of using language, "And I let the fish go." cannot be read or even misread as troublingly ambiguous or ironically deflating. She avoided verbal ambiguity and was not reticent about her dislike of irony. The casual sentence fragment that ends "The Fish" is plainly matter-of-fact, and matter-of-fact is precisely what she claimed the poem to be:

I *always* tell the truth in my poems. With *The Fish*, that's *exactly* how it happened. It was in Key West, and I *did* catch it just as the poem says. That was in 1938. Oh, but I did change *one* thing; the poem says he had five hooks hanging from his mouth, but actually he only had three. I think it improved the poem when I made that change. Sometimes a poem makes its own demands. But I always *try* to stick as much as possible to what really happened when I describe something in a poem.[64]

By claiming the poem to be a description of what happened just as it happened, she loosened it from the traditional story-telling mold, which presupposes the shape of a lesson arrived at through moral or psychological development, a shape predicted by the beginning of the poem and resolved by its conclusion. Reading "The Fish" according to the directive of "The Monument" to "Watch it closely," as the poet watches the creature she has caught, we can see that her observations do not have a linear design showing inner development, not even an unconventional one.

The last simile in the poem, by personifying the fish in the conventionally sympathetic role of the old fighter heroic in defeat, would in the teleological paradigm reflect a new and deeper understanding earned by patient observation. Yet this poem actually begins with the poet personifying the creature in a similar and already sympathetic way:

> He didn't fight.
> He hadn't fought at all.
> He hung a grunting weight,
> battered and venerable
> and homely.

All through the poem until the last line, the narrator goes on unthinkingly personifying the fish even when comparing it to something nonhuman, using some fifteen repetitions of *he, his, him*. This by itself could suggest that she found its features not difficult to think of in human terms, not unknowably other.

At the same time, a contrary sense of the nonhuman being of the fish, of its alien or even hostile otherness, intrudes at irregular intervals introduced by dashes. They signal heightenings of intensity that work against a pattern of development in the poet's empathy or fellow feeling for the fish. Watching "his gills" breathe in "the terrible oxygen," she is jolted into the sense of them as "—the frightening gills, / fresh and crisp with blood, / that can cut so badly"; "from his lower lip / —if you could call it a lip—" she sees the fishline hanging "weapon-like."

The most loaded of these sudden perceptions happens in a passage between these two, about halfway through the poem. It comes as the poet's interpretive comment on what she saw when she "looked into" the eyes of the fish as other poets—Wordsworth, Keats, Eliot, Frost come specially to mind—have *looked into* the depths of nature's secret places:

> I looked into his eyes
> which were larger than mine
> but shallower, and yellowed,
> the irises backed and packed
> with tarnished tinfoil
> seen through the lenses
> of old scratched isinglass.
> They shifted a little, but not
> to return my stare.

There is something almost grotesque in the intensity and exactitude of this scrutiny. The narrator must have been holding the fish nearer, its face close to her own, so that she could look into "his" eyes the way a lover gazes into the beloved's. Her looking did not discover something more of the depths, or even the reflection of her eyes in his, though the lenses of the fish's eyes looked like a mirror. Its backing was "tarnished" and further obscured by "scratched" lenses made of "isinglass," which a dictionary teaches (and Bishop insisted to students that looking up words was a prerequisite for reading poems) is a semitransparent gelatin manufactured from the bladder of a large fish. Violence jolts the comparison and the poet's looking.

When the fish's eyes "shifted a little, but not/to return my stare," the baffled sense of strangeness erupts again in a perception of the creature's inscrutable otherness: "—It was more like the tipping/of an object toward the light." This is radically different from the similes earlier in the poem, all of which describe something visible about the fish in terms of some also visible feature of another particular thing. Here the shift in the fish's eyes is compared to an act performed by an unseen agent on an unspecified "object," bringing back hints in earlier descriptions of some identified agency at work everywhere in "battered," "stained," "speckled," "packed," "backed and packed," "tarnished," "scratched." This strange perception is the only return the poet's baffled staring is granted, but it intensifies the seeing: a change of light happens, made by an unknown agent—not the divine power that shines like streaks of light from "shook foil" in Hopkins's "God's Grandeur"—and charged with mysterious force.

This instant of empowered seeing is not allowed to be climactic for a development of the narrator's consciousness because the momentary tilting "toward the light" is immediately readjusted as her "stare" relaxes for a while into a more ordinary way of perceiving the fish: "I admired . . . and then I saw. . . ."

The presence of all these inconsistencies, of pulls in contrary directions, of shifts in intensity, is too persistent in the poem to be argued away. With the traditionally heightened line "I stared and stared," the poem has reached its visionary climax, but it did not arrive there by a conventionally describable line of development. That is, there is no traceable growth in the poet's empathy or fellow feeling for the fish, nor is there a building of her guilty dismay at man's inhumanity to animals. Throughout "The Fish," the poet's observations and feelings about what she sees shift suddenly, back and forth, in kind and intensity, all of which is to say that the movement of the lines does not dramatize a moral or psychological development, or reflect the learning of a philosophical lesson. It gives no ground for the conclusion that the poet has come to the smug or sentimental decision to give up fishing.

Instead, the poem seems to remember an experience not retold according to a plan or to be made accountable to logic. That way it can end in monosyllabically simple narrative closure with an incomplete sentence that claims no causal connection with the climactic vision that comes before it: "And I let the fish go." What the narrator also lets go is the need to interrogate the fish or to describe it: for the first time in the poem she calls it "the fish."

The moment of vision is validated by the unconventional movement of the poem because that testifies to its faithful telling of the story. It verifies the vision because it just happened, somehow believable because the patient, scrupulously delicate description admits the mystery of things without ever straying from the vocabulary we use about everyday experience. The description of the vision itself—like Hopkins's of "the ooze of oil/ Crushed"—is made out of words for the physical phenomenon of light striking "the bilge/where oil had spread" so it made the "rainbow," and the ordinary objects it transformed are called by their ordinary names.

There is implied, then, some noncausal link between the poet's unplanned way of looking and the vision, which together make "The Fish" the kind of poem it is. In a letter of 1964 from Bishop to Anne Stevenson there is a much quoted sentence about reading Darwin that seems intended to describe the way of observing that characterizes "The Fish" and some of Bishop's other poems where she studies an object: "What one seems to want in art, in experiencing it, is the same thing that is necessary for creation, a self-forgetful, perfectly useless concentration."[65] But it is the sentence just before that seems to speak of something like what happens in "The Fish" when the poet's looking suddenly opens to a vision:

But reading Darwin, one admires the beautiful solid case being built up out of his endless heroic *observations*, almost unconscious and automatic—and then comes a sudden relaxation, a forgetful phrase, and one *feels* the strangeness of his undertaking, sees the lonely young man, his eyes fixed on facts and minute details, sinking or sliding giddily into the unknown.

"The Fish" probably earned its place in anthologies in large measure for its likeness to a traditional story-telling poem, which gives readers the pleasure of familiarity so often characteristic of anthology-pieces. The retrospective light cast by *Geography III* on the unified, recognizable, and coherent shape of Bishop's work has also made it possible to see "The Fish" as a narrative poem of a different order, as "a beginning" (to quote "The Monument") that pointed the direction for great later poems like "The End of March." Bishop's poems of this order are shaped by whatever happens, and what really happens includes uncaused moments of vision.

The recognition in retrospect of this wholeness has transformed Bishop's reception by readers, as it is described in the unsigned opening statement of a symposium held in 1984 to celebrate her work five years after her death:

Some readers have known and loved Bishop's poems for years. Others have discovered her very recently. The number of her admirers seems to be growing steadily. Ask them just what they especially prize about her poetry and you will get a host of different answers. . . . One fact seems clear: affection for her poems cuts right across lines of gender, region, school, fashion, or whatever else might make her the special spokesperson of a special group; the universality of her appeal is increasingly evident, and it is reassuring.[66]

She is no longer cast as a "writer's writer's writer" or as an "ideal poet for anthologies," but as a poet with something like the kind of appeal to varieties of readers that only Frost achieved in this country in this century.[67] Light on how this could be so might be cast by what is still her most widely known poem, "The Fish," which accommodates a familiar, popular storytelling form to a radically new and unconventional kind of poem, and does so without impatience and without deviating from what really happened.

The changes that *Geography III* brought about in the understanding of Bishop's work and of her stature as a poet have not dislodged what was from early on her best-known poem from its place in anthologies, any more than Frost's "Birches," or "Mending Wall," or "Stopping by Woods on a Snowy Evening" have been displaced by later readings of his work. Their accessibility to many readers, and of all sorts, marks them as representative poems by poets capable of achieving popularity in the genuine and most generous sense.

PART III

WHAT POETS MAKE OF ANTHOLOGIES

CHAPTER SEVEN

POETS AS ANTHOLOGY READERS

The poets of the early nineteenth century who read Percy's *Reliques of Ancient English Poetry* were the first writers to acknowledge their own and their generation's debts to an anthology. They expressed their gratitude in language that describes the book as if it had a combined effect beyond that of its components; as if it were a literary model in itself, capable like the work of an earlier poet of influencing the matter, language, and form of new verse writing. For a poet to acknowledge an anthology as a model was a phenomenon that could not have happened in the cultural situation of the early anthologists, who gathered the lyric poets that Percy revived in his collection.

In spite of the silence of authors in the first period of English verse anthologies, discussion of how poets have used them must begin, like most other matters to do with the history of this kind of book, with Tottel. Percy began there when he collected seven editions of Tottel's *Songes and Sonettes* to prepare for making a reprint of Surrey's poems.

TOTTEL'S PARADIGMATIC BOOK

Although in discussions of indebtedness in poetry the same critical vocabulary now serves for all periods, a crude sign that it is anachronistic when we apply it to the situation of poetry in the sixteenth century is that the *OED* gives no instances before 1600 of such key terms as: *adaptation, allusion, borrowing, imitation*. The modern use of *original* to mean *not derivative* entered English only in the eighteenth century (a meaning perhaps evolved from the earlier use of *original* to distinguish a poem written in the vernacular from a translation).

Of course the fact that these now current terms had not yet been invented does not mean that the practices they refer to did not exist; only that

they were differently conceived, and largely ignored as matters of indifference. Related questions of the authenticity of texts and the accuracy of attri-
butions were muddled or left unasked about poems in the sixteenth century,
and what is specially pertinent to the discussion here, there was no common
standard or practice of acknowledging sources. This very different cultural
situation is visible both in the ways anthologies gathered their contents from
unnamed sources, and in the ways they were themselves much used with
little recognition.

Sixteenth-century poets showed their personal knowledge of *Songes and
Sonettes* by unattributed borrowings from its contents or by praising contributors to it without acknowledging that their poems were gathered in a
special kind of book made by someone else. Even so, *Songes and Sonettes* as a
book made a direct impression on the formation of printed collections of
verse in mixed short forms by single authors. Built on its model, such gatherings of poems took their place among accepted kinds of poetry books
along side sonnet sequences and volumes of poems in classical forms like the
epigram.

The most extreme instance of imitation of Tottel's book is George
Turberville's collection of his own poems, *Epitaphes, Epigrams, Songs and
Sonets*, first published in 1567 and again as revised in 1570.[1] It is a mixture of
poems in the short forms listed in its allusive expansion of Tottel's simpler
title (with *Songs and Sonets* in much the largest letters on the title page).
Every poem in Turberville's book is given a title, one of Tottel's distinctive
practices, and Turberville's titles signal like kinds loosely grouped together
but not in wholly separated sections, as in *Songes and Sonettes*. The love poems dominate as in Tottel's anthology, and they are titled by the same formulas: some thirty of them begin "The louer."

Contrary to what we might expect, given our commitment to the prior-
ity of authorial presentation of poetry over an anthologist's treatment of it,
Turberville's borrowings not only from particular selections but from the
nature, structure, and arrangement of Tottel's book itself show that printed
anthologies prepared the way for arrangements of authorial collections of
poems in a variety of short forms, rather than the other way around.

There are few records until the later seventeenth century to tell us which
poets before that time had kept *Songes and Sonettes* in their libraries, but a
copy of the 1587 edition was owned by William Drummond of Haw-

thornden, along with *A Poetical Rapsody, Englands Parnassus*, and works by the most prestigious poets like Sidney, Spenser, and Shakespeare. Where *Songes and Sonettes* can be seen still persisting in the earlier seventeenth century as an influence on a collection of poems by a single author is in the 1635 edition of Donne's poetry.

Poems, By J.D. is a posthumous arrangement of short poems, possibly based at least partly on groupings in one or more manuscripts more or less directly reflecting decisions made by Donne himself. They were put together by the editor of the printed collection under headings according to their kinds, many classical but with love poems in the most prominent place at the beginning, as they were situated in Tottel's ordering of poems by Surrey and Wyatt. Almost all have individual titles very different from Tottel's, which probably by then seemed old-fashioned evocations of bygone social situations and language, but the heading for the opening group is "Songs and Sonets." Though both these formal terms could still be used either strictly or as a loose description of any short poem (even in the late eighteenth century Percy called Marlowe's "Come live with me" a "sonnet"), the choice of this unmistakably allusive heading for a group of love poems in 1635 is unexpected.

Sonnets, abundant in Tottel's collection and particularly associated with its heroes Surrey and Wyatt, had largely gone out of use for love poems—as Donne's avoidance of them illustrates—while other forms prominent in *Songes and Sonettes* like the poulter's measure had been dismissed altogether. The anthologies that included Tudor and Stuart verse were disappearing from print. What is more, English itself had greatly changed in grammar, spelling, punctuation, and vocabulary, making it inevitable that Tottel's modernizations of early sixteenth-century poems would seem more antiquated to Donne's readers after fifty years had passed than Wyatt's language unimproved would have seemed to Tottel's after half that length of time.

In the changed situation of poetry in Caroline society of the 1630s, the fact that the editor of Donne's *Poems* would choose to allude to *Songes and Sonettes* might mean only that Tottel's title had become a generic phrase. Still, that circumstance itself would point to the anthology's continuing influence as a model for a different kind of book after the poems it contained no longer attracted new writers as a source they could learn from.

"A POURING OUT OF THE SPIRIT":
PERCY'S 'RELIQUES'

Wordsworth made an extraordinary statement in 1815 in his *Essay, Supplementary to the Preface*:

I do not think that there is an able writer in verse of the present day who would not be proud to acknowledge his obligations to the Reliques; I know that it is so with my friends; and, for myself, I am happy in this occasion to make a public avowal of my own.[2]

This announcement is extraordinary on a number of counts, beginning with the fact that it is, so far as I have found, the first public declaration in the history of English poetry by a poet to the maker of an anthology for being an influence on his own poems

It is also surprising in its style. It seems to be almost a manifesto for a generation of poets, an announcement generalized as well as personal, as we can measure by comparing it with Sir Walter Scott's intimate expression of indebtedness in a letter he wrote to Percy in 1801. In it he remembered

the sensation I felt when the Reliques of Ancient Poetry were first put into my hands, an era in my poetical taste which I shall never forget. The very grass sod seat to which (when a boy of twelve years old) I retreated from my playfellows, to devour the works of the ancient minstrels, is still fresh and dear to my memory.[3]

While the affectionate detail describes a private response, "era" is a large public word, though not nearly as sweeping as the terms Robert Southey used in 1807 in the preface to his anthology *Specimens of the Later English Poets*. Tracing how "the growing interest in Shakespeare gradually brought our old writers into notice," he invoked Percy:

Warton aided in this good work, which was forwarded more effectually by the publication of the Reliques of Ancient Poetry, the great literary epocha of the present reign, which will prove to English poetry, what the discovery of the Pandects proved to jurisprudence.[4]

Switching from a legal to a religious comparison, Southey in 1814 attributed epoch-making power to Percy's book in a review of Chalmers's massive collection (sequel to the series prefaced by Johnson's *Lives*), *The Works of the*

English Poets: "To borrow a phrase from the Methodists, there has been *a great revival* in our days—a pouring out of the spirit. The publication of Percy's Reliques led the way."[5]

Wordsworth was also moved to use religious vocabulary when he preceded his avowal of obligation to Percy's book by another astonishing claim about the sweep of its influence: that "for our country, its poetry has been absolutely redeemed by it."[6] This was so, another passage in the *Essay* suggests, because the *Reliques* broke the confines dictated by "the most eminent English Poets" enshrined in the series that Johnson's *Lives* lent his name to, which consisted of authors chosen by the booksellers with reference "probably to the most popular miscellanies, and, unquestionably, to their books of accounts."[7]

Elizabeth Barrett Browning later described "the revival of poetry" in almost the same terms, perhaps having borrowed them straight from Wordsworth. She claimed "the *réveillé* of Dr. Percy's Reliques" to have sounded the call that opened a new "era, the putting down of the Dryden dynasty" and the "system" of Johnson, whose lives of the poets "left out the poets."[8]

Percy's collection did leave visible marks on poetry (German as well as English) in the late 1700s and early 1800s, and the variety of forms its influence took is a sign of the book's timeliness and richness as a source for poets working in that period. Beattie's "The Minstrel," itself an influence on Wordsworth's thinking about his poetic mission, was a dramatized version of Percy's romanticized version of the early minstrels' lives. Blake's "Mad Song" seems to have been suggested by a group of "Mad Songs" put together in the anthology by Percy. Chatterton's "Rowley" poems, Scott's narratives, Wordworth's longer poems "The Mad Mother" and "The White Doe of Rylestone" all used materials from ballads in Percy's collection (which Wordsworth read first in school, later borrowed from Coleridge, and purchased a copy of in 1798).[9] Coleridge in "The Rime of the Ancient Mariner" imitated Percy's archaizing vocabulary to enhance its spooky Gothic atmosphere: "beforne," "cauld," "eldritch," "pheere," "ween," "withouten" are examples.[10]

Wordsworth's large and emphatic declaration of indebtedness expresses a strong sense of affinity amounting to something like identification with Percy as the maker of the *Reliques*. He seems to have thought of the entries in it almost as if they were poems written by Percy and gathered by him in a collection of his own writing, or very nearly to have conceived of them as a single work of poetry. This is how he characterized them in a section of the *Essay* that is a descriptive catalogue of English poets leading up to his own generation:

Next in importance to the Seasons of Thomson, though at considerable distance from that work in order of time, come the Reliques of Ancient English Poetry; collected, new-modelled, and in many instances (if such a contradiction in terms may be used) composed by the Editor, Dr. Percy.[11]

The anthologist emerges in the same paragraph as a poet who followed "his genius into the regions of true simplicity and genuine pathos, (as evinced by the exquisite ballad of Sir Cauline and by many other pieces)," ancient ballads Wordsworth included among those "composed" by Percy. These were the very regions Wordsworth saw himself as having entered.

As author of the *Reliques*, Percy also appears in the same paragraph, somewhat inaccurately, in the role of a poet whose work was "ill suited to the then existing taste of city society," the position Wordsworth bitterly felt himself to be in when he wrote the *Essay*: "Dr. Johnson, 'mid the little senate to which he gave laws, was not sparing in his exertions to make it an object of contempt," and "the critic triumphed," in Percy's as in Wordsworth's situation as he saw it.

Wordsworth's resentment of Johnson's attitude toward Percy's "Compilation" is based on a confusion that uncovers more of his own feeling toward both the book and its editor or—in his view—its author. Johnson openly supported the making of the *Reliques*, as Percy tactically acknowledged in the preface to the first edition, and admired its accomplishment. He told Boswell in a letter written in 1778: "Percy's attention to poetry has given grace and splendour to his studies of antiquity. A mere antiquarian is a rugged being."[12] This was how the anthology was also received, perhaps partly due to Johnson's influence, by readers of the social class it hoped to please, who ignored the attacks on it led by the rugged antiquarian Joseph Ritson. Dodsley published four elegantly presented editions of Percy's multivolume collection between 1765 and 1794.

Wordsworth's confusion in the *Essay* about the reception of the *Reliques* and Johnson's part in it had roots in his treatment of the same painful subject in the *Preface to Lyrical Ballads* of 1800. He was clearly thinking back fifteen years to the section of that work following his defense of himself as poet for having "chosen subjects from common life, and endeavoured to bring my language nearer to the real language of men," which led him into an extended defense of the *Reliques*.[13] Having made that statement of his ideals, he shifted to protest against "a mode of false criticism which has been applied to Poetry in which the language closely resembles that of life and nature," that is, poetry like his own, which would be vulnerable to the same critical objections.

His one choice of example to illustrate this criticism was Johnson's parody of a modern imitation of an ancient ballad written by Percy, *The Hermit of Warkworth. A Northumberland Ballad. In three fits or cantos*, 1771. Here is Johnson's well-known stanza, as Wordsworth quoted it:

> "I put my hat upon my head,
> And walk'd into the Strand,
> And there I met another man
> Whose hat was in his hand."

To advance his argument that what made this stanza bad poetry was not simple form or natural language but rather its contemptible matter, Wordsworth quoted for contrast "one of the most justly admired stanzas of the '*Babes* in the Wood'"(actually titled "The Children in the Wood" in the *Reliques*):

> "These pretty Babes with hand in hand
> Went wandering up and down;
> But never more they saw the Man
> Approaching from the town."

There are unmistakable likenesses of language, matter, and tone between these lines and poems by Wordsworth in *Lyrical Ballads* such as "We Are Seven," "Lucy Gray," and most of all "Anecdote for Fathers," which begins:

> I have a boy of five years old;
> His face is fair and fresh to see;
> His limbs are cast in beauty's mold
> And dearly he loves me.[14]

Besides the larger resemblances in form, style, and subject, this stanza includes what seems to be an echo of particular language from another stanza in "The Children in the Wood":

> The one a fine and pretty boy
> Not passing three years olde;
> The other a girl more young than he,
> And fram'd in beautyes molde.[15]

The brilliant inanity of Johnson's parodic stanza in contrast with the sympathetic treatment of the subject in the lines from the *Reliques* makes Wordsworth's point, but by using a skewed comparison. The target of Johnson's parody was not one of the ancient ballads improved by Percy for inclusion in his anthology, but a modern ballad imitation entirely of Percy's own making. It was an instance of a current fashion in poetry that, according to Boswell, Johnson always treated with "ridicule" whenever the subject came up.[16]

The same slanted comparison is made even more distorting in the paragraph of Wordsworth's *Essay* that begins by accusing Johnson of making Percy's "Compilation . . . an object of contempt," but moves on to deplore that in consequence of the ridicule, Percy "adopted, as in the tale of the Hermit of Warkworth, a diction scarcely in any one of its features distinguishable from the vague, the glossy, and unfeeling language of his day."[17]

Wordsworth, it turns out here, had the same low opinion of Percy's own poems as Johnson—that the ballad imitations were essentially silly—though his critical vocabulary for stating that shared view was very different from Johnson's. The sympathetic blurring of the lines of argument in favor of Percy in Wordsworth's two discussions, separated in time by fifteen years (and the passage in the *Preface* is kept in the 1850 version), shows that Wordsworth had an enduring sense of affinity between Percy's *Reliques* and his own poetry. That helps to explain the nature of the indebtedness he felt so strongly and announced in such large terms. It did not inhere in adaptation, allusion, borrowing, imitation so much as in something like a perceived kinship of spirit or of sympathetic ideals that Wordsworth took to be Percy's, which were partly of his own imposition.

What Percy's poetic ideals for the *Reliques* actually were is implied in the Advertisement to the fourth edition (the one Wordsworth owned), which for tactical reasons was signed by his nephew. Published only four years before *Lyrical Ballads*, the Advertisement uses a critical vocabulary to describe the achievement of the *Reliques* which is much closer to Johnson's than to Wordsworth's. It invites the public to judge

how much they are indebted to the composer of this collection; who, at an early period of life, with such materials and such subjects, formed a work which hath been admitted into the most elegant libraries; and with which the judicious Antiquary hath just reason to be satisfied, while refined entertainment has been provided for every Reader of taste and genius.[18]

FROST'S "LAND OF 'THE GOLDEN TREASURY'"

In his utterly characteristic style of talking about himself, Frost said in 1956: "I must have been asked once years ago what I was doing in England, and I had forgotten what I was doing. . . . I said to somebody—I saw it in print somewhere—that I said I had come to the land of *The Golden Treasury*. That's what I went for."[19] The fairy-tale language of this explanation is an instance of playful and evasive myth-making, as is the offer in the next sentence of an alternative, matchingly fanciful, explanation: "that I went to live under thatch." We are not meant to believe that the sentences are telling facts: "must have been," "had forgotten," "somebody," and the sly "I saw it in print somewhere" see to that. At the same time the skepticism of such phrases, and they are everywhere in Frost's work, makes us trust the speaker, so that we can believe in the myth of his early entrance into a pastoral world of poetry represented by Palgrave's anthology.

This instance of Frost's reconsidering of his own life at the age of eighty-two is perfectly continuous with his imagining of it in the early years as he was writing the poems of *A Boy's Will*, published in 1913 in England soon after he brought his family to live there. Not just the act of weaving his experience into a myth, but the very form and matter of this particular myth of himself having sailed the seas and "come to the land of *The Golden Treasury*" (reversing the direction of Keats's traveler who left behind "the realms of gold" in the sonnet Frost could read in the anthology) illustrate the seamlessness of his lifelong imagining. The endurance of Palgrave's book, first published less than fifteen years before Frost was born, as a focus for Frost's mythologizing in his writings and sayings from the 1890s into his last years seems to be at once the reflection and the cause of its special power to nourish his literary life.

Tracing some of its recurrences, we can watch Frost turning fact into myth, and myth into material he could use: in making poems and in making a space for himself as a poet. Frost's early reading of *The Golden Treasury* was one of the most important things that happened to him in his literary life. The book was a shaping influence on his poetry at its beginnings in a remarkable variety of ways, and through all his life it was his chief instrument in measuring his distance from modernism. Beyond that, *The Golden Treasury* embodied what he understood poetic tradition to be, and by that embodying helped Frost to imagine a space for his poems in it. His encounter with it was an event in the history of modern poetry and in the history of modern criticism.

Some early matters of fact are that Frost in a letter of 1906 told of having discovered and bought a copy of Palgrave's alluringly titled anthology in 1892, and of "neglecting my studies" at Dartmouth to bask in its radiance "(Halcyon days!)."[20] In a letter of 1904 he listed as his "favorites" poems by Keats, Shelley, Tennyson, and Browning, and "Besides these I am fond of the whole collection of Palgrave's."[21] The same range of taste was displayed on the shelves of a parlor bookcase in the Frosts' house during these years: "Poe, Coleridge, Tennyson, Matthew Arnold, Jean Ingelow, Palgrave's *Golden Treasury*, and the *Songs of Shakespeare*."[22] Frost's own children learned poems by heart from this store, while his pupils in English I at Pinkerton Academy were more systematically required to memorize "Twenty poems from the Golden Treasury; basis of subsequent study of the history of English literature."[23]

Then in a letter written soon after leaving "*New* England" for "Old England" or Palgrave country, Frost described where he settled with his family in what his wife approved as "a dear little cottage," not literally thatched but at least vine-covered:[24]

Here we are between high hedges of laurel and red-osier dogwood, within a mile or two of where Milton finished Paradise Lost on the one hand and a mile or two of where Grey lies buried on the other. . . . If there is any virtue in Location—but don't think I think there is. I know where the poetry must come from if it comes.[25]

Between Wordsworthian hedgerows, between Milton and Gray, and, as he goes on to say in the letter, within seeing distance of the "lights" of Shakespeare's "London town," Frost imagined himself in a pastoral world mapped like *The Golden Treasury*, which Palgrave in its preface compares to a "landscape" measured out in "Books of Shakespeare, Milton, Gray, and Wordsworth."

Frost's youthful work celebrates Palgrave's claim in his preface that "Poetry gives treasures 'more golden than gold'": the poems in *A Boy's Will* are suffused with the golden pastoral diction that is everywhere the mark of the taste reflected in the anthology. So are other poems Frost wrote in this preparatory period but never included in his collected editions, where we come across "Gold flowers," "autumn gold," "golden autumn," "fainter gold behind the golden stars."[26] The poems Frost winnowed from the pile of loose pages he brought to England are all in the lyric forms allowed by Palgrave's rules for inclusion: sonnets, odes, ballads, songs, elegiac poems.

Much of Frost's early work shows that he had not only immersed himself in the diction and forms preferred in *The Golden Treasury*, but had deeply explored the poems in it by early writers it seems he met first there alongside many of his favorite nineteenth-century poets: Spenser, Shakespeare in songs and sonnets, Herrick, Marvell, and Milton particularly in "Lycidas," where an endnote of Palgrave's says the conventions of classical pastoral are "exhibited more magnificently . . . than in any other pastoral."[27] When, as so often in the public performances of Frost's later life, he dismissed academic study of poems, he seems to have been contrasting it in his mind with his adventure of "discovering on my own Palgrave's *Golden Treasury*" and privately reveling in its riches: "Goodness' sakes, the beauty of those poems at the top of everything," a metaphor of heights, of the summit that he used often for Palgrave's book, "is that some of them must be in your nature, you know, in your head. You can't hear them without their catching on to you without being studied."[28] The "Location" where he knew his poetry must come from was this internalized "land of *The Golden Treasury*."

In an interview with Richard Poirier in 1960, Frost, having caught his questioner "trying to trace" his "line of preference" among poets, ducked the question with a remembrance of his explorations in Palgrave's treasure trove:

Oh, I read 'em all. One of my points of departure is an anthology. I find a poet I admire, and I think, well, there must be a lot to that. Some old one—Shirley, for instance, 'The glories of our blood and state'—that sort of splendid poem. I go looking for more.[29]

Of all the selections in the anthology, this poem (along with Herrick's "To Daffodils") came to mind most often in Frost's letters and talks about poetry, lovingly remembered as if he still pictured it as he had first seen it on the page: "Now at the head of that it says in the Palgrave, if I remember rightly... 'Death the Leveller.'"[30]

Traces of Frost having assimilated particular poems in the anthology are everywhere in *A Boy's Will*, and take various forms. "Rose Pogonias" is itself a kind of anthology of effects borrowed from Palgrave's choices among poems by Herrick, Vaughan, and Marvell, with some remembrances of Keats's "To Autumn." In the later lines of "Waiting/Afield at Dusk," the "stubble field" and the progression of natural sounds catalogued by present participles more particularly evoke "To Autumn," with some reminders of Collins's "Ode to Evening." "Stars" owes the line "When wintry winds do blow" to one in a song by Shakespeare, "When all the winds doth blow." The sonnet "The Vantage Point" sets up its structure in the first line, "If tired of trees I seek again mankind," on the model of Shakespeare's sonnet "Tired with all these, for restful death I cry," but reverses the direction of the argument, pivoting on the playful rhyming substitution of "trees" for "these." In the last poem of the volume, "Reluctance," as the youthful poet moves "Out through the fields and the woods," the hopeful mood and simplified pastoral diction of that line call up the closing line of "Lycidas," where the young shepherd-poet moves "Tomorrow to fresh woods, and pastures new."[31]

Two instances of Frost's assimilations from *The Golden Treasury* constitute what might more precisely be called answer-poems. "Asking for Roses," dropped by Frost from the collected editions of his poems, includes a stanza rewriting Herrick's smilingly admonitory *carpe diem* song ("Gather ye rosebuds while ye may"). That poem was given a title by Palgrave, "Counsel to Girls," which, like Frost's stanza, tries for Herrick's lightness of touch:

> 'A word with you, that of the singer recalling—
> Old Herrick: a saying that every maid knows is
> A flower unplucked is but left to the falling,
> And nothing is gained by not gathering roses.'

More radical and surprising is the response to Shelley's "Ode to the West Wind" in Frost's "To the Thawing Wind," listed in a letter of 1913 among poems he thought "almost or quite as perfect" as "My November

Guest."[32] This is the volume's only poem of apostrophe—"Come with rain, O loud Southwester"—compressing into six couplets and a closing triplet its response to Shelley's long stanzaic ode with its opening apostrophe—"O wild West Wind, thou breath of Autumn's being."

The more layered relation to its source of this answer-poem may have to do with the fact that in "To the Thawing Wind" the youthful lover is for the first time explicit about being a poet, when he implores the wind to burst the walls of his self-enclosure: "Scatter poems on the floor;/ Turn the poet out of door." The allusions to Shelley's importunate "Drive my dead thoughts.../ Like withered leaves," "Scatter.../ ... my words among mankind" are at once tributes and distancing sounds of the new poet's different voice. His imperatives, acknowledging Shelley's double meaning of "leaves," turn into an amused evocation of domestic untidiness.

There is nothing particularly surprising about this lavish appropriation in Frost's early poems, as he may well have known when he was writing them, and certainly recognized in amused retrospect when in 1925 he contributed the introduction to an anthology of "Dartmouth Verse":

No one given to looking under-ground in spring can have failed to notice how a bean starts its growth from the seed. Now the manner of a poet's germination is less like that of a bean in the ground than of a waterspout at sea. He has to begin as a cloud of all the other poets he ever read.[33]

Still, what is remarkable about these traces of Frost's reading in his early poems is their being concentrated and focused by one book, which guided him by its own selective presentation of poets and poems.

In Frost's arrangement of *A Boy's Will* as it was originally published, the poem at the very center of the first and longest by far of its three parts is "Flower-Gathering." He rarely if ever recited or commented on it in his public performances, a reticence perhaps deliberately matched to the curious silences in the poem itself, but he did include it among his recommendations to William Braithwaite in 1915 of the best poems he and other friends should read in *A Boy's Will*.[34] Its importance here is that it is the first of several poems in the volume that go beyond assimilations from Palgrave's choices to use the book of *The Golden Treasury* itself as a focus for Frost's concerns about making his own poems, and about making a place for himself in poetic tradition.

In the first arrangement of *A Boy's Will*, the introduction of the lover as a poet in "To the Thawing Wind" is followed by "A Prayer in Spring" and "Flower-Gathering." In this grouping, love-making and verse-making come together, or pull apart, a pattern in Frost's work discussed extensively by Poirier.[35] The point to begin the related argument here is that the title "Flower-Gathering" is a translation into English of the literal meaning of *anthology* from its Greek root *anthos* [*flower*] + *legein* [*to gather*], and that this title introduces the first poem in *A Boy's Will* to use Palgrave's gathering of poems as a metaphor. Here, besides being a love-offering, the gathering of flowers makes a figure for the poem itself, for the other verses of the poet-lover, and for all poetry.

The first stanza of "Flower-Gathering" tells a balladlike story of how the youth, having left his beloved "in the morning glow," then returns "in the gloaming, / Gaunt and dusty gray with roaming," to be met by her unreadable silence: "Are you dumb because you know me not, / Or dumb because you know?" These unanswered questions raise their own questions about her silence and his inward separation from her: "because you know me not" as a poet to be taken seriously? "because you know" me to be a poet spurred to be a great poet by ambition that will keep me separate from you?

Her silence is then marked by the space between the stanzas, and during it, as we learn from the second stanza, the lover holds out the bunch of flowers he has gathered for his beloved, which it seems she does not take, perhaps turns away not to see?

> They are yours, and be the measure
> Of their worth for you to treasure,
> The measure of the little while
> That I've been long away.

Here his reassurance to the beloved raises more unanswered questions, not all of them about her unreadable silence. Offering what he has spent the day away from her to gather, he says simply, "They are yours," but what follows is not simply said. The explicit meaning intended for her seems to be that her treasuring of the gift will be the measure of its worth, but there are suggestions of meanings tugging in other directions in the insistent associations of "measure," "measure" with poems, of "treasure" and "Flower-Gathering" with Palgrave's anthology. These tensions seem to deflect the explicit meaning: there are suggestions that the poems are "treasure" in their own "worth" by virtue of their "measure." And though they are "faded flowers gay," once "gay" but "faded" now because he has picked and carried them home to her, he does not apologize for them. In a sense he takes away their fadedness, gives them back their "gay" freshness by his archaic poetical word order (Victorian leftovers called "straddled adjectives" by Pound) describing them.

Poirier, reading nearby poems in the volume concerned with the connections "between sexual love and poetic making," says the poems are "the stranger for *not* showing very much acknowledgement of their strangeness," as if the two kinds of making "were so naturally, so instinctively identified as not to call for comment."[36] Besides that strangeness in "Flower-Gathering," there is another kind that seems to surround the association, verging on identification, of the poem and others in *A Boy's Will* with the selections in *The Golden Treasury*. Unacknowledged in the poem is the possibility that these "flowers gay" are not "faded" because they have been gathered, but because they are the work of poets no longer living, so not responsive to the coming together, or pulling apart, of sexual and literary creation, which is the experience pressing its demands on the young lover's poetic making.

Frost originally placed "Waiting/Afield at Dusk" three poems after "Flower-Gathering," with "Rose Pogonias" and "Asking for Roses"—both to do with gathering flowers—in between. In "Waiting," as in "Flower-Gathering," the lovers are separated, but here she is the "one absent," and he is left "alone" in "my secret place" to dream on nature's changing lights; more especially on the motions and sounds of the nighthawks, the bat, and the swallow. Then, last in this catalogue of things in nature, joined simply by another "And" almost as if it were one among them, comes another source of sound to dream on:

> And on the worn book of old-golden song,
> I brought not here to read, it seems, but hold
> And freshen in this air of withering sweetness.

This book is certainly Palgrave's gathering of poems, here not faded from having been picked, but lovingly "worn" with handling which has rubbed it to a soft "old-golden" burnish. This poet has brought it "not to read, it seems, but hold" in his hand—but *hold* perhaps also with a slight trace of the biblical sense of *to keep, to treasure*—not needing to gather anything from it, not wholly preoccupied in dreaming on it, "But on the memory of one absent most, / For whom these lines when they shall greet her eye."

The poem is achieved, made out of what the poet's senses have gathered from natural sights and sounds into the "secret place" where he holds his beloved in "memory"; and those imaginative resources have the power to "freshen" the "book of old-golden song." The fullness and ease of the poem's articulation makes a turn away from the strangely spare or cramped manner of "Flower-Gathering," and that new direction seems to be focused by the poet's power to "hold" and "freshen" the "old-golden song" from within his own treasury of immediate and remembered experience.

The gloss of "Mowing," second from the end of the poems in Part I, announces another phase of the poet's growth: "He takes up life simply with the small tasks." Looking back in 1925, Frost may have suggested how he thought of this change of direction when he spoke of "Mowing" as his first "talk-song," a departure from "old-golden song."[37] The mower-poet, listening to the sound of the scythe he used "to make" the hay, was unsure what it was it did in "fact" whisper—whether about the sun's heat or the silence—but he was certain what it was not. "It was no dream of the gift of idle hours," what the poem "Waiting" could be said to be, "Or easy gold at the hand of fay or elf," which suggests Frost might have been hearing in his head lines he had read in *The Golden Treasury*, for instance about the "faery child" in her "elfin grot" in Keats's "La Belle Dame Sans Merci." Certainly the seductive power of these lines for the mower-poet, and for Frost, is felt as it is held off: "easy gold" is not rejected but resisted. Behind the mower, Frost refigures himself as a poet: he no longer imagines making poems as flower-gathering; he holds the "long scythe" as the instrument of his making, and not the "old-golden book of song."

In a public performance in 1958, Frost traced the course of his literary life to "Mowing," which he had said as early as 1914 was the best poem in *A Boy's Will*:[38]

There, way back very early, this little one. . . . Now you see that one line in there . . . 'The fact is the sweetest dream that labor knows.' That had a lot to do with my career. . . . The fact . . . not getting up fanciful things. I had no business to mention fay and elf in it. I always feel sorry about that.[39]

This reconsidering says a lot about why, after *A Boy's Will*, none of Frost's books came as close to being like "a cloud of all the other poets he ever read," or to imagining *The Golden Treasury* as a mythical place where his poems were to come from.

Even so, there is one much later and very beautiful poem, suggestively titled "Time Out," where it may be that *The Golden Treasury* is present, somewhere not far below the surface, as a metaphor for poetry. The poem is about—to state it most simply—an experience of reading (like "On First Looking into Chapman's Homer"). It is a sonnet, a form Frost closely associated with Palgrave's book, and it strictly follows the Shakespearean rhyme scheme, not typical among Frost's sonnets. In *A Witness Tree* of 1942, Frost placed this sonnet only two poems before "The Lost Follower," described by William Pritchard as "a crisply argued, ironic tribute to a fellow poet who gave his soul to politics."[40] "The Lost Follower" begins:

> As I have known them passionate and fine
> The gold for which they leave the golden line
> Of lyric is a golden light divine

misguiding them to seek the "Golden Age" in "state-manipulated pelf, / Or politics of Ghibelline or Guelph" instead of "right beside you book-like on a shelf."

This poem seems to be a kind of gloss on "Time Out," which celebrates a "pause" when the speaker in the sonnet escaped to a place above the clamor of "cause and sect"; a place where nature and poetry come together as metaphors for each other. He tells how he climbed a mountain that part way up he discovered to have the same slant as "a book held up before his eyes / (And was a text albeit done in plant)," like the "lovely leaves" we "may read" in Herrick's "To Blossoms," one of Palgrave's choices. This pastoral high place, described in "the golden line / Of lyric," grows flowers with seemingly mythological names—"Dwarf cornel, gold-thread, and maian-themum"—but what signified most to the climber was the angle the mountain gave to his seeing:

> The same for reading as it was for thought,
> So different from the hard and level stare
> Of enemies defied and battles fought.

He had climbed above party rancor and strife to a halcyon sphere freshened and calmed by the "obstinately gentle air / That may be clamored at by cause and sect, / But it will have its moment to reflect." Frost might have been listening to what seems to press against the explicit meaning of "Time Out" when, in a talk of 1956, he expanded on "what I think is the height of it all for me? I might sum it up in the word *Golden Treasury*—lyric poetry. A book almost without animus; all up in the spirit of high poetry; a book all the way up in the high guesses."[41]

Frost's praises lifted *The Golden Treasury* to a summit beyond the reach of rancorous opinion, while at the same time he was entirely aware of its actual situation as a focus of modernists' attacks on nineteenth-century poetry and criticism. Pound, as always, led the fight, and Frost, as characteristically, made sly counterattacks, using praises of Palgrave for the purpose.

Pound's intemperate opinion of *The Golden Treasury*—"that stinking sugar teat Palgrave"—was well-publicized, by him and by others.[42] Yeats in a letter to Lady Gregory of 1928 joked about it as if it had been declared by manifesto to be of public importance:

> He has most of Maud Gonne's opinions (political and economic) about the world in general. . . . The chief difference is that he hates Palgrave's *Golden Treasury* as she does the Free State Government, and thinks even worse of its editor than she does of President Cosgrave.[43]

Even when Pound did not mention "that doddard Palgrave" by name, he repeatedly defined his own critical positions by their opposition to all that *The Golden Treasury* stood for in the opinion of its still admiring public.[44] In 1915 in Pound's preface to *Poetical Works of Lionel Johnson* he wrote:

> I think I have been chosen to write this Preface largely because I am known to hold theories which some people think new, and which several people know to be hostile to much that hitherto has been accepted as 'classic' in English poetry; that is to say, I reverence Dante and Villon and Catullus; for Milton and Victorianism and for the softness of the 'nineties' I have different degrees of antipathy or even contempt.[45]

In letters of this period, when Frost's first two books were being published in England, Pound said of his own "*new* work" that it was "absolutely the *last* obsequies of the Victorian period," which he identified with the poetry and influence of Palgrave's friend and chief adviser on the choice of entries in *The Golden Treasury*: "no hindside-beforeness, no straddled adjectives (as 'addled mosses dank'), no Tennysonianness of speech."[46]

Frost's letters in this period describe his initial uneasiness hardening into resentment at Pound's patronizing patronage, and all through his later correspondence, conversations, and public performances he never stopped feeling pressed to distance his poems and critical opinions from Pound's. In this effort he enlisted on his side *The Golden Treasury* and its multiple associations, in a variety of countermoves to Pound's game of demonizing Palgrave.

In Frost's more general ways of praising the anthology, he identified his own taste in poetry with Palgrave's, and this implies the larger dimension of his difference with Pound. In a talk on "Attitudes toward Poetry" in 1960 he said:

Thinking of Tennyson again—he helped to make the most of a gem of a little book of poetry the world's ever seen—lyric poetry—Palgrave's *Golden Treasury*. It was his choices, a good part of it. It's beautiful—it's the top of the far of English literature. . . .[47]

Three weeks later Frost continued these remarks about Tennyson's shaping influence on the unity of taste in the selection of entries: "And it gets violated all the time. People are always putting in more poems, calling it Palgrave's," a desecration of the book "like throwing away Tennyson. It's the legacy of Tennyson."[48]

In more detailed comments scattered through his work, Frost used the anthology to counter specific positions associated with what he sometimes called "the new Movement" of which "Ezra Pound was the Prime Mover," or "Imagism" and "he was the first Imagist too," or "the free-verse people" and "Ezra Pound used to say that you've got to get all the meter out of it— extirpate the meter." Carrying *The Golden Treasury* as his shield (Frost once praised a student for making the metaphor "He is the kind that wounds with his shield"), he went to battle against Pound, most particularly over issues about poetry to do with obscurity, and with the values of using visual imagery, meter, and rhyme.[49]

Frost's commentary about poetry over the years includes many sly observations that there "have been works lately to surpass all records for hardness," where his term is a practical, workmanlike substitute for what he considered buzzwords like *obscurity* or *difficulty*.[50] To a discussion of the impenetrability of the ancient Eleusinian mysteries, "the real mysteries," he added as if parenthetically, "And that's so with some people's poetry."[51]

The celebration of difficulty as a criterion for poems that should be taken seriously Frost saw as the danger of "the general critical approach," of too complicated interpretive readings that at once overvalue and exaggerate or even manufacture difficulty. By contrast, "the anthology," meaning chiefly Palgrave's but also the genre of poetry book, "is the best form of criticism": "I was told, when I was young, let the anthologies alone. You might as well say, let all opinion in poetry alone, for the anthology is the best of all opinionation. It is a good form of criticism, just because it is pure example."[52]

Without acknowledging the target of the maneuver, he more particularly used the absence of footnotes in *The Golden Treasury* (overlooking, perhaps for the purposes of his argument, the notes at the end of the book) to challenge the worth of obscurity in poetry. Talking to an audience mainly of teachers, he asked them what they would "do with the Palgrave? It was published without a single note, if I'm not mistaken. . . . And what is there to be said about poetry like that?"[53] In another talk he marshaled the support to his side—and Palgrave's—of Emerson, Henry Dana (probably meaning Charles Anderson Dana), and Goldsmith, all makers of anthologies: "There've been anthologizing right down. Taking the top of poetry—interesting—there isn't anything in any of them that needs a note when you get up to that height of poetry."[54]

Paradoxically, the omission of notes was related for Frost to Palgrave's—and other anthologists'—addition of simple titles to untitled entries, or substitution of more explicitly explanatory titles for those already given. Both these decisions about how to present the poem to the reader seemed to Frost to be expressions of his own sense that poems should not be treated as mysteries inaccessible to the uninitiated. Referring to one of his most treasured examples from *The Golden Treasury*, Shirley's "The glories of our blood and state," he praised its explanatory title, "Death the Leveller": "Palgrave just added that—a smart addition."[55] Elsewhere, after reciting Shakespeare's sonnet "They that have power to hurt and will do none," he slipped it into his attack on obscurity, saying it "always has had my great admiration. But lately someone told me it is considered one of the great puzzles." Then approving Palgrave's dubious title for it, "Life without Passion," he concluded blandly, "That's my idea of it. But it's supposed to be controversial."[56] The titles regularly supplied by Palgrave and other anthologists are more like Frost's own apparently simple, declarative titles than like Pound's often elusively allusive titles, often untranslated from European languages.

Although Frost was less critical of Pound's imagist insistence "on clearer sharper less muddled half realized images (chiefly eye images)," he still felt the need to stake out his different interest: "Strange with all their modernity and psychology they didnt have more to say about ear images," or what he more often called "sentence-sounds," his own prerequisite for what makes a good poem.[57] On this issue he characteristically defended himself with examples from Palgrave's book. He declared in a letter of 1915: "The sentence is everything—the sentence well imagined. See the beautiful sentences in a thing like Wordsworth's To Sleep or Herrick's To Daffodils. . . . We will prove it out of the Golden Treasury some day."[58] In a letter of 1918 he made the same point with the same supporting example, that the roots of every good poem are "well within the colloquial as I use the word. And so is all the lyric in Palgrave's Treasury. Consider Herrick's To Daffodils."[59]

Frost took a more strenuous poke at Pound in his essay "The Constant Symbol" of 1946. This time the target was Pound's program as a "free-verser" to liberate poetry from meter—in Pound's idiom "the god damn iambic"—and from lyric forms constrained by fixed lineation and rhyme, an idea Frost often liked to say would make writing poems like playing tennis with the net down.[60] In the essay Frost pictured the poet playing a different game, jump rope (elsewhere it is hopscotch, and the poet-player is Pope writing "Ode on Solitude," the only one of his poems chosen by Palgrave, probably because it was almost unique among Pope's poetry in being both pastoral and short).[61] The rope skipper enters into the game "to make the most of his opportunities," which are the choices of: "two metres, strict iambic and loose iambic"; "any length of line up to six feet"; and "an assortment of line lengths for any shape of stanza, like Herrick in 'To Daffodils.'"[62]

The entries in *The Golden Treasury* that Frost returned to all his writing life in defining his poems and poetics, often in their differences from Pound's, are beautifully true to his own preferences in lyric forms: "my love of neatness, of a little poem, you know, the rhymes of it and the little bits."[63] His chosen examples are equally representative of Palgrave's commitment to meter, rhyme, and the lyric: the rules he explained in the preface to his anthology excluded "Blank verse and the ten-syllable couplet . . . as alien from what is commonly understood by Song, and rarely conforming to Lyrical conditions in treatment."[64]

Short stanzaic poems like Herrick's "To Daffodils," Shirley's "The glories of our blood and state," Pope's "Ode on Solitude," sonnets like Shakespeare's and Wordsworth's, and those of Frost's favorite poems of his own that he often affectionately called the "little ones" ("Stopping by Woods on a Snowy Evening" and "Mowing," for example) are described by an extended metaphor in a talk of 1958: "I have a little ivory box . . . a couple of inches—a little box with a slide cover, carved, and in two layers of pieces and they fitted together—a little puzzle. . . . they're very like a poem to me . . . and the poem is the box."[65] Not only particular favorites among Palgrave's choices were used by Frost as representations of his ideal poem. He even made such a figure out of the book of *The Golden Treasury* itself:

Here's this little book, Palgrave's *Golden Treasury*, which I admire—that little book—so much. . . . And I wouldn't have that book violated any more than I'd have one of Shakespeare's sonnets violated. And it gets violated all the time. People are always putting in more poems, calling it Palgrave's. . . . It's a pretty little sonnet of a book.[66]

In the interview of 1960 quoted earlier, Poirier, denying Frost's accusation that he had been "trying to trace" the poet to his sources, tried again by asking what Frost would say to the fact that "Eliot and Pound seem to many people to be writing in a tradition that's very different from yours." Frost's answer is much more importantly revealing than its playful naughtiness pretends:

Pound seemed to me very like a troubadour. . . . I never touched that. I don't know Old French. I don't like foreign languages that I haven't had. . . . I like to say dreadful, unpleasant things about Dante. Pound, though, he's supposed to know Old French.[67]

Asked next if Pound was a good linguist, Frost repeated what a teacher once told him (or so Frost said) about Pound's performance in a college Latin course: that he "never knew the difference between a declension and a conjugation." While delighting in his own mischief, Frost characteristically used it here to hint at essentially the same answer about his different understanding of poetic tradition from Pound's that he had given in 1942 in the head note he gave to the poems he chose for Whit Burnett's anthology *This Is My Best*. There his sense of profound difference between himself and Pound, though unmentioned, seems as usual to be somewhere behind Frost's way of placing himself as a poet:

It would be hard to gather biography from poems of mine except as they were all written by the same person, out of the same general region north of Boston, and out of the same books, a few Greek and Latin, practically no others in any other tongue than our own.[68]

This unspoken contrast with Pound's Europeanism expresses Frost's sense of belonging to the classic tradition of English poetry and his appreciation of its continuity, for which Palgrave's anthology was to him both an actual embodiment and a metaphor. He seems to have been imagining the tradition of poetry in English as *The Golden Treasury* hypostatized when, in the course of praising Hopkins, he spoke of a poet's immortality: "A very fine poet, and one of our poets. There'll always be some of him in the anthology, speaking of him that way—[in] the English Anthology."[69]

He seems also to have been picturing poems of his own inscribed forever among the pages of such an imaginary anthology when he made a wish for his own poetic immortality: "The utmost of ambition is to lodge a few poems where they will be hard to get rid of, a few irreducible bits."[70] Hardy must have imagined immortality in the same figure when in the last year of his life, Florence Hardy noted, he told her that "His only ambition, so far as he could remember, was to have some poem or poems in a good anthology like the *Golden Treasury*."[71]

AFTER "PALGRAVE"

Among poets classified as *modern* in anthologies, those who were born in the nineteenth century were marked almost inevitably by the influence of *The Golden Treasury*: for Hardy and Frost the embodiment of their ideal; for Pound anathema to his. Eliot treated Palgrave's continually reissued anthology with silence, or with his usual bland disdain as an instance of inconsequential Victorian criticism. Still chafing at its hold over public taste in poetry in 1933, he ranked it dismissingly with popular verse collections designed for the middle-class household of the late nineteenth century:

The instruments [of criticism] of Arnold's time appear now, of course, very antiquated: his was the epoch of Ward's *English Poets* [with introductions for the general reader including one by Arnold], and of *The Golden Treasury*, birthday albums and calendars with a poetical quotation for each day.[72]

When Edward Thomas wrote a letter in 1906 about his plan for his forthcoming "collection of ballads & songs, but especially folk songs" titled *The Book of the Open Air*, he implied that his anxiety was the inevitable feeling of any anthologist who must work still against Palgrave's tired influence: "Of course I must avoid the *Golden Treasury* obviousness, but that will mean hard work if I am to produce something very good."[73]

Georgian Poetry, the most influential on public taste of the poetry anthologies printed in the decade between 1912 and 1922, aimed to promote what its title announced as a new kind of poetry emancipated from all that the adjective *Victorian* implied. In 1915 Robert Graves wrote to his mentor Edward Marsh, the founder and editor of the series and patron of the poets who appeared in it: "when this ridiculous war is over, I . . . with the help of other young Georgians to whom I trust you will introduce me, will try to root out more effectively the obnoxious survivals of Victorianism."[74]

Five years after it was decided that the *Georgian Poetry* series had run its course—Edmund Gosse commemorated Marsh's achievement in producing the anthology with the valediction "He is with Tottel"—Graves described its aesthetic program in *The Survey of Modernist Poetry* (written in collaboration with Laura Riding):[75] "the discarding of archaistic diction such as 'thee' and 'thou' and 'floweret' and 'whene'er' and poetical constructions such as 'winter drear' and 'host on armèd host' and of the pomposities generally."[76] This comes close to Pound's call for a purge of all "Tennysonianness," but how dedicated the *Georgian Anthology* was to these tenets is called in question by a representative entry like one of de la Mare's poems in the 1920–22 volume, "Titmouse," which includes this stanza, the last of three:

> This tiny son of life; this spright,
> By momentary Human sought,
> Plume will his wing in the dappling light,
> Clash timbrel shrill and gay—
> And into time's enormous nought,
> Sweet-fed, will flit away.[77]

Certainly "spright," "timbrel," "nought" are pure instances of forbidden archaisms; inversion, as in "Plume will his wing," qualifies as an outlawed poetical construction; and though *pomposity* might not quite characterize the poem, *inflated importance* does.

Graves added to his account of the Georgians' aims "that their verse should avoid all formally religious, philosophic or improving themes"—in brief, didactic poetry—"in reaction to Victorianism."[78] Paradoxically, that precept perfectly harmonized with Palgrave's rules for the kind of poem admissible in *The Golden Treasury*, and so did the simple songlike form and the shortness of de la Mare's lyric which, though only fifteen lines, is longer than a considerable number of other entries in *Georgian Poetry*.

Richard Aldington recognized the Georgians' Palgravian love of "littleness" by burlesque: "They took a little trip for a little week-end to a little cottage where they wrote a little poem on a little theme."[79] Although the Georgian poets liked to live in little weekend cottages (Frost went to live among them), this generic formula seems to be a sly allusion to the "small cabin" in Yeats's ubiquitously anthologized "The Lake Isle of Innisfree." It also points to another likeness between Marsh's anthology and Palgrave's: their elevation of the pastoral lyric.

Georgian Poetry was in its day, and still is, thought to have been responsible for a new burst of public interest in poetry, and for its corollary, the proliferation of anthologies. In the same beginning phase, *Georgian Poetry* also promoted the sales of individual books by its contributors, but the glut of contemporaneous anthologies encouraged by its success began to have the opposite effect. By the 1920s, poets were becoming hostile critics of the very books that brought their work to the attention of the most readers. Eliot was among them, but Graves was the most vociferous, although he had enthusiastically approved the series while it was appearing (and paying its contributors generously), praising Marsh as "the Father of modern English Poetry with fillets and palm leaves and a grateful flock of poetry lovers at your knees."[80]

In 1928, Graves published *A Pamphlet Against Anthologies* (again with Riding, who became known for refusing to contribute to any such collections). Its title announces it as almost a political manifesto. It takes a public stand against a whole class of book for its inherently damaging features and its debased practices, but Graves was most interested in its influence on the present situation of poetry.

The historical survey in the early part of the book takes aim at the two still most powerful collections: *The Golden Treasury*, "the Dean of Anthologies, its original liberalism ossified beyond recognition," and its "one serious rival in circulation," *The Oxford Book of English Verse*.[81] They are accused of being ultimately responsible for enfeebling effects on modern criticism and modern poetry as they were being brought together in modern anthologies.

Graves protested the objectionable effects of anthologies on poets and poems in two different but related lines of argument illustrated by descriptions and examples of the perfect modern anthology-piece:

It must be fairly regular in form and easily memorized, it must be a new combination of absolutely worn-out material, it must have a certain unhealthy vigour or languor, and it must start off with a simple and engaging statement of a sentimental character.[82]

The examples of course include "The Lake Isle of Innisfree" as an "invaluable" anthology-piece; de la Mare's "Arabia"; Robert Bridges's "I love all beauteous things"; Rupert Brooke's "famous *England* sonnet *If I should die think only this of me*"; John Masefield's "Cargoes." Of the last Graves said:

It is his most anthologized poem, one that has even been included by Dr. Bridges in his *Chiswell Book of English Verse* (a collection, by the way, that omits Donne, Marvell, Vaughan, Marlowe, Skelton and the three Fletchers, for the benefit of Newbolt, Moore, Lang, Longfellow, Arnold, Kipling, Campbell, R. W. Dixon who has four, Scott who has six, Byron who has eight and Tennyson who has ten pieces included).[83]

Graves made another protest against a different though related kind of damage done to poems and poets by the creation of anthology-pieces, illustrating it first with a poem of his own written when he was nineteen. (He liked it enough not to expunge it from editions of his collected poems, where it is titled "In the Wilderness.") The idea for it came from a reproduction of Holman Hunt's "Scapegoat"; it tells a simple story; it makes an equation between Christ in the wilderness and a ritual scapegoat wandering there; it rhymes; "it is a 'Shorter Lyric of the Twentieth Century'"; it was included in at least seventeen English anthologies and more in America (in 1929 he upped the figure to seventy or more). Graves stated in conclusion that its "author has written no other successful anthology-piece, and so remains the author of 'that poem about the Goat.'"[84]

The irritating effect that the overanthologizing of a poem can have on its author's reputation is expectable. Graves also argued a less self-evident point that such treatment does harm to the poem itself. He discussed the "slow spiritual breakdown" of a poem overexposed in anthologies as the hypnotizing effect of repetition, its capacity to obliterate meaning, and he used his own youthful poem to make another, more subtle, argument.[85] Though "muddled" and "silly," his early effort was not "originally dishonest in its conception, but it certainly is made to appear so" by turning up too often in anthologies, presumably along with other poems too much like it, as if made to measure for the purpose. As a result, what might have been the "genuine feelings" that initiated it are undiscoverable.[86]

Graves continued this line of argument by introducing "The Lake Isle of Innisfree" as another instance of a poem that began "in innocence, but the progress of which from anthology to anthology suggests that of the "'simple village maiden' of the ballad" who comes to no good end.[87] Yeats himself lamented the overanthologizing of "The Lake Isle of Innisfree," when in a letter of 1911 he deplored a request for permission to set it to music arranged for use by the Boy Scouts: "Imagine 'Innisfree' as a marching song—poor island."[88]

The supreme silliness of the popular treatment given to this most famous—or infamous—of anthology-pieces was still a joke in 1982 when Larkin complained about his own anthology-piece "This Be the Verse" after too much attention was paid to it during a celebration of his sixtieth birthday: "'They fuck you up' will clearly by my Lake Isle of Innisfree. I fully expect to hear it recited by a thousand Girl Guides before I die."[89]

CHAPTER EIGHT

POETS AS ANTHOLOGY MAKERS

The permanent situation of the anthology, that it is a book made by the compiler of work made by others, creates an odd relationship between the parties concerned (unless the book includes only poets safely dead before it was made). Montaigne condensed this situation into a sentence often alluded to in the titles of anthologies, or quoted as a motto. Vicesimus Knox used it to conclude the preface to *Elegant Extracts*: "*I have here only made a nosegay of culled flowers, and have brought nothing of my own but the thread that ties them together.*"[1]

The humility professed in these simply described acts of gathering and binding is called in question because the sentence disregards the gardener who originally planted the flowers (the poet as gardener was a traditional trope) while the maker of the posie (a common figure for poetry itself) is granted full powers to pick and choose the flowers and to arrange them in a new design. This may be a much more suspiciously charged analysis than Montaigne's commonplaces invite or deserve, but it draws a usefully simple diagram of inevitable tensions built into the anthology as a special kind of book.

Its peculiar character encourages the compiler to assume the status of author, and the poet to be restive about that appropriation, even while seeming to comply or collaborate with it. In the changing cultural situations that have unfolded in the history of anthologies, these tensions have always been there, but closer to the surface in the last hundred years. A telling example is Hardy, a dedicated admirer and user of Palgrave's anthology, who even so distrusted such books and their makers as a class, and for the reason that they had acquired powers hard for the poet to combat:

I have found that one has to overcome one's first instinct not to allow any of these people to use poems, etc., for if they are refused the reading public invariably conclude that one's work is not good enough to be in such anthologies, and that it is therefore negligible by a purchaser.[2]

There have always been poets who protested the authority of anthologists, and others who have appropriated that power by exerting influence, behind the scenes or openly, over the choices of poems to represent them in anthologies they did not make.[3] The most resourceful moves have been made by poets who have themselves become makers of anthologies suited to their own literary intentions.

SHOWCASES AND MANIFESTOS

Writers in the early period who were still alive when their work found its way into anthologies had occasions for complaint about the appropriation and presentation of their work, but within the literary system the ownership and authenticity of poems—particularly short pieces—were treated so laxly that abused authors had little effective recourse. Besides these hindrances, attitudes toward the social standing of poets complicated the relations between authors and anthologies. Writers like George Gascoigne, who aspired to be accepted in courtly circles, needed a place to display their wit as an essential qualification for entrance, but would risk being snubbed if they stooped to present their poems in print. Seeing the opportunities for respectable appearance before the public that an anthology might offer (since Tottel's had named the Earl of Surrey on its title page), Gascoigne arranged (while innocently abroad) to have work of his published in 1573 in a book with a title announcing it to be an anthology, *A Hundreth sundrie Flowres bound vp in one small Poesie.* Gascoigne's name is not on the title page.

Its contents are prefaced by a fake letter from "G.T." to "H.VV." angling for the publication "of *Sonets*, layes, letters, Ballades, Rondlets, verlayes and verses, the workes of your friend and myne master *F.I.* and diuers others, the which . . . I had with long travayle confusedly gathered together."[4] A group of poems under the running head "The deuises of sundrie Gentlemen" have titles in third-person forms naming Gascoigne—as in "Gascogne his passion," "Gascoines libell of diuorce"—designed to signal the presence of someone other than the poet doing the work of arranging the poems and preparing them for presentation in print. Gascoigne was the earliest of many poets to seize on the usefulness of the anthology for an author's self-presentation.

A century after Gascoigne's experiment, it was possible for poets to be involved in the publication of their own poems, though self-presentation required tact to give it a self-effacing look. Dryden, who early showed skill in finding his way in the literary system, was the first poet to involve himself directly, and in a short time publicly, in the making of an anthology of poetry that would offer a variety of entries of a quality that educated readers would appreciate as serious literature. This character distinguished it from collections of light-hearted verse of the sort performed at court or in theaters, one such being the *Covent Garden Drolery* (1672) with the name of its compiler, Aphra Behn, appearing thinly disguised as A.B.

Dryden entered discretely into collaboration with Jacob Tonson, already the respected publisher of Dryden and other poets well thought of, among them Behn, Nathaniel Lee, and Nahum Tate. The collaboration of Dryden and Tonson produced the model for the miscellany largely of Pope's work published by Bernard Lintot—Pope called him "the redoubtable rival of Mr. Tonson"—and for collections produced by Tate, William Wycherly, Sir Richard Steele, and Jonathan Swift.[5]

For Dryden's purposes, *Miscellany Poems* gave him a space to publish his current work, and by its instant success helped to promote the notion that translation, his present absorption, was a dignified mode of displaying a poet's own talent (on the title page of *Miscellany Poems* the words *NEW TRANSLATION* are in larger type than *ORIGINAL POEMS*). Once the interest or fashion of verse translation had been established by the first volume, Dryden apparently felt free to let his part in making the anthology be publicly acknowledged in the second. The preface is signed "John Dryden."

Predictably, poets since have often turned to making anthologies for the display of their writing when they thought it likely to find no place among prevailing styles and schools. That seems to have been Robert Southey's impulse in bringing out *The Annual Anthology*, which appeared only twice, in 1799 and 1800. Or at least that is how Coleridge perceived their situation when he wrote to Southey in 1799 about what would be the most effective placing of his "Christabel" in the anthology:

It ought I think to be last.—The first ought, me judice, to be a poem in couplets, didactic or satirical—such as the lovers of genuine poetry would call sensible and entertaining, such as the Ignoramuses & Pope-admirers would deem genuine Poetry.[6]

No compiler was named on the title page, but authors who so wished were acknowledged beside their poems, Southey prominent among them. The contributors, mostly friends of his and of each other (including George Dyer, Charles Lamb, and Charles Lloyd), were not greatly given to couplets, didacticism, or satire, but wrote largely in short songlike stanzas or blank verse. Their poems, lyrical rather than discursive, belonged more to the 1800s than to the century before.

At the other end of the 1800s, the members of the Rhymers' Club—Yeats, Ernest Rhys, Ernest Dowson, Arthur Symons, Lionel Johnson among them—anthologized two volumes of their own work as *The Book of the Rhymers' Club* in 1892 and 1894. In this self-presentation they seem to have been acting on the same awareness of writing against the grain of currently appreciated poetry that informed *The Annual Anthology*. They thought of themselves as living in what was even then described by the stock phrase "an age of transition," and positioned themselves in it by their "revolt against Victorianism," which—Yeats explained in retrospect—meant for these young poets

a revolt against irrelevant descriptions of nature, the scientific and moral discursiveness of *In Memoriam*—'when he should have been broken-hearted,' said Verlaine, 'he had many reminiscences'—the political eloquence of Swinburne, the psychological curiosity of Browning, and the poetical diction of everybody.[7]

Their ideal of poetry—"speech of gold" hammered in "golden rhyme"—found expression in "The Lake Isle of Innisfree," which was among Yeats's contributions to the first volume.[8]

Ezra Pound, the most effective showman of the next self-styled revolutionary generation, brought out an anthology conceived less pacifically as a showcase than as what he called "a sort of group manifesto": *Des Imagistes* of 1914.[9] The group it manifested included Amy Lowell, Richard Aldington, H.D., F. S. Flint, and William Carlos Williams. It was followed by a salvo of such anthologies made by other poets to defend their not always distinct schools: most promptly in 1915 by Amy Lowell's imitative (in Pound's view diluted or degraded) sequel. Its title was translated from Pound's as *Some Imagist Poets*, and its list of contributors partly duplicated his by including Lowell, Aldington, H.D., and Flint. Next came *Others*, edited by Alfred Kreymborg and Williams in collaboration, with Pound, Williams, and Kreymborg heavily represented and Eliot by "Portrait of a Lady." In the same year *Wheels* began to appear, edited by Edith Sitwell as an anti-Georgian showcase for family and friends.

Virtually every school or movement of poetry after the Pound era has been anthologized by one or several of its own. As is true of all anthologies, this revisionist sort has evolved its own tradition of forms and conventions typically focused in and by their titles. Anthologies designed to be showcases or manifestos for more recent movements have lavishly used *new* as their defining descriptive term in their titles. The adjective has carried different meanings but usually the same suggestion of countering whatever is at the time considered the dominant and dominating kind of poetry (whereas in titles similar in form and dating to *New Court-Songs and Poems* of 1672, the adjective *new* describes the latest fashionable poems, never before printed).

In the early 1930s, the poets grouped around the dominating presence of Auden, whose poems appeared in magazines like *New Verse* and *New Writing*, were being simultaneously gathered for display in two anthologies made by their fellow poet Michael Roberts: *New Signatures* (1932) and *New Country* (1933). Besides Roberts himself, and of course Auden, they included C. Day Lewis, Stephen Spender, Charles Madge, and John Lehmann, the editor of *New Writing*. Speaking for them in the preface to *New Signatures*, Roberts announced: "The poems in this book represent a clear reaction against esoteric poetry in which it is necessary for the reader to catch each recondite allusion."[10] The preface to *New Country* is a manifesto in the most strictly political sense. It is a call to bring about radical reform of society by educating "you, the readers of the *Observer*, *The Times*, you, Garvin, Gould, Squire" meaning J. C. Squire, whose successful anthologies of modern verse published between 1921 and 1934 embodied the taste of what his critics called the "Squirearchy" for the established Georgian mode of "buttercup lyricism."[11] In the titles of these two anthologies, *New* paradoxically carries the sense of reactionary: "reaction to" modernist exclusiveness and obscurity, and to poetry "more concerned with making 'literature'" than with "trying to make something, to say something as clearly as may be, to express an attitude."[12]

Larkin said that the poets of his generation styled in *The Spectator* as the "Movement" were first actually brought together by the poet Robert Conquest in his anthology *New Lines*, published in 1956 and in a second volume in 1963. Besides Larkin and Conquest, the group included D. J. Enright and Edward Lucie-Smith, each of whom made an anthology of recent poetry. In his 1963 introduction, Conquest said that both volumes of *New Lines* aimed to show how "as against much of the work of the past few decades, a good deal of contemporary poetry had returned to the cardinal traditions of English verse." The collections were designed to illustrate "the persistence and variety of the central current of English verse, in its present manifestations, at a time when a great deal is still being written which affects to be founded upon new, or at least different, attitudes."[13] In the title *New Lines*, the adjective means something like traditional, the opposite of "new, or at least different" in the sense of experimental. The phrase "still being written" underscores the intended paradox that the self-styled "new" writing not in the anthology was leftover modernism.

Three American poets together made *New Poets of England and America*, first published in 1957 and in four more printings up to 1960: Donald Hall, Robert Pack, Louis Simpson. The anthology does not openly present itself as a showcase for any particular school or kind of poetry: some fifty poets—American and British, born between 1917 and 1935 and listed in alphabetical order—are included. "What characteristics are to be discovered in this poetry we leave to the reader to determine" is the only directive from the editors.[14]

Still, the discovery is not hard to make. Following the one-page "Editors' Introduction" is an "Introduction by Robert Frost," a choice that gives away more than it may have been meant to do, or gives it away more easily. Frost was the great American formalist of twentieth-century poetry. His presence presides over the anthology, which he endorsed in the typically Frostian closing statement of his introduction: "As I often say a thousand, two thousand, colleges, town and gown together in the little town they make, give us the best audiences for poetry ever had in all this world. I am in on the ambition that this book will get to them—heart and mind."[15] This, then, is an anthology of formalist verse made by poets who, like the editors and indeed like Frost himself, had academic connections or who wrote like those who did: in rhyme and meter, and in such forms as song- and ballad-stanzas, sonnets, sestinas, villanelles; using such titles as "Autumn: An Ode," "Epithalamium," "Elegy for my Father," "The Green Shepherd."

Here *New* in the title means young or younger, the generation coming into its own as the mainstream, which can help to explain the appeal of the anthology to many or some beginning poets. For example, Mark Strand testified to its shaping effect on his poetry in an interview he gave in 1971: "I look back now and I read it, and I'm bored by a lot of the stuff, and some of it seems so forced and decorative. But I can still see why I was excited. There was an awful lot of 'technical authority' in many of those poems, and it's something that I, as a beginning poet, lacked."[16] Otherwise the importance of *New Poets of England and America* seems to be that it probably started what has been called "the war of anthologies" by constituting a challenge to Donald Allen to put together *The New American Poetry 1945–1960*.

This anthology was designed as an attack on formalism on behalf of poetry in open forms (also the aim of Stephen Berg and Robert Mezey in *Naked Poetry* of 1969). As such it made perhaps the most prominent contribution to the "literary revolts and poetic vendettas" that Elizabeth Jennings designed *An Anthology of Modern Verse* of 1961 to cut across.[17] Looking back in 1969, Strand in the preface to his anthology *The Contemporary American Poets* minimized this "brief skirmish" between ideologies of poetry as "more a part of the sociology of poetry than an accurate description of what in fact was being written."[18] By 1990, J. D. McClatchy in *The Vintage Book of Contemporary American Poetry* further disparaged such overglamorized critical episodes as mere "pot shots" and "sniper fire" only briefly interrupting poets' abilities to ignore the "battle lines."[19]

Allen planned his book as a showcase and manifesto for poets he grouped in five schools, who had "shown one common characteristic: a total rejection of all those qualities typical of academic verse."[20] His ideal was of poems that would give a sense of temporal immediacy, that would bring about what Frank O'Hara, one of Allen's new poets, famously joked would be "the death of literature as we know it."[21] Although not a poet, Allen's achievement as anthologist has been ranked as a major event in poetry of its time with Allen Ginsberg's *Howl* of 1956 and Robert Lowell's *Life Studies* of 1960: an effective instrument in turning numbers of poets in a new direction from the kind of contemporary writing represented in the three poets' rival anthology.[22]

The title of Allen's book calls its contributors *The New* generation of poets in America, meaning they are new in the sense of being the only true innovators, the sole originators of what is genuinely experimental in contemporary American poetry. As James Breslin has pointed out, there is "irony," unperceived by Allen, in his claim that his *new* poets constitute "our avantgarde, the true continuers of the modern movement in poetry."[23]

LITERARY HISTORIES

The first anthology in the prestigious Oxford series to collect twentiethcentury poems, *The Oxford Book of Modern Verse*, was made by Yeats and published three years before he died in 1939. In that year, Auden grieved over his death as a dark moment in history in his elegy—since become an anthology-piece—"In Memory of W. B. Yeats." In the same year, Auden wrote an essay titled "The Public v. the Late Mr. William Butler Yeats," in which he prosecuted his hero for the kind of anthology he made (where Auden is represented with others of his school). Coming from such an admirer as Auden, the attack shows what passionate irritation (some of it on aesthetic grounds, some on political) the anthology could provoke:

I challenge anyone in this court to deny that it is the most deplorable volume ever issued under the imprint of that highly respected firm which has done so much for the cause of poetry in this country, The Clarendon Press.[24]

Auden was only one of many contributors to the uproar that Yeats, one supposes knowingly, brought on by his choices of poems to put in or leave out, and by his introduction only obliquely explaining those choices. The anthology was described in various pitches of indignation or interest, but almost invariably with some irritation as "inexplicable," "eccentric," "perverse," or at best "extremely personal."[25]

Auden was also not alone in his judgment that Yeats's anthology constituted a breach of trust by its betrayal of readers' expectations for an *Oxford Book*. The series had from its beginning, when Quiller-Couch was invited to edit the comprehensively retrospective first volume, been guided by the principle that its "anthologies must include anthology pieces, old favourites the public would expect to find there."[26] From then on, the editors—professional anthologists or scholars, not poets—had acted on their understanding of what was also told to Yeats when he agreed to take on the modern anthology: that "a popular book for ordinary people to enjoy was intended."[27]

The officials of the press, one again assumes knowingly, took an uncharacteristic step when they decided to add a modern collection to their series, but the retrospective form and generalizing title lifted it out of the category of the anthology designed as a showcase for the work of a specialized group of immediately contemporary poets, or as a manifesto promoting the few only true practitioners of truly modern poetry.

The officers of the press could not have fully known the risk they were taking when they invited Yeats to make the anthology, but though they were handed a very different book from the kind they ordered, they were pleased that its provocation of controversy did not prevent it from selling well. Only a few months after its publication Yeats wrote to Dorothy Wellesley, whose poems filled a controversially large number of its pages: "The Oxford University Press has congratulated me on my 'courage' in stirring up 'such a hornet's nest' & offers me a further advance on royalties. Most of my critics are very vindictive, a sure sign that I have some where got down to reality."[28]

Although the intensity of the hostile response to the anthology may have surprised Yeats, there are convincing signs inside it and out—in his correspondence while he was working on it—of his intentions not to make it in the image of the expected *Oxford Book*. In his introduction we learn that he assumed authority to make it his book—one critic said it should have been titled "Mr. Yeats's Book of Modern Verse"—by virtue of having been chosen because he was a poet, and one almost at the end of a writing life that spanned the period of the anthology itself.[29] He wrote in the second sentence of the introduction: "Even a long-lived man has the right to call his own contemporaries modern."[30] Some reviewers granted Yeats the right to his assumed authority, and, in spite of their annoyance at his liberties in exercising it, welcomed the anthology as an "autobiography" by the century's greatest practitioner of poetry.[31]

In a letter to Olivia Shakespear written early in 1935, Yeats outlined his plan of "work as editor of *The Cambridge Book of Modern Verse*" (a curious lapse or else a joke, either suggesting he was not overawed by Oxford precedents):

I can never do any kind of work (apart from verse) unless I have a clear problem to solve. My problem this time will be: 'How far do I like the Ezra, Eliot, Auden school and if I do not, why not?' Then this further problem 'Why do the younger generation like it so much? What do they see or hope?' I am to write a long introduction.[32]

There is something very moving about the seventy-year-old poet searching in himself, and in the work of his contemporaries, for a way of understanding the period he was acknowledged to be master of, although it seems in this quotation that he might not always have felt assured of that eminence. He made his work as anthologist an occasion for introspection as well as prodigious reading, that would lead to a presentation of the history of modern poetry as he envisioned it.

Inside the anthology the procession of authors—their order dictated, or seeming to be, solely by their birth dates—makes a chronology of the period, but the choices of poets and poems (and the ghostly presences of those not chosen), along with some manipulations of sequence, turn chronology into critical interpretation. The temporal line becomes a personally conceived history of modernity from the chosen date of "three years before the death of Tennyson"—a convenient but as it happens also symbolic or magical figure—to three years before the death of Yeats.

The space belonging to Yeats's own poems is on pages about a fifth of the way into the book. This spatial sequence measures a temporal situation charged with meanings that could have prompted the aside he made in his introduction when discussing the last—that is, the youngest—poets in the anthology: "I too have tried to be modern."[33]

He could not point to the poets who preceded him in the century—who wrote fifty years before the making of the anthology and were unquestionably not his equals—as the leaders of a movement or advancers of a poetic tradition that nourished the work of his maturity. To find such a line or lineage, he had somehow paradoxically to project it into the future of poetry, represented by the pages in the anthology that followed his self-presentation.

The introduction begins with Yeats's youthful memories of Hopkins, Hardy, Bridges, Wilfred Scawen Blunt, William Henley, Oscar Wilde, all poets included in the earlier pages of the anthology, who were thought by Yeats's generation to be "Victorian, and the new generation was in revolt" against the discursiveness, diction, and rhetoric of Victorian poetry. Then "in 1900 everybody got down off his stilts," so proving that "Victorianism had been defeated," though Rudyard Kipling in particular seemed not to notice.[34]

As it happens, Kipling was born the same year as Yeats, who saw to it in arranging the contents that he and Kipling, his chief poetic rival early in the century, were not forced by the chronological order of authors' birth dates to appear side by side as exact contemporaries. He separated them by two authors also born in 1865. Kipling, branded a belated Victorian, of course comes first, represented by only two entries. He is followed by Arthur Symons, a member of the Rhymers' Club, with three translations, two of them from Verlaine (said by Yeats in the introduction to have been a hero of the first modern generation for his rallying cry "Wring the neck of rhetoric").[35] Then comes Henry Trench's balladlike "John Richepin's Song," representing the rescue by Yeats's generation of ballads and folk songs from Victorian misconception and neglect. Thirteen entries by Yeats—two of them ballads—follow, then nine by Dowson, another Rhymer, born in 1867.

After the first moderns, Yeats loosely, and with some inconsistencies and even contradictions, sorted out three later modern schools, the first of poets who "with much loss of self-control and coherence force language against its will into a powerful, artificial vividness."[36] These forcers of language in question are, in order of the introductory discussion, Edith Sitwell, Pound, Eliot.

Sitwell, it appeared to Yeats, was modern in transforming "exaggerated metaphors into mythology" to create "a nightmare vision like that of Webster, of the emblems of mortality." He saw her affinity with Eliot in that both were "haunted once again by the Elizabethan image" of bones, of skeletons, as in her "terrible Gehenna of the bone" and two lines from Eliot's "Whispers of Immortality": "No contact possible to flesh / Allayed the fever of the bone."[37]

In the body of the anthology, Yeats gave Sitwell's work twenty pages to Eliot's thirteen, though in the introduction he acknowledged, reluctantly and sardonically, that Eliot was the more influential: "Eliot has produced his great effect upon his generation because he has described men and women that get out of bed or into it from mere habit; in describing this life that has lost heart his own art seems grey, cold, dry."[38] This aspect of Eliot's early modernism is illustrated in Yeats's choice and placing first of "Preludes"; in his selection of later poems—"The Hollow Men," "Journey of the Magi," a passage from "The Rock." His only full-hearted praise was for lines from "Sweeney Among the Nightingales" where "The nightingales are singing near/The Convent of the Sacred Heart." For once only he heard Eliot's work speak "in the great manner" of "poems that descend from Shakespeare and the translators of the Bible":

> And sang within the bloody wood
> When Agamemnon cried aloud,
> And let their liquid siftings fall
> To stain the stiff dishonored shroud.[39]

These lines, one might say, are also in the manner of Yeats.

Pound's forcing of language consisted for Yeats in "more deliberate nobility" than he found in any other poet of that generation, but "constantly interrupted, broken, twisted into nothing" or into "flux" or "fragments" by "lack of form." Yeats probably attributed this "loss of self-control" in large part to Pound's "vers libre," although he did not quite say so, content to illustrate both formal attributes by a difficult fragment from "The Cantos." While crediting Pound in the introduction with "great influence, more perhaps than any contemporary except Eliot," Yeats again played it down in the text of the anthology by including, besides the fragment, only two more entries by Pound: "The River Merchant's Wife: a Letter" and a passage from "Homage to Sextus Propertius."[40]

A reader who skipped the introduction and turned directly to the poems, and many anthology readers favor such books precisely because they invite intermittent or scattered attention, would not know from the choice or arrangement of entries that "Auden, Day Lewis, and their school" of younger moderns were closely affiliated with the school of Pound and Eliot, and strongly influenced by them. Only comments dispersed through the last third of the introduction allow glimpses of this main line of development that Yeats was, intermittently, tracing.

He saw Pound's influence in the tendencies of these youngest modern poets to "lack of form and consequent obscurity"; from Eliot he said, wryly, they learned to combine with "the modern vocabulary" an "accurate record of the relevant facts."[41] Yet he could "admire" these young moderns for their "intellectual passion," their interest in "associations hitherto untravelled."[42] Though he admitted being unable to "find more than a half a dozen lyrics that I like, yet in this moment of sympathy I prefer them to Eliot, to my-self—I too have tried to be modern."[43] He felt in puzzled sympathy with Auden and the others in his movement, perhaps because they appeared to him to be modern heroic figures who have cast off "the manner writers hith-erto assumed," like "Shelley in relation to his dream, Byron, Henley to their adventure, their action."[44] In Yeats's credo, heroism is the property of all great poetry, including, he wanted to believe, his own.

This article of belief informs what many critics of the anthology found to be its most inexplicable and infuriating idiosyncrasy. That was its eleva-tion of the writings of W. J. Turner and—to even greater height—Dorothy Wellesley, as embodiments of another major movement in twentieth-century poetry; one that, "but for a failure of talent," Yeats claimed he would most like to have been part of. He felt stirred on looking into the po-ems of Turner and Dorothy Wellesley—he had just discovered her in an anthology made by Squire while reading for his own—by a sense that their work would help him to make a new beginning, to locate his own poems among the new ways of being modern.

About Turner's particular claim to importance Yeats had little to say in the introduction beyond that it was Turner who raised the rallying "cry, to gain upon the instant a control of plastic material, a power of emotional construction Pound has always lacked."[45] In the text Turner follows Eliot with only one entry between them, an arrangement that makes easily visible Yeats's priorities in displaying Turner's work over five more pages than Eliot's.

Dorothy Wellesley's entries fill only three more pages than Eliot's, but would have been given an even larger space if Yeats had not felt the uneasi-ness he explained to her in a letter written while the anthology was still in the making: "I found I had given more from you than from anybody else and this would not do, people would think it was friendship, especially as, I think, you come immediately before T. S. Elliot."[46] His memory here in-terfered with more than his spelling. It was Sitwell whose poems he placed just before Eliot's, but he admired Wellesley's work more than any other. It was distinguished for Yeats by the strength of its "new positive belief," whereas Sitwell, like Eliot, achieved "intensity from a deliberate re-molding or checking of past impulse, Turner much of his from a deliberate rejection of current belief."[47]

The poem of Wellesley's he admired most and placed to introduce her in the anthology, "Fire," seems to suggest what he meant by her "new positive belief." Opening with a Yeatsian line of stark lament—"The great stone hearth has gone"—over the destruction of tradition by "Modern man," it draws toward its conclusion with an exultant ceremony that returns "dead man" to his indestructible elements:

> Run with the torches, blaze the pyre,
> Far from town and street:
> Burn his body on the shore
> Where Earth, Air, and Water meet,
> As all poets know,
> As all dead men know.[48]

Yeats was inventing his own literary history by making Wellesley the leading figure of some sort of movement or school that seems to cohere only by virtue of its differences from the two modern schools of Pound and Eliot and of Auden. In a letter Yeats wrote to Wellesley while he was looking over the anthology in galley proof, he gave her so-called school a name: "Most of the moderns—Auden, Spender etc. seem thin beside the more sensuous work of the 'romantics.'"[49]

What he meant by the name, and where he placed the "romantics" on his map of modern verse is clarified by a passage in the introduction that the letter seems to be thinking about:

Edith Sitwell with her Russian Ballet, Turner with his *Mare Tranquillum*, Dorothy Wellesley with her ancient names—'Heraclitus added fire'—her moths, horses, and serpents, Pound with his descent in Hades, his Chinese classics, are too romantic to seem modern. . . .[50]

Within the construct of this personal literary history, Yeats made his choice and arrangement of his own poems, and fitted them into the space he had elaborately and circuitously prepared for them among the "romantics."

Perhaps by fine calculation, Yeats gave his own work almost exactly the amount of space he allowed for Eliot's, but he treated his own poems altogether differently. Eliot's are arranged in chronological order by the books they appeared in up to 1934, so that earlier and later examples of his poetry are distinct, allowing readers to find development, or disjunction, among them. The presentation of Yeats's poetry ignores chronology, except that it excludes everything written before 1913, so that his early poems trailing their clouds of Victorian poetic diction and rhetoric are expunged, even the elsewhere inescapable anthology-piece "The Lake Isle of Innisfree." Yeats placed four poems written between 1913 and 1919 in the approximate middle of the selection; the opening entry was written in 1929, the fragment that serves as an envoy in 1926, with two poems from the 1930s somewhere in between. Instead of chronology, which is the professed organizing principle of the anthology itself, in the order of Yeats's poems a unity of attitude within formal diversity seems to be the aim, as if the poems were fashioned to deny or defy time and loss.

The voice in the opening entry, "After Long Silence," is an old poet's, who delivers a "Speech" to the beloved of his youth as they sit together in the semidarkness that shields them from both the lamplight within and the outer darkness. His speech, taking up all but one word in seven of the eight lines that constitute the poem's single sentence, is structured as a logical discourse—"it is right / . . . That"—supporting "the supreme theme of Art and Song: / Bodily decrepitude is wisdom." The syntactical tightness of the formally punctuated lines, the pompously capitalized entities of "Art" and "Song," the desiccated abstractness of "Bodily decrepitude" make the speech sound almost like parody of the Victorian discursive moralizing and inflated rhetoric that modern poetry in all its varieties tried to escape. But the poem is not the speech, which comes to a stop just before the end of line 7:

> Bodily decrepitude is wisdom; young
> We loved each other and were ignorant.[51]

Oration gives way to intimate speaking, in simple words filled with sadness: we hear it most in the pause at the unpunctuated end of the line that briefly suspends "young." Now the complacent celebration of "Bodily decrepitude" seems, not only to the reader but to the poet, to be a euphemism meant, like the drawn curtains of what seems to be a Victorian parlor, to hide the actuality of old age and coming death. The unctuous rhyme in "supreme theme" sounds like self-mockery, which is at the same time a form of bravado in the face of what the old poet knows, what young lovers because "ignorant" ignore.

Bravado, or bravery, in the face of fatal knowledge—of age, loss, defeat, death—is celebrated one way or another in every one of the poems Yeats chose to represent him in his anthology. The actors are a woman speaking from the grave; another to her sleeping lover, Paris; heroes of the Irish struggle; an Irish airman who goes to death driven by "A lonely impulse of delight"; a "Friend whose Work has come to Nothing," who was "bred" to "Be secret and exult" in defeat.

Most of all, the actors are old poets like the maker of the anthology. They are sometimes self-deceiving and self-mocking, in "After Long Silence" and in the best-known of the entries, "Sailing to Byzantium." They are defiant and angry, disappointed and sad, or proud in their resignation in the elegiac closing stanza of the last poem before the envoy, "Coole Park and Ballylee, 1931":

> We were the last romantics—chose for theme
> Traditional sanctity and loveliness;
> Whatever's written in what poets name
> The book of the people; whatever most can bless
> The mind of man or elevate a rhyme;
> But all is changed, that high horse riderless,
> Though mounted in that saddle Homer rode
> Where the swan drifts upon a darkening flood.[52]

In the poem "We" are Yeats and his fellow Irish poets Synge and Lady Gregory. In the space of the anthology these "last romantics" are represented by Dorothy Wellesley. Yeats wrote in the introduction to the book of her verse that he persuaded her to collect, "When face to face with the problem that has perplexed us all, she unites a modern subject, a modern vocabulary with traditional richness."[53]

Yeats's choice and arrangement of his own poems in the anthology constitute a valediction formally closed by an envoy of lines from his translation of "Oedipus at Colonus," presented here as the last words spoken by an old hero at the threshold between life and death: "Never to have lived is best, ancient writers say, / / The second best's a gay goodnight and quickly turn away."[54] The anthology itself is valedictory, made that way by the autobiographical cast of the introduction and the treatment of Yeats's own poems in it.

Without contradicting this reading, letters written while he was in the last stages of putting together the collection tell us that his work on it turned into an act of rejuvenation. To Wellesley he wrote: "I have asked Macmillan to send my new book [*A Full Moon in March*]. I don't like it—it is a fragment of the past I had to get rid of," like all the poems written before 1913 that he kept out of the self-presentation he had just prepared. "The swift rhythm of 'Fire,' and the study of rhythm my work on the anthology entailed, have opened my door."[55]

It seems that the "clear problem" he had set himself to solve as anthologist—"How far do I like the Ezra, Eliot, Auden school, and if I do not, why not?"—led him to a sense of new possibilities for a poet writing in the present moment of literary history, and therefore changed his valedictory mood. The same letter begins an explanation of his personal reading of modern literary history with a phrase from a villanelle by Dowson placed in the anthology just after the envoy to Yeats's own poems: "'Bitter and gay,' that is the heroic mood. . . . a sense of something steel-like and cold within the will, something passionate and cold."[56]

Yeats wrote this letter in July of 1935, the same month he wrote "Lapis Lazuli," one of the greatest of his poems, which he included in a volume with the far from valedictory title *New Poems*. The poem celebrates the passion and coldness of artists who contemplate the "tragic scene": "Their eyes mid many wrinkles, their eyes, / Their ancient, glittering eyes, are gay." Its tone is not the valedictory sadness sounded in "We are the last romantics," but "Gaiety in the face of all that dread."[57]

When *The Oxford Book of Twentieth Century Verse* edited by Philip Larkin was published in 1973, Auden wrote one of the few favorable reviews of it. By contrast, Donald Hall, who had helped to make Larkin better known to American readers by including seven of his poems in *New American Poets of England and America*, condemned Larkin's anthology as severely as Auden had judged its predecessor: "Doubtless it is the *worst* anthology of modern poetry, with the possible exception of Yeats's."[58]

The *T.L.S.* reviewer, another contributor to the outcry that greeted Larkin's book, said that it "is an individual, even polemical, selection masquerading as a parade of the spirit of the age." While "not being preposterous, like Yeats's, it manages to be eccentric and institutional at the same time," perhaps meaning that it paid far less attention to experimental poets than to the Georgians and their little-known descendants.[59]

Larkin, in a letter of 1966, sketched an outline for his prospective editor of his approach to making the anthology that reads as if meant to encourage this hope:

I am sure my ideas concerning such a collection would develop in the course of its assemblage, but I should begin at any rate with the notion that it is not the business of an Oxford book of this character to be eccentric—in other words, I should aim to represent all verse writers who have made respectable reputations in this century, though the degree to which they were represented would depend on my own personal assessment of them.[60]

Words like "respectable" and "degree" must have sounded reassuring to the officers of the press after the outrage stirred by Yeats's scandalous omissions of some poets and immoderate offerings of others. The publishers could take as a further sign of moderation Larkin's statement of interest in how far the Georgians "represented an 'English tradition' that was submerged by the double impact of the Great War and the Irish-American-continental properties of Yeats and Eliot."[61] The English tradition was what Oxford anthologies were famous for representing.

Larkin's suggestion in the same letter for changing the title of the anthology was also calming to the fear that by choosing another poet as its editor the press was repeating its earlier risk-taking:

There is, I think, still a special overtone in the phrase 'modern poetry' (primarily one of experimentalism), but to concentrate on it would only impoverish choice, and I should prefer to interpret the phrase as 'twentieth century English verse.' Indeed the Delegates might like to consider substituting this form of words to distinguish this volume from its predecessor.[62]

Indeed, they did welcome the change, since experimentalism in poetry was not a specialty Oxford anthologies were expected to offer readers, and since the different title would widen the distance between their two overlapping collections of poems written in the twentieth century. So far as they hoped Larkin would give them a very different anthology from Yeats's, the publishers got what they wanted.

Dates dictated one large, unopinionated difference: *The Oxford Book of Modern Verse* spanned only the first third of the century, while *The Oxford Book of Twentieth Century Verse* was responsible for three quarters of it. Chronology also determined another difference, this one loaded with critical implications. While dating located Yeats's proper place about a fifth of the way along in the procession of poets in his book, in the sequence again determined by birth dates of poets in Larkin's (he turned fifty while working on it), his poems filled pages 537 to 542, only eighty pages from the end. Unlike Yeats, Larkin could discover a lineage for his poems by looking back through the century's poetry to trace its influences on his work up to the present. The two poets' different presentations of themselves were shaped by these determinations of time and space in the chronological arrangement of their anthologies.

The contrast between the two introductions is so starkly absolute as to be comical, as it seems likely Larkin intended. In the place of the colorful, digressive, opinion-filled autobiography that Yeats spread over some forty pages, Larkin gave his readers four paragraphs, only one saying anything— and that entirely general and evasive—about his grounds for choosing poems. His close friend and literary ally Kingsley Amis later hinted this might have been a practical joke that failed of its intended effect: that Larkin's "procedure" of "having no, or virtually no introduction at all" did "no good" in sidestepping the reviewers' game of contesting why Poet A was in and B out.[63]

The last sentence of Larkin's laconic introduction also dodges that sort of criticism by an innocent-seeming claim to have acted in his role as anthologist "not so much critically, or even historically, but as someone wanting to bring together poems that will give pleasure to their readers both separately and as a collection."[64] The readers, as distinct from the reviewers, were in fact pleased with *The Oxford Book of Twentieth Century Verse*. Like Yeats's anthology, Larkin's sold well in the midst of the critical uproar its unrevealing introduction failed to stave off.

The contrast of anthology makers in their contrasting introductions has its consequences in the very different arrangements the two poets gave to the selections in their books. By comparing their presentations up to and including their selections from Yeats's work, we can see Larkin, without ever saying so, giving his book the shape of an argument with its Oxford predecessor. His choices constitute an unspoken definition of his personal perspective, from which he rewrote the literary history of the period.

In the sequence of poets that fills the main body of each anthology, the first that the reader meets is Blunt, who died in 1922, the year Larkin was born. (By contrast, *The Faber Book of Modern Verse*, published the same year as Yeats's *Oxford Book* and in fourteen more impressions by 1948, begins with Hopkins, then Yeats.) Yeats presented four of Blunt's sonnets, one other short lyric, and a three-page fragment from a longer poem, prejudged in the introduction by the general understanding "that certain sonnets, lyrics, and stanzas of his were permanent in our literature."[65] Larkin, who made no comments on any poets in his radically short introduction, opened his anthology abruptly with a single sonnet by Blunt, likely to have been a surprise to readers in the 1970s, even to those who had heard the name.

The poet immediately following Blunt in each anthology is Hardy, who was born the same year. Yeats prepared readers for Hardy's four short entries by praising while mildly damning him for having mastered "the impersonal objective scene" though his work "lacked technical accomplishment."[66] The meager selection of Hardy's poems is then quickly outspaced by larger representations of Bridges, Hopkins, Lady Gregory, A. E. Housman, Rabindranath Tagore, and "Michael Field," and then by Yeats with thirteen poems, much the amplest selection to that point in the book.

After Larkin's strange opening with the one sonnet by Blunt, he offered what must also have been unexpected for its lavishness, a spread of twenty-seven poems by Hardy. Its abundance makes a clear and loud statement for itself, as if saying that there is an inexhaustible number of other Hardy poems as good that could have been chosen. Larkin might more intelligibly have opened the book and century with Hardy's poems, but by preceding them with Blunt's solitary entry he could pointedly invite a critical comparison of his literary history with Yeats's.

Hardy towers not only over Blunt, but above the other most heavily represented poets in Larkin's anthology. Yeats (an early master Larkin abandoned after having written "a great many" of what he looked back on as "sedulous and worthless Yeats-y poems") is represented by nineteen poems;[67] Auden (who also shifted allegiance from Yeats to Hardy) by sixteen; Sir John Betjeman by twelve; Graves by eleven; Eliot by nine (but they included "The Waste Land" and "Little Gidding"). Larkin's opening arrangement of poems declares Hardy the most powerful formative influence on twentieth-century poetry: not Yeats, and—as Yeats also tried, more nervously, to persuade in his anthology—not Eliot.

Larkin was as reticent, sometimes to the point of evasion, in answering interviewers' questions about his anthology as he was in the introduction to it. For example:

You only included six of your own poems in *The Oxford Book of Twentieth Century Verse* (as opposed, say, to twelve by John Betjeman). Do you consider these to be your half-dozen best, or are they merely 'representative'? I was surprised not to find 'Church Going,' arguably your single most famous poem.[68]

Larkin's response gives nothing away, by choosing to misunderstand or ignore what the interviewer was trying to find out:

My recollection is that I decided on six as a limit for my generation and anyone younger, to save hurt feelings. Mine were representative as you say—one pretty one, one funny one, one long one, and so on. As editor, I couldn't give myself much space, could I?[69]

Here by invoking his impartial limit of six poems, and willfully simplifying what the questioner meant by "representative," Larkin skirted the suggestion that there might be critical designs in his choice of poems to represent himself.

Nor does the selection he made show the kind of internal unifying preoccupation that holds together Yeats's self-presentation. Larkin arranged his six entries in order of the books they appeared in, but like Yeats he excluded his earlier work, the poems in *The North Ship* (in a letter he explained his preference for those that followed as being "much less poetic," that is, "much freer of the late Mr. W. B. Yeats").[70] Also like Yeats in his self-presentation, Larkin left out what the interviewer called his "single most famous poem," although he said about "Church Going" in another interview that "I certainly haven't revolted against the poem. It hasn't become a kind of *Innisfree*, or anything like that."[71]

It may be that he did not explain why he left out "Church Going" because to do so would have given away the design of his selection. The explanation seems to be implicit in the parts of his anthology so far discussed. They give extra emphasis to the presentation of Hardy as the embodiment of poetic tradition by diminishing the influence of Yeats, whereas "Church Going," though written later than the other poems Larkin banished, still shows the "poetic" influence of "the late Mr. W. B. Yeats" in its ascent to high rhetorical celebration of the empty church "where so many dead lie round,"

> because it held unspilt
> So long and equably what since is found
> Only in separation—marriage, and birth,
> And death, and thoughts of these—
>
> . . .
>
> A serious house on serious earth it is,
> In whose blent air all our compulsions meet,
> Are recognised, and robed as destinies.[72]

Yeats might have called this "Traditional sanctity," such as he celebrated in the penultimate stanza of "Coole Park and Ballylee" as he found it embodied in Lady Gregory's house:

> A spot whereon the founders lived and died
> Seemed once more dear than life; ancestral trees,
> Or gardens rich in memory glorified
> Marriages, alliances and families,
> And every bride's ambition satisfied.[73]

Inclusion of "Church Going" could have muddied what seems to have been Larkin's design to make the selection of his poems demonstrate his pure line of descent from Hardy.

Two pairs of quotations from poems by Hardy and Larkin can show the connections drawn between them in Larkin's selections, connections deeper and more pervasive than the echoes of Yeats in "Church Going." We can hear them in the quiet cadences, simple vocabulary, almost ordinary spoken syntax, underplaying of first-person pronouns, and the avoidance of esoteric and obscure effects in these lines from Hardy's "Where the Picnic Was":

> Where we made the fire
> In the summer time
> Of branch and briar
> On the hill to the sea,
> I slowly climb
> Through winter mire,
> And scan and trace
> The forsaken place
> Quite readily.[74]

and in these from Larkin's "Coming":

On longer evenings,
Light, chill and yellow,
Bathes the serene
Foreheads of houses.
A thrush sings,
Laurel-surrounded
In the deep bare garden,
Its fresh-peeled voice
Astonishing the brickwork.[75]

The quietness is not violated by the remembrance of Hardy's "The Dar-kling Thrush."

We can recognize in both poets what Yeats without enthusiasm called Hardy's mastery of "the impersonal objective scene," a common interest in observing the texture of detail in ordinary, modern English life. For instance in Hardy's "On the Departure Platform":

We kissed at the barrier; and passing through
She left me, and moment by moment got
Smaller and smaller, until to my view
    She was but a spot;

A wee white spot of muslin fluff
That down the diminishing platform bore
Through hustling crowds of gentle and rough
    To the carriage door.

Under the lamplight's fitful glowers,
Behind dark groups from far and near,
Whose interests were apart from ours,
    She would disappear[76]

and in Larkin's "The Whitsun Weddings":

At first, I didn't notice what a noise
    The weddings made
Each station that we stopped at: sun destroys
The interest of what's happening in the shade,
And down the long cool platforms whoops and skirls
I took for porters larking with the mails,
And went on reading.[77]

The unrhetorical style supports a cast of mind, an emotional tone that seems an expression of like temperaments, either natural or fashioned to present a poetic self. Even the sardonically funny titles of Hardy's "He Never Expected Much" and Larkin's "Nothing to be Said" epitomize their authors' dryly antisentimental, antipretentious skepticism.

Paradoxically, the contrasts between Larkin's treatment of poetry in this century and Yeats's expose odd likenesses. Neither poet produced what their publishers mainly wanted in an Oxford anthology, an uncontroversial retrospective representation of famous poets by their already well-known poems. Yeats made no apology for his extremely personal book; Larkin ruefully admitted to a friend while he was working on his that he was uneasy about it because, "as I feared, I am drawing English poetry in my own image."[78] He thought the book looked "very shaky" and vulnerable to attack: "It *is* a 'good bedside book,' and that's what people will hate. It's really the Oxford Book of *Nineteen & a Half Century's Right-Wing Animal-Lovers Verse*."[79] Still, a year after it appeared he exulted that Amis was to revise or remake *The Oxford Book of Light Verse* as a successor to Auden, saying "We shall have stamped our taste on the age between us in the end."[80]

What the anthologies by Yeats and Larkin have also in common is that their otherwise unlike readings of literary history push the revolutionary movement in twentieth-century poetry to the margins. They both made it seem an unEnglish aberration outside the main current, an ephemeral experiment, by contrast with *The Faber Book of Modern Verse* with its focus on advances in technical experimentation and consequent interest in American poets. What Larkin said in defense of his own anthology might almost as well have been said by Yeats, though without the opening mock-deprecation: "At any rate, I made a readable book. I made twentieth-century poetry sound nice. That's quite an achievement in itself."[81] By "readable" he meant easily accessible to the "ordinary people" postulated as readers of anthologies.

CODA

T. S. ELIOT'S IMAGINARY ANTHOLOGY

Auden reflected on the importance of retrospective anthologies to the making of poetry and of literary history in a lecture he gave as Professor of Poetry at Oxford in 1956. His view is informed by his fruitful personal use of anthologies both as reader and compiler:

Even a young poet knows or very soon will realize that, but for scholars, he would be at the mercy of the literary taste of a past generation, since, once a book has gone out of print and been forgotten, only the scholar with his unselfish courage to read the unreadable will retrieve the rare prize. How much Donne, even, would he have read, had it not been for Professor Grierson?[1]

To which many literary histories have in effect added the corollary question: how much would a young poet have read of Donne if it were not for Eliot's review of Grierson's anthology *Metaphysical Lyrics and Poems of the Seventeenth Century*?

Counter to the assumption implied in Auden's rhetorical question, Eliot as a young poet had read Donne well before 1921, the year he reviewed Grierson's newly published anthology, which in its preface proposed a revision of literary history by pronouncing Donne "the great master of English poetry in the seventeenth century."[2] Countering the many discussions that have credited Eliot's review as the initiating moment in the Donne revival, we have evidence of various earlier preparations for it. The particular evidence to the point here is in Eliot's poetry and criticism written before his public praise of Grierson's anthology.

Unlike Auden, Eliot never made an anthology, and he typically refused to let his poems be anthologized except by friends. In a letter he wrote to the *T.L.S.* in 1921 he complained of his inclusion in an anthology (Untermeyer's

Modern American Poetry) without permission: "On previous occasions, when compilers of such works have asked my consent, there have always been personal reasons for my willing compliance: here there would have been none."[3] In the same letter he made a public protest against the damage done by anthologies of living poets, which directly encouraged Graves's crusade against virtually all such collections of poetry.

Eliot's reviews of some anthologies that promoted contemporary poetry uncongenial to his own were in their more oblique way equally hostile. In 1917 in a review of Harriet Monroe's and Alice Corbin Henderson's *The New Poetry*, he made a gleefully parodic pronouncement on the importance of anthologies to the shaping of literary history:

> An anthology of contemporary verse can be a document of great importance for future generations. It ought not to contain many good poems, but a few; it ought to embalm a great many bad poems (but bad in a significant way) which would otherwise perish. Bad poems, from this point of view, need to be as carefully chosen as good; Miss Monroe and Mrs. Henderson have chosen wisely.[4]

His comments—in a less playful, sarcastic style—on *Georgian Poetry* in the *Dial* do not assign it even a ludicrous part in literary history, but banish it as a social phenomenon unassimilable by poetic tradition, and therefore beneath the contempt of criticism:

> I cannot see in the Georgian anthology any such influence as Wordsworth, Keats, and Shelley had upon Arnold, Tennyson, and Browning. The dulness of the Georgian Anthology is original, unique; we shall find its cause in something much more profound than the influence of a few predecessors. The subtle spirit . . . is not the shattered Keats but. . . . the insurgent middle class, Mr. Monro's General Reading Public.[5]

In the same year as this criticism and his letter of protest, Eliot wrote his unsigned review of Grierson's "excellent" anthology for the *T.L.S.* It became one of the best known and most influential of his critical writings, which must have been his intention for it when he had it reprinted in *Homage to John Dryden* in 1924 and again in *Selected Essays* in 1932 with the title "The Metaphysical Poets."

The chance to review the anthology may have been given to him by his editor because of Eliot's contributions in his capacity as the *T.L.S.* reviewer of books about Elizabethan and Jacobean drama, and because of his known interest in other writings of the period, or possibly he asked for the assignment. Whichever happened, the essay shows that he saw the publication of Grierson's book as an occasion to argue before an important group of readers for a realignment of poetic tradition that would serve him as poet: "May we not conclude, then, that Donne, Crashaw, Vaughan, Herbert and Lord Herbert, Marvell, King, Cowley at his best, are in the direct current of English poetry."[6] Eliot's magisterial "we" was supported by the power and prestige of the *T.L.S.*: he later recorded having felt "overawed" when he was interviewed for a position as one of its reviewers, because "to be invited to write for it was to have reached the top rung of the ladder of literary journalism."[7]

It is entirely in keeping with his habits of obliqueness and reserve, and more importantly with his early critical positions, for Eliot to have chosen not to make an anthology that would be a showcase for his own poems set among his personal choices of work by his contemporaries. Instead he chose to argue for his kind of poetry by promoting a collection of much earlier verse gathered by a scholar who wanted to reshape poetic tradition disinterestedly. Grierson did that, but in a way Eliot could describe in terms that located his own poems along a traditional line. This appropriation of Grierson's collection made it do the work for Eliot that other poets, Yeats and Larkin above all, have done by designing an anthology that writes literary history so that it accommodates their sense of their own poems in it.

Eliot's most famous essay, "Tradition and the Individual Talent," was placed first and dated 1917 in *Selected Essays* but was originally published in the *Egoist* in 1919.[8] In it he had spelled out some of the guiding premises his review of Grierson is specially predicated on: that the "poet must be very conscious of the main current, which does not at all flow invariably through the most distinguished reputations"; that "not only the best, but the most individual parts of his work may be those in which the dead poets, his ancestors, assert their immortality most vigorously"; and that only individual work so informed can be incorporated into the "ideal order" made by already "existing monuments" which is then "modified by the introduction of the new (the really new) work of art among them." This arrangement of monuments, what Eliot imagined *tradition* to be—"the whole of the literature of Europe" and "within it the whole of the literature of his own country"—has "a simultaneous existence and composes a simultaneous order."[9]

In the review Eliot acted on the first critical premise by retracing "the direct current" of English poetry so that it would be seen to flow through the poets demonstrated in Grierson's anthology and quoted in Eliot's discussion of it. He brought the second premise to bear on his own poetry only implicitly and retrospectively in the review: by the remarkable likenesses in one of his recently published poems to some of his most charged critical phrases in the review and to the quotations he chose in support of them. He acted out in his writings of this period the incorporation of his own work into the tradition, the literature of his own country.

The preparatory poem, "Whispers of Immortality," written contemporaneously with "Tradition and the Individual Talent," was first published three years before Grierson's anthology in the *Little Review*. It is built in two groups of four stanzas each that draw a sardonic contrast of Donne and the dramatist John Webster (who was included in the review as a metaphysical poet) with "our lot," a slang phrase referring in the poem most particularly to modern poets.

Looking back at the poem from the perspective allowed by its intimacy with the essay on tradition and the review of Grierson's anthology, the title "Whispers of Immortality" may suggest among its many innuendoes that in this early poem of Eliot's, "the dead poets, his ancestors, assert their immortality most vigorously." It may even hint that this new poet's inheritance descends to him from poetry of the seventeenth century and not from Wordsworth's ode on the "Intimations of Immortality."[10]

The simultaneous existence of the past in the present asserts itself in the first part of the poem by its remembrances of Donne's "The Relique," which Eliot admiringly quoted one line of in the review: "A bracelet of bright hair about the bone." He chose this line to illustrate how Donne got his "most successful and characteristic effects" by "brief words and sudden contrasts," by "telescoping of images and multiplied associations," devices of language that Donne shared with dramatists of his time, Webster named among them.[11]

The line from "The Relique" evokes "that effect of terror" Eliot associated with metaphysical poetry, and clearly wanted in the four opening stanzas of "Whispers of Immortality." There it is achieved most powerfully in the lines imagining Webster sexually "possessed" by the skeletons of "breastless creatures" leaning "backward" in the grave with a seductive "lipless grin":

> Daffodil bulbs instead of balls
> Stared from the sockets of the eyes![12]

The joining of "Daffodil bulbs" to eye "balls" missing from the "sockets" of a skull depends for its power to shock on the same sort of "sudden contrasts of associations" that Eliot found in Donne's joining of "bright hair" woven as a love token with the "bone" of a skeleton. That union, the triumph of sexuality that transcends death, figures what Eliot in the review described as "heterogeneity of material compelled into unity by the operation of the poet's mind." His discussion of the line from "The Relique" is his famous defense against D. Johnson's famous objection to metaphysical poetry: that in its conceits the "most heterogeneous ideas are yoked by violence together."[13]

The presence of "The Relique" in "Whispers of Immortality" shows more generally in the setting, diction, and grammar of Eliot's poem, and in the argument they express. This is the opening stanza of "The Relique":

> When my grave is broke up againe
>   Some second ghest to entertaine,
>   (For graves have learn'd that woman-head
>   To be to more then one a Bed)
>   And he that digs it, spies
> A bracelet of bright hair about the bone,
>   Will he not let'us alone,
> And thinke that there a loving couple lies,
> Who thought that this device might be some way
> To make their soules, at the last busie day,
> Meet at this grave, and make a little stay?[14]

Here, as in "Whispers of Immortality," the setting is a grave, fantasized as a bed where skeletons couple. Donne's poet-lover, speaking in the present and in the first person about "my grave," uses the future tense to imagine what a voyeuristic grave digger will someday spy on when he breaks open the grave: the poet's bones joined to his lady by her hair, making a "loving couple." The poet is both the passionate skeleton and a playful visionary who can see into the future as far as it will go, to "the last busie day." His two roles are united in the poem.

In Eliot's poem the dead poets do not speak. They are described by their modern descendant in the past tense and third person, but the description gives them a double role like the poet who speaks for himself in "The Relique." They are skeleton lovers: "Webster was much possessed by death" in the senses of being owned by it and erotically enslaved to it; Donne "knew the anguish of the marrow," knew of it but also knew it in the biblical sense of sexual penetration. At the same time—and the grammar in this first part of the poem carefully blurs their experience in death and life—Webster could see "the skull beneath the skin" and the "breastless creatures" buried "under ground" as if he were, like Donne, able to see and know "beyond experience."

In death or in life they are granted the visionary powers of the poet in "The Relique," while the modern poet who describes them in these stanzas demonstrates no more than that he has read them comprehendingly. He does not offer himself as a parallel figure. He uses the first person only in the self-deprecating, parenthetical "I suppose," and at the end of the poem in the modern, contemptuous phrase "our lot."

Still, Eliot's poem implies by the contrast between the first four stanzas and the last four that this modern poet's imaginative sympathy with the metaphysical writers allows him, in the first part, to re-create something like what he described in the review as the "rapid association" of their figures, using a diction that is characteristically "simple and pure," while the "*structure* of the sentences" is at times "far from simple; but this is not a vice; it is a fidelity to thought and feeling."[15]

By contrast the second part of Eliot's poem, all in the present tense, is a sardonic representation of modern experience rendered in a modern poem with a prostitute as muse: "Grishkin is nice," "Uncorseted, her friendly bust / Gives promise of pneumatic bliss" to be enjoyed in her modern bower, "a maisonnette." Far from expressing a sense of strangeness and terror, "Grishkin is nice" sounds like a smirking hint of salacious satisfactions; the "pneumatic" attractions of her "bust" prompt automatic lust.

She does not stir the deep and insatiable desires aroused by the "breastless creatures" who tormented Webster and Donne. They "knew that thought clings round dead limbs," whereas "our lot," the last two lines of

the poem tell us, "crawls between dry ribs / To keep our metaphysics warm."
As Eliot wrote in one of the most often quoted passages of his review:

A thought to Donne was an experience; it modified his sensibility. When a
poet's mind is perfectly equipped for its work, it is constantly amalgamating disparate experience; the ordinary man's experience is chaotic, irregular, fragmentary. . . . in the mind of the poets these experiences are always forming new
wholes.[16]

This power to "feel their thought" was lost to poets since the seventeenth
century, and with it the gift of association that brings together heterogeneous materials in a new and strange unity. The division of the last four stanzas
of "Whispers of Immortality" from the first four represents this too much
discussed "dissociation of sensibility."

In my reading of the poem as it is situated in the imaginary anthology,
the loss of associative power is acted out in the middle two of the last four
stanzas in the language of the modern poet representing "our lot":

> The couched Brazilian jaguar
> Compels the scampering marmoset
> With subtle effluence of cat . . .
>
> The sleek Brazilian jaguar
> Does not in its arboreal gloom
> Distil so rank a feline smell
> As Grishkin in a drawing room.

These lines, coming after the portrayal of Grishkin with all her synthetically
heightened attractions, link the two descriptions like terms in an implicit
simile in which heterogeneous materials are "yoked but not united" (as Eliot
granted Johnson to be true in some metaphysical poems, particularly
Cleveland's failures). The rubbery artificiality of Grishkin's bosom and her
"rank" animal smell (where we might expect seductively "strange synthetic
perfumes" like those of the woman in Part II of "The Waste Land") are
forced into proximity by the poet, so that the comparison—and pointedly
there are none in the stanzas about Webster and Donne—is made not to
work. That is, it fails to unite disparate materials as they are conjoined in
"bright hair about the bone" or "Daffodil bulbs . . . / Stare from the sockets
of the eyes."

Paradoxically, though, in the context of the poem and its place in the imaginary anthology, this failed comparison does work: as an effective representation of the failure, the dissociation, of modern poetic sensibility, from which English poetry could be rescued by recognition and appreciation of the metaphysical poets in the main tradition.

The extraordinary closeness of Eliot's language in his review to his earlier poem shows that he had formulated the revision of literary history argued in what became his famous essay "The Metaphysical Poets" well before Grierson's anthology gave him an occasion to announce it. The form of the review itself as it appeared in the *T.L.S.* suggests the possibility that Eliot had planned or written some or all of an essay on metaphysical poetry, and then seized the opportunity to adapt it as a review by referring to the anthology in a few sentences of the opening paragraph and then not again until the closing phrase of the last paragraph.

We know that Eliot had studied Donne as an undergraduate at Harvard; that he had recently been reviewing the dramatists of the period and had written an article on Donne's sermons; that he had poet friends who also read seventeenth-century poetry and recognized it the way Eliot described in a letter to Aldington, as an "excellent instrument."[17] He may also have known H. J. Massingham's *A Treasury of Seventeenth Century Verse* published by Macmillan in 1919. It contained eleven of Donne's love poems (nine of them including "The Relique" repeated among Grierson's nineteen), along with a generous presentation of Herbert's poems and more of Marvell's than Grierson included.

Massingham's introduction follows the pattern conventional in anthologies of justifying this one by its differences from others, for once genuine and important differences. His first purpose was to gather little-known poems and some "entirely new to the modern anthology"—"at a rough guess more than a fourth" of his choices—which were elsewhere available almost exclusively in "expensive, out of print, old, special or otherwise not easily accessible collections."[18] This was the kind of rescue operation that Auden valued in retrospective anthologies like Grierson's.

After explaining this antiquarian purpose of making the period "most neglected of any in English literature" better known, Massingham more apologetically proposed the critical aim of accomplishing a revision in literary history:

Donne, Spenser, and Jonson . . . all left their mark upon the age, and all were in point of time pretty strict Elizabethans. But Spenser and Jonson were a tradition; Donne a direct and overmastering influence. I therefore, and I believe legitimately, sallied forth and brought Donne into the fold.[19]

The introduction leads its defense—"sallied forth" suggests if not a battle at least a skirmish—of the "metaphysical lyric" or "Metaphysical School," "experimental in rhythm, rapidly transitional in effect, and uncertain in technique"—to the conclusion that the twentieth century has an "intimate fellowship with the seventeenth": "We can understand the *malaise* of many of these poets, the complex questionings and frustrations of some, the unrest and bitter awakening . . . in others."[20]

The resemblances between Grierson's realignment of poetic tradition and Massingham's earlier, more modest proposal show that an interested audience was preparing for a revival of Donne, and that anthologies could both reflect and contribute importantly to such a development. It helps to explain the reception of Eliot's essay "The Metaphysical Poets," although he at least pretended no awareness of its influence in a lecture he gave in 1926:

We have seen in the present century and increasingly within the last few years, an awakening of interest in this seventeenth-century poetry. However this arose, it undoubtedly contains besides pure literary appreciation, a consciousness or a belief that this poetry and this age have some peculiar affinity with our own poetry and our own age, a belief that our own mentality and feelings are better expressed by the seventeenth century than by the nineteenth or even the eighteenth. Donne is more frequently used as a critical measure than ever before.[21]

And by that critical measure, Eliot's poems could be folded into tradition.

Despite his mild disavowal, Eliot's use of Grierson's anthology as an instrument to refashion poetic tradition became itself an event in literary history. Although G. M. Young in 1936 (reviewing Yeats's revisionary anthology of modern verse) rightly protested the critical commonplace that Eliot initiated the revival of Donne, he reluctantly acknowledged its persistence as a myth. Contrary to general knowledge of "widespread interest in Donne towards the beginning of this century," he wrote, "it is one of the illusions of our age that Donne was invented by Mr. Eliot."[22]

What Eliot did invent was a way of shaping literary history in his own image by creating an imaginary anthology. The materials he used to make it are the interchanges among acts of criticism close in time of performance but different in kind: Grierson's choice and presentation of the seventeenth-century poems in his actual anthology; Eliot's own poem about those poems; and his prestigiously located review of them when they were situated in a retrospective collection that was itself one of a long line of respected anthologies with the Oxford imprint. The preface to this imaginary anthology was "Tradition and the Individual Talent."

Following the conventional practice of anthologists to justify their work, Eliot prepared for his imaginary anthology in the argument of "Tradition and the Individual Talent" that tradition is an "existing order" of poems "complete before the new work arrives," which must be "altered" as the new arrival "fits in" the order. In the same essay Eliot also justified the new order he created in his imaginary anthology by the different—in Donald Davie's view incompatible—figure of tradition as a "main current" that flows through an earlier and not necessarily major talent into the new one.[23]

In "The Poet in the Imaginary Museum," Davie asked what he called "the thousand-dollar question," how it is possible to "detect a main current through a simultaneous order?"[24] The answer, the response to Davie here proposed, may be in the nature of the anthology as a special kind of book actually embodied in Grierson's and conceptualized in Eliot's.

In one reading of the revisionary moment in literary history articulated in Eliot's imaginary anthology, the new arrival was Donne. A place in the order is made for his poems in Grierson's anthology, which is a selection from the whole of the literature of Donne's country (and Eliot's), where "The Relique" is judged as "fitting in." The timeless order is modified, and that readjustment is reified by retrospective anthologies beginning with Massingham's, where Donne now fills more space than Herrick. In another reading, only implicit in Eliot's review, the new arrival was Eliot, through whose poem "Whispers of Immortality" the "main current" flows from Donne.

It is to the point, to Eliot's point in his elaborate interweaving of texts, that these two readings are not contradictory. They are simultaneous, like the order of tradition and like poems in anthologies. Eliot's imaginary anthology is itself a figure that can reconcile his language for describing tradition as a simultaneous order and a flowing current, because in an anthology poems exist together in a space where there is no before or after except as they locate places in the book. This means that the current can flow backward and forward in the ordered disposition of the space that includes both Eliot's poem and Donne's. The anthology as a special kind of book is a paradigm for what Eliot understood tradition to be when he made his imaginary anthology: "an order which," to borrow Frank Kermode's words, "can be discerned in history but actually transcends it, and makes everything timeless and modern."[25]

Frost would not like to be caught in agreement with Eliot, but his figure for the tradition of poetry he claimed as his was an actual anthology, *The Golden Treasury*, and an imaginary one, "the English anthology."[26] Larkin, who kept a volume of Frost on a nearby shelf reserved for the poets who meant most to him, often expressed his opposition to Eliot by putting derogatory quotation marks around "tradition" and once famously calling it a "myth-kitty."[27] Even so, he arranged *The Oxford Book of Twentieth Century English Verse* to rescue from "the Irish-American-continental properties of Yeats and Eliot" what he called "an 'English tradition.'" This was the conceptual order he constituted in his actual anthology to make room for himself as the new "new arrival."

NOTES

NOTES

Introduction

1. W. H. Auden, *Edgar Allan Poe: Selected Prose, Poetry, and Eureka* (New York: Holt, Rhinehart and Winston, 1950), v.

2. John Stuart Mill, *Dissertations and Discussions* (London, 1859), I: 85.

3. Ezra Pound, *The Letters of Ezra Pound 1907–1941*, ed. D. D. Paige (London: Faber and Faber, 1951), 252.

4. Ezra Pound, *Poetry* 3 (1914): 137.

5. Robert von Hallberg, *American Poetry and Culture 1945–1980* (Cambridge, Mass.: Harvard University Press, 1985), 9.

6. John Wesley, ed., *A Collection of Moral and Sacred Poems* (Bristol, 1744); Henry Hobbs, ed., *Any Soldier to His Son*, 3d. ed., rev. (Calcutta: T. Spink, 1944); Laura Holloway, ed., *The Home in Poetry* (New York, 1884); Owen Moon, ed., *The Daffodil* (Woodstock, Vt.: Elm Tree Press, 1949); Robert Hass and Stephen Mitchell, eds., *Into the Garden* (New York: Harper Collins, 1993).

7. Frank McAlpine, ed., *Popular Poetic Pearls* (Philadelphia, 1887).

8. Geoffrey Grigson, ed., *The Gambit Book of Popular Verse* (Boston: Gambit, 1971).

9. Oliver Goldsmith, *Poems for Young Ladies* (London, 1767); Marguerite Wilkinson, ed., *Contemporary Poetry* (New York: Macmillan, 1923), xiv.

10. For a few examples of the various approaches to this area of study see: Richard Altick, *The English Common Reader* (Chicago: University of Chicago Press, 1957); Patricia Anderson, *The Printed Image and the Transformation of Popular Culture* (Oxford: Clarendon Press, 1991); John Barrell, *Poetry, Language, and Politics* (Manchester: Manchester University Press, 1988); Raymond Irwin, *The English Library* (London: George Allen and Unwin, 1966); Levin Schüking, *The Sociology of Literary Taste*, tr. Brian Battershaw (Chicago: University of Chicago Press, 1966); John Taylor, *Popular Literature and the Construction of British National Identity* (San Francisco: International Scholars Publications, 1997).

11. Craig Abbott, "Modern American Poetry: Anthologies, Classrooms and Canons," *College Literature* 17 (1990): 209–21; Alastair Fowler, "Genre and the Literary Canon," *New Literary History* 11 (1979): 97–119; Alan Golding, *From Outlaw to Classic* (Madison: University of Wisconsin Press, 1995), 3–40; Frank Lentricchia, *Modernist Quartet* (Cambridge, Mass.: Harvard University Press, 1994); Arthur Marotti, *Manuscript, Print, and the English Renaissance Lyric* (Ithaca, N.Y.: Cornell University Press, 1995); Douglas Patey, "The Eighteenth Century Invents the Canon," *Modern Language Studies* 18 (1988): 17–37.

12. Barbara Benedict, *Making the Modern Reader: Cultural Mediation in Early Modern Literary Anthologies* (Princeton: Princeton University Press, 1996), 28.

13. Sabine Haass, "Victorian Poetry Anthologies: Their Role and Success in the Nineteenth-Century Book Market," *Publishing History* 17 (1985): 51–64; Natalie Houston, "Valuable by Design: Material Features and Cultural Value in Nineteenth-Century Sonnet Anthologies" and Linda Peterson, "Anthologizing Women: Women Poets in Early Victorian Collections of Lyric," *Victorian Poetry* 37 (1999): 243–72, 193–209.

14. Elizabeth Pomeroy, *The Elizabethan Miscellanies* (Berkeley: University of California Press, 1973).

15. Raymond Havens, "Changing Taste in the Eighteenth Century: A Study of Dryden's and Dodsley's Miscellanies," *PMLA* 44 (1929): 501–36; James Tierney, "Relics from the cave of Dodsley," *T.L.S.* (Oct. 9, 1998): 27–28 [a review of Dodsley's *A Collection of Poetry By Several Hands*, ed. Michael Suarez (London: Routledge/Thoemmes, 1997)].

16. Robert McDowell, "The Poetry Anthology," *Hudson Review* 42 (1990): 594–608; Robert Ross, *The Georgian Revolt* (Carbondale: Southern Illinois University Press, 1965).

17. Dennis Taylor, "Hardy's Copy of *The Golden Treasury*," *Victorian Poetry* 37 (1999): 1–57.

18. Arthur Case, ed., *A Bibliography of English Poetical Miscellanies 1521–1750* (Oxford: Oxford University Press, 1935).

Chapter 1

1. Samuel Johnson, ed., *A Dictionary of the English Language* (London, 1755).

2. Martin Elsky, *Authorizing Words* (Ithaca, N.Y.: Cornell University Press, 1989), 112.

3. *Tottel's Miscellany*, ed. Hyder Rollins, rev. ed. (Cambridge, Mass.: Harvard University Press, 1965), I: 2.

4. Ruth Hughey, ed., *The Arundel Harington Manuscript of Tudor Poetry* (Columbus: Ohio State University Press, 1960). For discussions of manuscript anthologies, see: Julia Boffey, *Manuscripts of English Courtly Love Lyrics in the Later Middle Ages* (Dover, N.H.: D. S. Brewer, 1985); Mary Hobbs, *Early Seventeenth-Century Verse Miscellany Manuscripts* (Aldershot: Scholar Press, 1992).

5. Robert Dodsley, *A Collection of Poems in Six Volumes By Several Hands* (London, 1758), 333.

6. James Boswell, *Life of Johnson* (London: Oxford University Press, 1960), 979; Richard Wendorf, *Sir Joshua Reynolds* (Cambridge, Mass.: Harvard University Press, 1996), 30.

7. Thomas Warton, ed., *The Union: Or, Select Scots and English Poems* (London, 1753), preface.

8. William Cowper's library is a representative example documented by Geoffrey Keynes, *Transactions of the Cambridge Bibliography Society*, 3 (1959): 47–69. Along with Chapman's *Iliad*, some works by Shakespeare and Milton, and numerous volumes by eighteenth-century poets, Cowper's library included all six volumes of the Dryden/Tonson series, eleven of the Pope/Swift miscellany, and a volume of Vicesimus Knox's *Elegant Extracts*.

9. John Clarke, *An Essay Upon Study* (London, 1731).

10. Amelia Edwards, *A Poetry-Book of Elder Poets*, 1st ser. (Leipzig, 1878), viii.

11. William Shenstone, *Letters of William Shenstone*, ed. Duncan Mallam (Minneapolis: University of Minnesota Press, 1939), 277, 401.

12. Thomas Warton, ed., *The Oxford Sausage* (London, 1764). In the preface, the editor offers a reward of twelve sausages to anyone who will discover "the *Collector's* REAL Name," vii.

13. Peter Sutcliffe, *The Oxford University Press* (Oxford: Clarendon Press, 1978), 119.

14. F. Brittain, *Arthur Quiller-Couch* (Cambridge: Cambridge University Press, 1948), 39.

15. Paul Fussell, *The Great War and Modern Memory* (London: Oxford University Press, 1975), 159.

16. Sutcliffe, *Oxford University Press*, 119.

17. Ibid., 120.

18. Ibid.

19. Edmund Clarence Stedman, ed., *A Victorian Anthology* (Boston, 1895), xi.

20. Edmund Clarence Stedman, ed., *An American Anthology* (Boston, 1900), xxii.

21. Gaston Bachelard, *The Poetics of Space*, tr. Maria Jolas (Boston: Beacon Press, 1969), 85.

22. Roger Chartier, *The New Cultural History*, ed. Lynn Hunt (Berkeley: University of California Press, 1989), 167.

23. Marotti, *Manuscript and the Renaissance Lyric*, 288.

24. William Cullen Bryant, ed., *A Library of Poetry and Song* (New York, 1874), xxiv.

25. W. J. T. Mitchell, *The Language of Images* (Chicago: University of Chicago Press, 1980), 274.

26. Thomas Campbell, ed., *Specimens of the British Poets* (London, 1819), I: 195.

27. Compare comments on these titles by Wendy Wall, *The Imprint of Gender* (Ithaca: Cornell University Press, 1993), 103–4.

28. George Crabbe, *The Library* (London, 1781), 10.

29. Bertrand Bronson, *Facets of the Enlightenment* (Berkeley: University of California Press, 1968), 352.

30. Robert Dodsley, *The Correspondence of Robert Dodsley 1733–1764*, ed. James Tierney (Cambridge: Cambridge University Press, 1988), 135.

31. Elizabeth Cooper, *The Muses Library* (1737).

32. Sir Walter Besant, *Autobiography of Sir Walter Besant* (London: Hutchinson, 1902), 37–38.

33. Charles Lamb, *The Letters of Charles Lamb*, ed. E. V. Lucas (New Haven: Yale University Press, 1935), II: 48–49.

34. D. F. McKenzie, *Bibliography and the Sociology of Texts* (London: British Library, 1986), 8. See also: D. F. McKenzie, *Buch und Buchhandel in Europa*, ed. Giles Barber and Berhard Fabian (Hamburg: Ernst Hauswedell, 1981), 81–126; Stanley Morison, *Politics and Script*, ed. Nicolas Barker (Oxford: Clarendon Press, 1972); Roger Stoddard, *Printing History*, 9 (1987): 2–14.

35. Elizabeth Bishop, *Questions of Travel* (New York: Farrar, Straus, Giroux, 1965), 80–81.

36. Elizabeth Bishop, *Geography III* (New York: Farrar, Straus, Giroux, 1976), 3–8.

37. John Frederick Nims, ed., *The Harper Anthology of Poetry* (New York: Harper and Row, 1981), 652. Bishop's letter, written the day of her death, is quoted in part in *One Art*, ed. Robert Giroux (New York: Farrar, Straus, Giroux, 1994), 638–39.

38. Robert Frost, *The Letters of Robert Frost to Louis Untermeyer* (New York: Holt, Rhinehart and Winston, 1963), 183; Wallace Stevens, *Letters of Wallace Stevens*, ed. Holly Stevens (New York: Alfred Knopf, 1966), 250.

39. Helen Vendler, ed., *The Harvard Book of Contemporary American Poetry* (Cambridge, Mass.: Harvard University Press, 1985), 414.

40. Stuart Freibert and David Young, *The Longman Anthology of Contemporary American Poetry* (New York: Longman, 1989), 39.

41. Seamus Heaney and Ted Hughes, eds., *The Rattle Bag* (London: Faber and Faber, 1982), 19.

42. William Thynne, *The workes of Geffray Chaucer* (London, 1532), preface.

43. Gwenllian Palgrave, *Francis Turner Palgrave* (London, 1899), 66.

44. Ibid.

45. These are the titles of books by: Barnabe Googe, Alexander Pope, Elizabeth Barrett Browning, Marianne Moore, Robert Browning, George Meredith, Seamus Heaney, Edmund Spenser, Abraham Cowley, Walt Whitman, Imamu Amiri Baraka.

Chapter 2

1. Francis Turner Palgrave, ed., *The Treasury of Sacred Song* (Oxford, 1889), viii.

2. Richard Chenevich Trench, ed., *A Household Book of English Poetry* (London, 1868), v.

3. Ferdinand Earle, ed., *The Lyric Year* (New York: Mitchell Kennerly, 1912), vii.

4. Ernest Rhys, ed., *The New Golden Treasury of Songs and Lyrics* (London: J. M. Dent, 1914), vii.

5. T. Earle Welby, ed., *The Silver Treasury of English Lyrics* (New York: Dial, 1925), viii.

6. Louis Untermeyer, ed., *The Book of Living Verse* (New York: Harcourt, Brace, 1932), vi.

7. Helen Gardner, ed., *The New Oxford Book of English Verse 1250–1950* (Oxford: Oxford University Press, 1972), v.

8. C. Day Lewis, ed., *The Golden Treasury* (London: Collins, 1954), 5.

9. Laurence Binyon, ed., *The Golden Treasury* (London: Collins, 1924), 15; Oscar Williams, ed., *F. T. Palgrave's The Golden Treasury* (New York: New American Library, 1953); John Press, ed., *The Golden Treasury* (London: Oxford University Press, 1964, 1994); Walter Barnes, ed., *Palgrave's The Golden Treasury* (Chicago: Row, Peterson, 1915).

10. Day Lewis, *Golden Treasury*, 15.

11. Christopher Ricks, ed., *The Golden Treasury* (London: Penguin, 1991).

12. Francis Turner Palgrave, ed., *The Golden Treasury* (London, 1883), 10.

13. Francis Turner Palgrave, *The Golden Treasury* (London, 1861), preface. Unless otherwise specified, all references to *The Golden Treasury* are to this first edition. All prose quotations from it are cited in the end notes; the locations of poems are indicated in the text by the roman numeral given them in this edition in all its reprints.

14. John Churton Collins, *Ephemera Critica* (New York: E. P. Dutton, 1902), 251.

15. Palgrave, *Golden Treasury*, preface.

16. Ibid.

17. Churton Collins, *Ephemera Critica*, 251.

18. Palgrave, *Golden Treasury*, preface. Herbert Tucker has suggested to me that *fitness* here may refer also to Spencerian and Darwinian discussions of evolution.

19. Ricks, *Golden Treasury*, 468.

20. Palgrave, *Golden Treasury*, preface.

21. Ibid., 309, 311; 309, 321; 309, 319.

22. Ibid., dedication.

23. Ibid., preface.

24. Haass, "Victorian Poetry Anthologies," 55, 53.

25. Charles Mackay, *The Home Affections* (London, 1858), vii–viii.

26. G. Palgrave, *Palgrave*, 65.

27. Palgrave, *Golden Treasury*, preface.

28. G. Palgrave, *Palgrave*, 71.

29. Anonymous review, *Fraser's Magazine* 64 (Oct. 1861), reprinted in Ricks, *Golden Treasury*, 459–60.

30. Day Lewis, *Golden Treasury*, 15–16.

31. Matthew Arnold, *Essays Literary and Critical* (London: J. M. Dent, 1907), 45. One might dispute Arnold's own delicacy of feeling in singling out from the many much more richly suggestive juxtapositions this unsubtle pairing of contrasting moods as the poets contemplate the end of "life" just before the end of *The Golden Treasury*.

32. Palgrave, *Golden Treasury*, preface.

33. Charles Anderson Dana, ed., *The Household Book of Poetry* (New York, 1858), preface.

34. Charles Graves, *Life and Letters of Alexander Macmillan* (London: Macmillan, 1910), 170.

35. Amy Woolner, *Thomas Woolner, R.A.* (London: Chapman and Hall, 1917), 199.

36. Giraldus [William Allingham], ed., *Nightingale Valley* (London, 1860), v.

37. Palgrave, *Golden Treasury*, preface.

38. Ibid.

39. Woolner, *Thomas Woolner*, 199.

40. Palgrave, *Golden Treasury*, preface.

41. Ibid., 308.

42. Ibid.

43. Ibid., 311.

44. Ibid.

45. Ibid., 316.

46. Ibid., 316–17.

47. Francis Turner Palgrave, *Quarterly Review* 112 (1862): 157.

48. Palgrave, *Golden Treasury*, preface.

49. Thomas Warton, *The History of English Poetry* (London, 1774–83), III: 490; Robert Southey, ed., *Specimens of the Later English Poets* (London, 1807), I: xxiii; John Churton Collins, *Studies in Poetry and Criticism* (London: George Bell, 1905), 6.

50. Palgrave, *Golden Treasury*, 320.

51. Walter Jackson Bate, *John Keats* (Cambridge, Mass.: Harvard University Press, 1963), 88.

52. Palgrave, *Golden Treasury*, 320.

53. T. S. Eliot, *Selected Essays* (New York: Harcourt, Brace, 1932), 7.

54. Robert Graves, *Collected Writings on Poetry*, ed. Paul O'Prey (Manchester: Carcanet Press, 1995), 400.

55. A. T. Quiller-Couch, ed., *The Oxford Book of English Verse 1250–1900* (Oxford: Clarendon Press, 1900), vii–viii. All prose quotations from this edition are cited in end notes. The locations of poems are indicated in the text by the number given to them in this edition in all its reprints.

56. Ibid., x.

57. Robert Bridges, *The Correspondence of Robert Bridges and W. B. Yeats*, ed. Richard Finneran (London: Macmillan, 1977), 24.

58. Robert Bridges, *The Selected Letters of Robert Bridges*, ed. Donald Stanford (Newark: University of Delaware Press, 1984), II: 661, 675, 661.

59. Bridges, *Correspondence with Yeats*, 28.

60. Ibid., 29.

61. Robert Bridges, ed., *The Spirit of Man* (London: Longmans, 1916), preface.

62. Ibid. The omission of page numbers throughout the entire book was perhaps another, and still more extreme, effort to avoid distracting the reader's attention from the pure text.

63. Walter de la Mare, *T.L.S.* (Feb. 3, 1916), 49.

64. Bridges, *Spirit of Man*, note to entry 135.

65. De la Mare, *T.L.S.*, 50.

66. Theresa Whistler, *Imagination of the Heart* (London: Duckworth, 1993), 322.

67. Day Lewis, *Golden Treasury*, 15.

68. Walter de la Mare, *Come Hither* (New York: Alfred Knopf, 1923), 17, 281.

69. Elizabeth Bishop, *Poetry* 93 (1958): 51.

70. W. H. Auden, *The Dyer's Hand* (New York: Random House, 1962), 36; Humphrey Carpenter, *W. H. Auden* (Boston: Houghton, Mifflin, 1981), 34.

71. Bishop, *Poetry*, 53.

72. Ibid., 51, 53.

73. George Moore, *Pure Poetry* (London: Nonesuch, 1924); Ezra Pound, *Profile* (Milan: Typograffi Card. Ferrari, 1932); Aldous Huxley, *Texts & Pretexts* (London: Chatto and Windus, 1933); W. H. Auden, *A Certain World* (New York: Viking, 1970).

74. F. O. Matthiessen, ed., *The Oxford Book of American Verse* (New York: Oxford University Press, 1950), ix–xii.

75. Mill, *Dissertations and Discussions*, 85.

76. Gardner, *New Oxford Book*, vii.

77. Ibid., v.

78. Palgrave, *Quarterly Review*, 146.

79. Palgrave, *Golden Treasury*, 316–17.

80. Ibid., 308.

Chapter 3

1. George Gascoigne, *A Hundreth Sundrie Flowres* [from the 1st ed., 1573] (London: Frederick Etchells and Hugh Macdonald, 1926), 10, 31.

2. George Gascoigne, *Certayne Notes of Instruction* in *Elizabethan Critical Essays*, ed. G. G. Smith (Oxford: Clarendon Press, 1904), I: 55.

3. Gascoigne, *Hundreth Sundrie Flowres*, 8.

4. All quotations from poems in *Songes and Sonettes* are taken from Rollins's revised edition. Their locations are indicated by the Arabic numeral given in this edition. Prose quotations are cited in endnotes.

5. Gardner, *New Oxford Book*, 946.

6. John Skelton, *The Poetical Works of John Skelton*, ed. Alexander Dyce (New York: AMS Press, 1965), 378.

7. George Puttenham, *The Arte of English Poesie,* ed. Gladys Willcock and Alice Walker (Cambridge: Cambridge University Press, 1970), 60.

8. *Tottel's Miscellany*, II: 94.

9. Richard Harrier, *The Canon of Sir Thomas Wyatt's Poetry* (Cambridge, Mass.: Harvard University Press, 1975), 101.

10. *Tottel's Miscellany*, II: 94.

11. Thomas Percy, ed., *Reliques of Ancient English Poetry*, 4th ed. (London, 1794), I: xvii. Except where otherwise noted, the fourth edition has been used throughout this discussion because it is the most fully corrected and improved.

12. John Hales and Frederick Furnivall, eds., *Bishop Percy's Folio Manuscript* (London, 1867), I: xvii.

13. Thomas Warton, *The Correspondence of Thomas Percy and Thomas Warton*, ed. M. G. Robinson and Leah Dennis, in *The Percy Letters*, ed. David Nichol Smith and Cleanth Brooks (Louisiana State University Press, 1951), 113.

14. Anonymous writer, *Gentleman's Magazine* 63 (Aug. 1793): 704.

15. Percy, *Reliques*, I: xiv.

16. Ibid.

17. Ibid., 232–33.

18. *England's Helicon*, ed. Hyder Rollins (Cambridge, Mass.: Harvard University Press, 1935), I: 184–85.

19. Thomas Percy, *Reliques of Ancient English Poetry* (London, 1765), I: 199–200.

20. Percy, *Reliques*, I: 234–35.

21. Charles Gayley and Clement Young, eds., *The Principles and Progress of English Poetry* (New York: Macmillan, 1904), xii.

22. W. H. Auden and Norman Holmes Pearson, eds., *Poets of the English Language* (New York: Viking, 1950), I: vii.

23. Christopher Ricks, ed., *The Oxford Book of English Verse* (Oxford: Clarendon Press, 1999), preface.

24. Arthur Eastman et al., eds., *The Norton Anthology of Poetry* (New York: W. W. Norton, 1970), x.

25. Sir Thomas Wyatt, *Collected Poems of Sir Thomas Wyatt*, ed. Kenneth Muir and Patricia Thomson (Liverpool: Liverpool University Press, 1969), 1–2. I have quoted Wyatt's poems from this edition rather than Harrier's (but with some emendations based on Harrier's transcription) because the markings used by him in reproducing the text of the Egerton manuscript are not familiar to readers untrained in transcription.

26. *Tottel's Miscellany*, II: 94.

27. Ibid., 95.

28. Wyatt, *Collected Poems*, 27.

29. John Thompson, *The Founding of English Metre* (New York: Columbia University Press, 1989), 15–29.

30. Sir Thomas Wyatt, *The Works of Henry Howard and of Sir Thomas Wyatt*, ed. G. F. Nott (London, 1816), II: 23.

31. Ibid., 546.

32. Palgrave, *Golden Treasury*, preface.

33. For comments on Palgrave's omissions see the notes to Ricks, *Golden Treasury*, 470–512.

34. Thomas Carew, *Poems* (London, 1640), 29.

35. Percy, *Reliques*, III: 247.

36. Agnes Replier, ed., *A Book of Famous Verse* (Boston, 1894), 62; Burton Stevenson, ed., *The Home Book of Verse*, 3d ed., rev. (New York: Henry Holt, 1918), II: 2836.

37. Hales and Furnivall, *Percy's Folio Manuscript*, I: xx.

38. Ibid., II: xxix–xxx.

Chapter 4

1. John Dryden, *The Letters of John Dryden*, ed. Charles Ward (New York: AMS Press, 1965), 23.

2. He retained the dedication even after the death of the countess, probably at least in part to preserve the suggestion of a family connection, having changed his name from Piercy to Percy. See Bertram Davis, *Thomas Percy: A Scholar-Cleric in the Age of Johnson* (Philadelphia: University of Pennsylvania Press, 1989), 109.

3. Southey, *Specimens*, I: iii.

4. Henry Headley, ed., *Select Beauties of Ancient English Poetry* (London, 1787), I: vii.

5. Sir Egerton Brydges, *Censura Literaria*, 2d ed. (London, 1815), I: iii.

6. Trench, *Household Book*, vi–vii.

7. Quiller-Couch, *Oxford Book*, ix.

8. Ibid., ix–x.

9. Walter Learned, ed., *A Treasury of Favorite Poems* (New York, 1893), xi.

10. J. Churton Collins, ed., *A Treasury of Minor British Poetry* (London, 1896), vii–viii.

11. Ibid., ix.

12. Ibid., viii.

13. H. J. Massingham, ed., *A Treasury of Seventeenth Century English Verse* (London: Macmillan, 1919), ix–x.

14. R. S. Forsythe, *PMLA* 40 (1925): 701.

15. See: Millar Maclure, *The Poems of Christopher Marlowe* (London: Methuen, 1968), xxxvii; Suzanne Woods, *Huntington Library Quarterly* 34 (1970): 25–33.

16. *England's Helicon*, 3.

17. Percy, *Reliques*, I: 234.

18. Brydges, *Censura Literaria*, ix.

19. Percy, *Reliques*, I: xiv.

20. Ibid, II: 332.

21. *England's Helicon*, 5.

22. Sir Philip Sidney, *An Apologie for Poetrie* in *Elizabethan Critical Essays*, I: 203.

23. Palgrave, *Golden Treasury*, 309.

24. William Empson, *Some Versions of Pastoral* (New York: New Directions, 1974), 22.

25. Paul Alpers, *What is Pastoral?* (Chicago: University of Chicago Press, 1996), 223.

26. *Tottel's Miscellany*, II: 82.

27. Sidney, *Apologie for Poetrie*, 201.

28. John Cotgrave, *The English Treasury of Wit and Language* (London, 1655), To the Courteous Reader.

29. Clarke, *Essay on Study*, 223.

30. Vicesimus Knox, *The Works of Vicesimus Knox* (London, 1824), II: 390.

31. John Greenleaf Whittier, ed., *Songs of Three Centuries* (Boston, 1877), iii, vi.

32. Robert Bell, ed., *Art and Song* (London, 1868), xi.

33. Palgrave, *Golden Treasury*, preface.

34. Ibid.

35. Derek Attridge, *Rhythms of English Poetry* (London: Longman, 1982), 83.

36. Ibid.

37. Ibid., 82.

38. John Hollander, *Vision and Resonance*, 2d ed. (New Haven: Yale University Press, 1985), 41.

39. Sidney, *Apologie for Poetrie*, 159.

40. Ibid., 156.

41. Palgrave, *Golden Treasury*, preface.

42. The texts of the poems quoted are: Thomas Carew, *Poems* (London, 1640), 180–81; George Herbert, *The Temple* ([facsimile of the first edition], 1633); Robert Herrick, *Hesperides* (London, 1648), 144; Ben Jonson, *Cynthias Revels* (V: vi), in *The workes of Beniamin Jonson* (London, 1616), 254; Edmund Waller, *Poems* (London, 1645), 48–49.

43. Hollander, *Vision and Resonance*, 247.

44. Renato Poggioli, *The Oaten Flute* (Cambridge, Mass.: Harvard University Press, 1975), 41.

45. Massingham, *Treasury*, 347.

46. David Daiches and William Charvat, eds., *Poems in English* (New York: Ronald Press, 1950), 660–61.

47. Oscar Williams, ed., *Master Poems of the English Language* (New York: Trident, 1966), 149.

48. Massingham, *Treasury*, xii; Herbert Grierson, ed., *Metaphysical Lyrics and Poems of the Seventeenth Century* (Oxford: Clarendon Press, 1921), xxxviii.

49. Karl Shapiro, *Poetry* 135 (1979), 38.

50. Cleanth Brooks and Robert Penn Warren, eds., *Understanding Poetry* (New York: Henry Holt, 1960), 20.

51. Ibid., 309–10.

52. Grierson, *Metaphysical Lyrics*, xxxvii–xxxviii, xxi.

53. Robert Penn Warren and Albert Erskine, eds., *Six Centuries of Great Poetry* (New York: Dell, 1972), 257–58.

54. Ibid., 258–59.

Chapter 5

1. Edward Thomas, ed., *This England* (London: Oxford University Press, 1915); Dorothy Carrico Wood, *This Nation* (Cleveland: World, 1969).

2. G. S. Rousseau, ed., *Goldsmith: The Critical Heritage* (London: Routledge and Kegan Paul, 1974), 244.

3. John Foster, *The Life and Adventures of Oliver Goldsmith* (London, 1848), 538.

4. George Hill, ed., *Johnsonian Miscellanies* (Oxford, 1897), II: 2.

5. Knox, *Elegant Extracts*, vii.

6. James Prior, *The Life of Oliver Goldsmith* (London, 1837), II: 264.

7. Ralph Waldo Emerson, *Emerson in His Journals*, ed. Joel Porte (Cambridge, Mass.: Harvard University Press, 1982), 43.

8. Foster, *Life of Goldsmith*, 537.

9. Dodsley, *Collection of Poems*, VI: 333.

10. Shenstone, *Letters*, 277.

11. Ibid., 400.

12. Ibid., 401.

13. Oliver Goldsmith, *Collected Works of Oliver Goldsmith*, ed. Arthur Friedman (Oxford: Clarendon Press, 1966), I: 112.

14. Ibid., 317.

15. Oliver Goldsmith, ed., *The Beauties of English Poesy* (London, 1767), I: i, iii.

16. Richard Altick, *Bulletin of the New York Public Library* 66 (1962), 403.

17. Knox, *Elegant Extracts*, vi–vii.

18. Ibid., iv, vi.

19. Samuel Johnson, *Lives of the Poets* (London: Oxford University Press, 1964), II: 460.

20. Ibid., 463–64.

21. Empson, *Some Versions of Pastoral*, 5. Pierre Bourdieu's phrase gave the title and focus to John Guillory, *Cultural Capital* (Chicago: University of Chicago Press, 1993), 133.

22. Rousseau, *Goldsmith: Critical Heritage*, 243, 244, 111, 295, 295–96, 109, 336, 244.

23. Edward McAdam, "Goldsmith, the Good-Natured Man," in *The Age of Johnson*, ed. Frederick Hilles (New Haven: Yale University Press, 1949), 45.

24. Rousseau, *Goldsmith: Critical Heritage*, 295.

25. Goldsmith, *Collected Works*, IV: 287–304. All quotations from the poem are from this edition and are located in the text by line numbers.

26. Prior, *Life of Goldsmith*, II: 243–44.

27. Edward Casey, *Senses of Place*, ed. Stephen Feld and Keith Basso (Sante Fe: School of American Research Press, 1996), 27.

28. Foster, *Life of Goldsmith*, 543; Prior, *Life of Goldsmith*, II: 251.

29. Thomas Percy, *The Life of Dr. Oliver Goldsmith* (London, 1777), 26.

30. James Boswell, *Boswell's Life of Johnson* (London: Oxford University Press, 1960), 918; Foster, *Life of Goldsmith*, 537.

31. Matthew Arnold, *Reports on Elementary Schools 1852–1882*, ed. Sir Francis Sandford (London, 1889), 227–28.

32. Matthew Arnold, *Essays in Criticism* (London: Macmillan, 1903), III: 331–33.

33. Raymond Williams, *Culture and Society* (New York: Harper and Row, 1958), 33–34.

34. Carl Dawson, ed., *Matthew Arnold: The Poetry: The Critical Heritage* (London: Routledge and Kegan Paul, 1973), 193, 266, 319.

35. Ibid., 163, 185.

36. Ibid., 265, 256.

37. Ibid., 291.

38. Ibid., 384.

39. Ibid., 433.

40. Ibid., 392.

41. Ibid., 403.

42. Matthew Arnold, *The Poems of Matthew Arnold*, ed. Sir Arthur Quiller-Couch (Oxford: Oxford University Press, 1920), iv.

43. Geoffrey and Kathleen Tillotson, *Mid-Victorian Studies* (London: Athlone Press, 1965), 154.

44. Stedman, *Victorian Anthology*, xi–xii.

45. Gardner, *New Oxford Book*, v.

46. Untermeyer, *Book of Living Verse*, v.

47. Max Eastman, ed., *Anthology for the Enjoyment of Poetry* (New York: Charles Scribner's Sons, 1939), xv, xiii.

48. Lionel Trilling, ed., *The Experience of Literature* (New York: Holt, Rhinehart and Winston, 1967), 900.

49. Dawson, *Arnold: Critical Heritage*, 267.

50. Ibid., 186.

51. Ibid., 210.

52. Ibid., 282.

53. Ibid., 385.

54. Ibid., 203.

55. Ibid., 229.

56. Stephen Kern, *The Culture of Time and Space* (Cambridge, Mass.: Harvard University Press, 1983).

57. Dawson, *Arnold: Critical Heritage*, 331.

58. Ibid., 210.

59. Ibid., 262–63.

60. T. S. Eliot, *The Use of Poetry and the Use of Criticism* (London: Faber and Faber, 1933), 105–6.

61. Richard Poirier, *Critics on Robert Lowell*, ed. Jonathan Price (Coral Gables: University of Miami Press, 1972), 92.

62. Kenneth Allott, ed., *Matthew Arnold* (London: G. Bell, 1975), 65.

63. William Lisle Bowles, *The Poetical Works of William Lisle Bowles*, ed. George Gilfillan (Edinburgh, 1855), 12.

64. William Wordsworth, *Poetical Works*, ed. Thomas Hutchinson, rev. Ernest de Selincourt (Oxford: Oxford University Press, 1978), 243. Keats's parody is quoted by Robert Graves, *Collected Writings*, 445.

65. Wordsworth, *Poetical Works*, 276–77.

66. Dwight Culler, *Imaginative Reason* (New Haven: Yale University Press, 1966), 399n14.

67. Matthew Arnold, *The Poems of Matthew Arnold*, 2d ed., ed. Miriam Allott (London: Longman, 1979), 254–57.

68. What is here described as a broken metaphor is called an "illegitimate metaphor" by Graves, *Collected Writings*, 443.

69. Culler, *Imaginative Reason*, 41.

70. C. B. Tinker and H. F. Lowry, *The Poetry of Matthew Arnold* (London: Oxford University Press, 1940), 174–75.

71. Matthew Arnold, *The Letters of Matthew Arnold*, ed. Cecil Lang (Charlottesville: University Press of Virginia, 1998), I: 337.

72. Ibid., III: 347.

73. James Stephens et al., eds. *Victorian and Later English Poets* (New York: American Book, 1937), 503.

74. Arnold, *Letters*, I: xiii.

75. Christopher Levinson, *delta* 8 (1956): 27; Barbara Everett, *Poets in Their Time* (London: Faber and Faber, 1986), 245–56; Donald Hall, *Shenandoah* 7 (1956): 50; G. S. Fraser, *Vision and Rhetoric* (London: Faber and Faber, 1959), 261; J. R. Watson, *Critical*

Quarterly 17 (1975): 224; Anthony Thwaite, *The Survival of Poetry*, ed. Martin Dodsworth (London: Faber and Faber, 1970), 48–49.

76. David Timms, *Philip Larkin* (Edinburgh: Oliver and Boyd, 1973), 81.

77. Joseph Epstein quoted by John Augustine, *Philip Larkin: The Man and His Work*, ed. Dale Salwak (London: Macmillan, 1989), 112; John Press quoted by R. N. Parkinson, *Critical Survey* 5 (1971): 224.

78. Anonymous reviewer, *T.L.S.* (March 12, 1964): 216; Herbert Peschmann, *English* 24 (1975): 51.

79. A. Alvarez, *Partisan Review* 25 (1956): 606.

80. Philip Larkin, *Collected Poems*, ed. Anthony Thwaite (New York: Farrar, Straus, Giroux, 1989), 97–98.

81. Peschmann, *English*, 50.

82. W. H. Auden, *The Collected Poetry of W. H. Auden* (New York: Random House, 1945), 57–59.

83. Ibid., 54.

84. Philip Larkin, *Required Writing* (New York: Farrar, Straus, Giroux, 1984), 124.

85. Quoted by David Wright, *Encounter* 7 (1956): 77.

86. Larkin's statement introducing the selection of his poems in *Poets of the 1950's*, ed. D. J. Enright (Tokyo: Kenkyusha, 1955), 78.

87. Larkin, *Required Writing*, 69.

88. Ibid., 48.

89. Interview with Ian Hamilton, *London Magazine* n.s. 4 (1964): 74.

90. Barbara Everett, *Philip Larkin*, ed. George Hartley (London: Marvell Press, 1988), 141.

91. Larkin, *Required Writing*, 47.

Chapter 6

1. C. K. Doreski, *Elizabeth Bishop: The Restraints of Language* (New York: Oxford University Press, 1993), ix.

2. Tony Schwartz, *New York Times* (Oct. 8, 1979): B13.

3. Howard Moss, *Kenyon Review* 28 (1966): 262.

4. Selden Rodman, *New York Times Book Review* (Oct. 27, 1946): 18; M. L. Rosenthal, *New York Herald Tribune Book Review* (May 18, 1947): 2; Coleman Rosenberg, *New York Herald Tribune Book Review* (Sept. 4, 1955): 2.

5. David Kalstone, *Becoming a Poet* (New York: Farrar, Straus, Giroux, 1989), x–xi.

6. Ann Winslow, ed., *Trial Balances* (New York: Macmillan, 1935).

7. Randall Jarrell, *Poetry and the Age* (New York: Ecco Press, 1980), 173.

8. Lloyd Frankenberg, ed., *Pleasure Dome* (Columbia Records, c.1949–50).

9. Kalstone, *Becoming a Poet*, 133.

10. Anonymous reviewer, *Kirkus* 14 (Aug. 1, 1946) quoted by Diana Wylie, ed., *Elizabeth Bishop and Howard Nemerov: A Reference Guide* (Boston: G. K. Hall, 1983), 1.

11. Elizabeth Bishop, *North & South* (Boston: Houghton, Mifflin, 1946), 1.

12. Bishop's statement in *Mid-Century American Poets*, ed. John Ciardi (New York: Twayne, 1950), 267.

13. Marianne Moore, *The Complete Prose of Marianne Moore*, ed. Patricia Willis (New York: Viking, 1986), 406–7; Rosenthal, *Tribune Book Review*, 2; Edward Weeks, *Atlantic*

(Aug. 1946): 148; Randall Jarrell, *Partisan Review* 13 (1946): 498; Robert Lowell, *Sewanee Review* 55 (1947): 497; Barbara Gibbs, *Poetry* 69 (1947): 229.

14. Oscar Williams, *New Republic* 115 (Oct. 21, 1946): 525.

15. Louise Bogan, *New Yorker* (Oct. 5, 1946): 121–22.

16. Weeks, *Atlantic*, 146; Arthur Mizener, *Furioso* (1949): 75.

17. Rosenthal, *Tribune Book Review*, 2.

18. Weeks, *Atlantic*, 148.

19. Moore, *Complete Prose*, 408.

20. Rosenthal, *Tribune Book Review*, 2.

21. Rodman, *Times Book Review*, 18.

22. Jarrell, *Partisan Review*, 498–99.

23. Lowell, *Sewanee Review*, 496–99.

24. Ibid., 497.

25. Ibid., 498.

26. Interview with Elizabeth Spires, *Writers at Work*, ed. George Plimpton, 6th ser. (New York: Viking, 1984), 145.

27. W. B. Yeats, *The Letters of W. B. Yeats*, ed. Allan Wade (London: Rupert Hart-Davis, 1954), 353.

28. Auden, *Edgar Allan Poe*, v.

29. Bishop, *One Art*, 515.

30. Philip Booth, *Village Voice* (Jan. 25, 1956): 7; Lorrie Goldensohn, *American Poetry Review* 7 (1978): 18; Edward Honig, *Partisan Review* 23 (1956): 115; Nathan Scott, *Virginia Quarterly Review* 60 (1984): 266.

31. H. T. Kirby-Smith, *Sewanee Review* 80 (1972): 483; Anthony Hecht, *Hudson Review* 9 (1956): 458; Louis Martz, *Yale Review* 55 (1966): 458.

32. Rosenberg, *Tribune Book Review*, 2.

33. William Jay Smith, *Harper's Magazine* (Aug. 1966): 89.

34. Helen Vendler, *Yale Review* 66 (1977): 420.

35. Helen Vendler, *Part of Nature, Part of Us* (Cambridge, Mass.: Harvard University Press, 1980), 136.

36. M. L. Rosenthal, *Nation* (Sept. 19, 1959): 154; William Meredith, *New York Times Book Review* (June 15, 1969): 119; Irwin Ehrenpreis, *Critics on Robert Lowell*, 22, 33.

37. Christopher Ricks, *New Statesman* (Mar. 26, 1965): 496.

38. Poirier, *Critics on Robert Lowell*, 92.

39. Honig, *Partisan Review*, 115.

40. Moss, *Kenyon Review*, 261–62.

41. Schwartz, *New York Times*, B13.

42. Peter Prescott, *New York Times Book Review* (Nov. 13, 1994): 60.

43. John Ashbery, *World Literature Today* (1977): 9.

44. Kirby-Smith, *Sewanee Review*, 483.

45. Jerome Mazzaro, *Shenandoah* 20 (1969): 100.

46. Jarrell, *Poetry and the Age*, 208.

47. Ibid., 219.

48. Howard Nemerov, *Poetry* 87 (1955): 181.

49. Robert Mazzacco, *New York Review of Books* (Oct. 12, 1967): 4.

50. Robert Pinsky, *New Republic* (Nov. 10, 1979): 32; *Newsweek* (Oct. 22, 1972): 72.

51. Interview with George Starbuck, *Conversations with Elizabeth Bishop*, ed. George Monteiro (Jackson: University Press of Mississippi, 1996), 86.

52. Elizabeth Bishop, Letter to Robert Lowell, July 11, 1951 (Houghton Library Bms 1905).

53. Kalstone, *Becoming a Poet*, 85.

54. Bishop, Letter to Lowell, Houghton Bms 1905.

55. Denis Donoghue, *Connoisseurs of Chaos* (New York: Columbia University Press, 1984), 270.

56. Alfred Corn, *Georgia Review* 31 (1977): 533.

57. J. D. McClatchy, *Canto* I (1977): 167–68.

58. Bishop, *North & South*, 23–25; *Geography III*, 42–45.

59. Bishop, *Geography III*, 177.

60. David Bromwich, *New York Times Book Review* (Feb. 27, 1983): 7.

61. Jarrell, *Poetry and the Age*, 235.

62. Rodman, *Times Book Review*, 18; Richard Eberhart, *Reading the Spirit* (London: Chatto and Windus, 1936), 64–65.

63. Bishop, *North & South*, 44–46.

64. Interview with Wesley Wehr, *Antioch Review* 39 (1981): 324.

65. Elizabeth Bishop, Letter to Anne Stevenson, *T.L.S.* (March 7, 1980): 261.

66. Anonymous writer, *FIELD* 31 (1984): 7.

67. The description of Bishop as "an ideal poet for anthologies" is by Mazzaro, *Shenandoah*, 100.

Chapter 7

1. The only earlier example of an authorial collection of poems modeled, less closely, on Tottel's anthology is Barnaby Googe, *Eglogs, Epitaphes, and Sonettes* of 1563.

2. William Wordsworth, *The Prose Works of William Wordsworth*, ed. W. J. B. Owen and Jane Smyser (Oxford: Clarendon Press, 1974), III: 78.

3. Sir Walter Scott, *The Letters of Sir Walter Scott*, ed. Sir Herbert Grierson (London: Constable, 1932), I: 108.

4. Southey, *Specimens*, I: xxxii.

5. Robert Southey, *Quarterly Review* 12 (1814): 90.

6. Wordsworth, *Prose Works*, III: 78.

7. Ibid.

8. Elizabeth Barrett Browning, *The Complete Works of Elizabeth Barrett Browning* (New York: AMS Press, 1973), VI: 297–99.

9. Davis, *Thomas Percy*, 331.

10. John Livingston Lowes, *The Road to Xanadu* (Boston: Houghton, Mifflin, 1927), 331–32.

11. Wordsworth, *Prose Works*, III: 75.

12. Boswell, *Life of Johnson*, 937.

13. Wordsworth, *Prose Works*, I: 150–54.

14. Wordsworth, *Poetical Works*, 67.

15. Percy, *Reliques*, III: 172.

16. Boswell, *Life of Johnson*, 510.

17. Wordsworth, *Prose Works*, III: 75–76.

18. Percy, *Reliques*, I: 12.

19. Reginald Cook, *Robert Frost: A Living Voice* (Amherst: University of Massachusetts Press, 1974), 109–10.

20. Robert Frost, *Selected Letters of Robert Frost*, ed. Lawrance Thompson (New York: Holt, Rhinehart and Winston, 1964), 37.

21. Ibid., 20.

22. Lawrance Thompson, *Robert Frost: The Early Years 1874–1915* (New York: Holt, Rhinehart and Winston, 1966), 304.

23. Ibid., 347.

24. Robert Frost, *Collected, Poems, Prose, & Plays*, ed. Richard Poirier and Mark Richardson (New York: Library of America, 1995), 686; Frost, *Selected Letters*, 54.

25. Frost, *Selected Letters*, 52.

26. Frost, *Collected Poems*, 503, 511, 514, 874. All quotations of Frost's poems are from this edition where they are located in the table of contents, listed by volume and title.

27. Palgrave, *Golden Treasury*, 313.

28. Elizabeth Sergeant, *Robert Frost: The Trial by Existence* (New York: Holt, Rhinehart and Winston, 1960), 28; Cook, *Robert Frost*, 56.

29. Frost, *Collected Poems*, 881, 879.

30. Cook, *Robert Frost*, 58.

31. For a discussion of "Lycidas" as a shaping influence of *A Boy's Will*, see Anne Ferry, *The Title to the Poem* (Stanford: Stanford University Press, 1996), 25, 27, 28–29.

32. Frost, *Selected Letters*, 76–77.

33. Frost, *Collected Poems*, 709.

34. Ibid., 684.

35. Richard Poirier, *Robert Frost: The Work of Knowing* (New York: Oxford University Press, 1977), esp. 62–72. In discussing poems in *A Boy's Will*, Poirier points out some of the allusions to choices in *The Golden Treasury* that are expanded on here.

36. Ibid., 64.

37. Sergeant, *Robert Frost*, 423.

38. Frost, *Selected Letters*, 141.

39. Cook, *Robert Frost*, 123. Frost omitted "Spoils of the Dead" with its "fairies" from collected editions.

40. William Pritchard, *Frost: A Literary Life Reconsidered* (New York: Oxford University Press, 1984), 239.

41. Cook, *Robert Frost*, 109.

42. Ezra Pound, *Ezra Pound: Letters to Ibbotson, 1935–1952*, ed. Vittoria Mondolfo and Margaret Hurley (Orono: University of Maine, 1979), 24.

43. Yeats, *Letters*, 739.

44. Ezra Pound, *Literary Essays of Ezra Pound*, ed. T. S. Eliot (New York: New Directions, 1968), 18.

45. Ibid., 362.

46. Ezra Pound, *The Letters of Ezra Pound 1907–1941*, ed. D. D. Paige (New York: Harcourt, Brace, 1950), 23, 49.

47. Cook, *Robert Frost*, 144.

48. Ibid., 159.

49. Frost, *Collected Poems*, 734–35, 856.

50. Ibid., 786.

51. Cook, *Robert Frost*, 39.

52. Frost, *Collected Poems*, 768–69.

53. Cook, *Robert Frost*, 46.

54. Ibid., 58.

55. Ibid. Palgrave himself could have discovered this song in Percy's *Reliques* or in an anthology he acknowledged in his preface, Robert Bell's *Songs from the Dramatists* (1854), where the poem is titled "The Equality of the Grave."

56. Ibid., 156.

57. Frost, *Collected Poems*, 735.

58. William Evans, ed., *Robert Frost and Sidney Cox* (Hanover, N.H.: University Press of New England, 1981), 61.

59. Frost, *Selected Letters*, 228.

60. Pound, *Letters 1907–1941*, 260.

61. Sergeant, *Robert Frost*, 410–11; Cook, *Robert Frost*, 146–47.

62. Frost, *Collected Poems*, 788.

63. Cook, *Robert Frost*, 122.

64. Palgrave, *Golden Treasury*, preface.

65. Cook, *Robert Frost*, 122.

66. Ibid., 159.

67. Frost, *Collected Poems*, 881.

68. Ibid., 783.

69. Cook, *Robert Frost*, 63.

70. Frost, *Collected Poems*, 744.

71. Florence Emily Hardy, *The Later Years of Thomas Hardy 1892–1928* (New York: Macmillan, 1930), 263.

72. Eliot, *The Use of Poetry*, 110.

73. Edward Thomas, *Letters from Edward Thomas to Gordon Bottomley*, ed. R. George Thomas (London: Oxford University Press, 1968), 113.

74. Robert Graves, *In Broken Images: Selected Letters of Robert Graves 1914–1946*, ed. Paul O'Prey (London: Hutchinson, 1982), 30.

75. Christopher Hassal, *Edward Marsh Patron of the Arts* (London: Longmans, 1959), 533.

76. Laura Riding and Robert Graves, *A Survey of Modernist Poetry* (Garden City, N.Y.: Doubleday, Doran, 1928), 118–19.

77. *Georgian Poetry 1920–1922* (New York: G. P. Putnam's Sons, 1923), 51.

78. Riding and Graves, *Survey of Modernist Poetry*, 119.

79. Richard Aldington, *Life for Life's Sake* (New York: Viking, 1941), 110.

80. Graves, *In Broken Images*, 90.

81. Laura Riding and Robert Graves, *A Pamphlet Against Anthologies* (London: Jonathan Cape, 1928), 44.

82. Ibid., 94–95.

83. Ibid., 110.

84. Ibid., 93.

85. Ibid., 83.

86. Ibid., 92.

87. Ibid., 95.

88. Yeats, *Letters*, 561.

89. Larkin, *Selected Letters*, 674.

Chapter 8

1. Knox, *Elegant Extracts*, viii; this quotation is used for both title and motto in A. P. Wavell, *Other Men's Flowers: An Anthology of Poetry* (London: Jonathan Cape, 1944).

2. Thomas Hardy, *The Collected Letters of Thomas Hardy 1920–1925*, ed. Richard Purdy and Michael Millgate (Oxford: Clarendon Press, 1987), VI: 183.

3. One method poets have used for controlling the choices of their poems by anthologists is behind-the-scenes collaboration such as Frost's with Untermeyer. Another opportunity was first offered by anthologists in the late nineteenth century and has become more common since: collections that announce their selections to be entirely of the poets' choices. Examples are: Jeannette Leonard Gilder, ed., *Representative Poems of Living Poets American and English* (New York, 1886); William Rose Benét, *Fifty American Poets: An American Autobiography* (New York: Duffield and Green, 1933); Whit Burnett, ed., *This Is My Best* (New York: Dial Press, 1942) and its sequel, *The World's Best* (New York: Dial Press, 1950); Paul Engle and Joseph Langland, eds., *Poet's Choice* (New York: Dial Press, 1962); James Gibson, ed., *Let the Poet Choose* (London: Harrap, 1973).

4. Gascoigne, *Hundreth sundrie Flowres*, 10.

5. Alexandre Beljame, *Men of Letters and the English Public in the Eighteenth Century*, ed. Bonamy Dobrée, tr. E. O. Lorimer (London: Kegan Paul, Trench, Trubner, 1948), 368.

6. Samuel Taylor Coleridge, *Collected Letters of Samuel Taylor Coleridge 1785–1800*, ed. Earl Griggs (Oxford: Clarendon Press, 1966), I: 545.

7. W. B. Yeats, *The Oxford Book of Modern Verse 1892–1935* (New York: Oxford University Press, 1936), ix.

8. *The Book of the Rhymers' Club* (London, 1892), 92, 94. The quoted phrases are from the last poem in the book, written by G. M. Greene for the "First Anniversary of the Rhymers' Club."

9. Pound, *Letters 1907–1941*, 82.

10. Michael Roberts, ed., *New Signatures* (London: Hogarth Press, 1932), 12.

11. Michael Roberts, ed., *New Country* (London: Hogarth Press, 1933), 14.

12. Ibid., 17.

13. Robert Conquest, ed., *New Lines* (London: Macmillan, 1963), xiii.

14. Donald Hall, Robert Pack, and Louis Simpson, eds., *The New Poets of England and America* (New York: Meridian, 1960), 9.

15. Ibid., 12.

16. Robert Shaw, ed., *American Poetry Since 1960* (Cheadle: Carcanet Press, 1973), 194.

17. Elizabeth Jennings, ed., *An Anthology of Modern Verse 1940–1960* (London: Methuen, 1961), 8.

18. Mark Strand, ed., *The Contemporary American Poets* (New York: World, 1969), xiii.

19. J. D. McClatchy, ed., *The Vintage Book of Contemporary American Poetry* (New York: Random House, 1990), xxi–xxii.

20. Donald Allen, ed., *The New American Poetry: 1945–1960* (New York: Grove Press, 1960), xi.

21. Frank O'Hara, *The Collected Poems of Frank O'Hara*, ed. Donald Allen (New York: Alfred Knopf, 1971), 499.

22. James Breslin, *From Modern to Contemporary* (Chicago: University of Chicago Press, 1984), xiv.

23. Ibid., 12–13.

24. W. H. Auden, *Partisan Review* 6 (1939), 47.

25. A. Norman Jeffares, ed., *W. B. Yeats: The Critical Heritage* (London: Routledge and Kegan Paul, 1977), 386, 379.

26. Sutcliffe, *Oxford University Press*, 120.

27. Ibid., 208.

28. W. B. Yeats, *Letters on Poetry from W. B. Yeats to Dorothy Wellesley* (London: Oxford University Press, 1940), 121–22.

29. Jeffares, *Yeats: Critical Heritage*, 379.

30. Yeats, *Oxford Book*, v.

31. Laurence Binyon, *English* I (1936): 339.

32. Yeats, *Letters*, 833.

33. Yeats, *Oxford Book*, xxxvi.

34. Ibid., xi–xii.

35. Ibid., xii.

36. Ibid., xviii.

37. Ibid., xix–xx.

38. Ibid., xxi.

39. Ibid., xxii–xxiii.

40. Ibid., xxiv–xxvi.

41. Ibid., xvi, xxxv.

42. Ibid., xvi, xxxvi.

43. Ibid., xxxvi.

44. Ibid.

45. Ibid., xxviii.

46. Yeats, *Letters to Wellesley*, 34.

47. Yeats, *Oxford Book*, xxxii.

48. Ibid., 309, 314.

49. Yeats, *Letters to Wellesley*, 81.

50. Yeats, *Oxford Book*, xxxv.

51. Ibid., 80.

52. Ibid., 90.

53. Yeats, *Letters to Wellesley*, 27.

54. Yeats, *Oxford Book*, 91.

55. Yeats, *Letters to Wellesley*, 44.

56. Ibid., 7–8.

57. W. B. Yeats, *The Collected Poems of W. B. Yeats*, 2d ed. (New York: Macmillan, 1950), 291–93.

58. Donald Hall, *Larkin: The Man and His Work*, 166.

59. Anonymous reviewer, *T.L.S.* (April 13, 1973): 405, 407.

60. Larkin, *Letters*, 380.

61. Ibid.

62. Ibid., 380–81.

63. Kingsley Amis, *The Amis Collection* (London: Penguin Books, 1990), 172.

64. Philip Larkin, ed., *The Oxford Book of Twentieth Century English Verse* (Oxford: Clarendon Press, 1973), vi.

65. Yeats, *Oxford Book*, vi.

66. Ibid., xiv.

67. Larkin, *London Magazine*, 72.

68. Larkin, *Required Writing*, 71.

69. Ibid., 72.

70. Larkin, *Letters*, 162.

71. Larkin, *London Magazine*, 74.

72. Larkin, *Collected Poems*, 98.

73. Yeats, *Oxford Book*, 90.

74. Larkin, *Oxford Book*, 11.

75. Ibid., 538.

76. Ibid., 5–6.

77. Ibid., 541.

78. Larkin, *Letters*, 434.

79. Ibid., 471–72.

80. Andrew Motion, *Philip Larkin: A Writer's Life* (London: Faber and Faber, 1993), 434.

81. Larkin, *Required Writing*, 73.

Coda

1. Auden, *Dyer's Hand*, 43.

2. Grierson, *Metaphysical Lyrics*, xvi; T. S. Eliot, *The Letters of T. S. Eliot 1898–1922*, ed. Valerie Eliot (London: Faber and Faber, 1988), 84n2.

3. T. S. Eliot, *T.L.S.* (Nov. 24, 1921): 771.

4. T. S. Eliot, *Egoist* (Nov. 1917): 151.

5. T. S. Eliot, *Dial* 70 (1921): 450–51.

6. T. S. Eliot, *Selected Essays 1917–1932* (New York: Harcourt, Brace, 1932), 250.

7. T. S. Eliot, *T.L.S.* (Jan. 13, 1961): 17.

8. Eliot complained of its repeated appearances in anthologies in the 1964 preface to *The Use of Poetry and the Use of Criticism*. See John Paul Riquelme, *Harmony of Dissonances* (Baltimore: Johns Hopkins University Press, 1991), 28.

9. Eliot, *Selected Essays*, 4–6.

10. For other suggestions made by this title, see Ferry, *Title to the Poem*, 227–28.

11. Eliot, *Selected Essays*, 242–43.

12. T. S. Eliot, *Poems* (New York: Alfred Knopf, 1920), 31–32.

13. Johnson, *Lives of the Poets*, I: 14.

14. John Donne, *The Poems of John Donne*, ed. Herbert Grierson (London: Oxford University Press, 1951), I: 62. The first edition was published in 1912.

15. Eliot, *Selected Essays*, 245.

16. Ibid., 247.

17. Eliot, *Letters*, I: 596.

18. Massingham, *Treasury*, xi.

19. Ibid., xii.

20. Ibid., xxi.

21. T. S. Eliot, *The Varieties of Metaphysical Poetry*, ed. Ronald Suchard (London: Faber and Faber, 1993), 43.

22. G. M. Young, *London Mercury* 35 (Dec. 1936): 114.

23. Eliot, *Selected Essays*, 5.

24. Donald Davie, *The Poet in the Imaginary Museum*, ed. Barry Alpert (Manchester: Carcanet, 1977), 52.

25. Frank Kermode, *History and Value* (Oxford: Clarendon Press, 1988), 116.

26. Cook, *Robert Frost*, 63.

27. Larkin, *London Magazine*, 31; Larkin, *Poets of the 1950's*, 78.

INDEX 1

ANTHOLOGIES

In this index and the following, an "f" after a number indicates a separate reference on the next page, and an "ff" indicates separate references on the next two pages. A continuous discussion over two or more pages is indicated by a span of page numbers, e.g., "57–59." *Passim* is used for a cluster of references in close but not consecutive sequence.

INDEX 2

AUTHORS